MUNGO PARK, THE AFRICAN TRAVELER

Mungo Park
the
African Traveler

Kenneth Lupton

OXFORD   NEW YORK   TORONTO   IBADAN
OXFORD UNIVERSITY PRESS
1979

Oxford University Press, Walton Street, Oxford OX2 6DP

OXFORD LONDON GLASGOW NEW YORK
TORONTO MELBOURNE WELLINGTON
IBADAN NAIROBI DAR ES SALAAM CAPE TOWN
KUALA LUMPUR SINGAPORE JAKARTA HONG KONG TOKYO
DELHI BOMBAY CALCUTTA MADRAS KARACHI

© Kenneth Lupton 1979

British Library Cataloguing in Publication Data

Lupton, Kenneth
  Mungo Park.
  1. Park, Mungo   2. Explorers, British – Biography
  916.6'04   DT356.P37   78–40200
  ISBN 0–19–211749–1

Printed in Great Britain by
Hazell Watson & Viney Ltd,
Aylesbury, Bucks

TO MY PARENTS

Preface

———— ∞ ————

This book explores the life of Mungo Park. I hope that the reader can easily discover in it the boundary between fact and interpretation, and that what was known of Africa in Park's time has been sufficiently clearly distinguished from what has been learnt subsequently. Park's own investigations were mainly geographical and social, and he obtained little historical information. Except where the text indicates otherwise, later studies have provided nearly all of the historical material here used.

In quotations I have kept the original spelling. Where a place-name has a modern English form I have used it, and failing that a modern French form. For places that have vanished or will not be found even in good atlases, it seemed pointless to change from Park's form of the name. Personal names have, for the most part, been kept as he used them. I do not see that any confusion should result from this, or over the different titles used at different times for office-holders.

Where it seemed useful to add a note to enlarge on a point, this has been placed on the page of text. The numbered notes at the end of the book are primarily source-references, with only a few comments on points of attribution, dates, etc.

I wish to thank all those who have helped me, many of whom are named in the notes. I have received help and encouragement, including comments on drafts, from Professors Lalage Bown and Michael Crowder, both formerly of Ahmadu Bello University, Zaria, but now at Lagos University, and from Professor George Shepperson of the University of Edinburgh. At Selkirk, previously unpublished material, local knowledge, and help in tracing or preparing illustrations were all kindly made available. My thanks in this regard are offered especially to Mr J.B.Baxter, Mrs. N.Marshall, Mr. W.McL.Mitchell, the Librarian of the Public Library (Mr. James Smith), and the Selkirkshire Antiquarian Society. Mr. and Mrs. G.Ogilvie, and the Revd.

R.I.Johnstone have also generously allowed me to use previously un-published letters. A number of Librarians have assisted in collecting material, and the Bodleian Library, Oxford, also in the preparation of illustrations.

Transcripts of Crown-copyright records in the Public Record Office and the reproduction of Captain Clapperton's sketch-map of Bussa appear by permission of the Controller of Her Majesty's Stationery Office. I am grateful to the Trustees respectively of the British Library, the National Library of Scotland, the National Maritime Museum, and the British Museum (Natural History) for permission to quote from their collections. In the case of the last-named, this extends to the reproduction of Park's own painting of a Sumatra fish. Permission has also been gratefully received to reproduce the portraits of Mungo Park by Henry Edridge, on the book jacket, from Mr. J.Mungo Park; of Sir Joseph Banks, from the Royal Society; of Mungo Park by Thomas Rowlandson, of Major James Rennell, and of the 1st Marquess Camden, from the National Portrait Gallery; and of James Dickson, from the Linnean Society of London. The drawing of Foulshiels is reproduced by permission of the Royal Scottish Academy. Reproductions have been made of copyright photographs with the permission of Messrs. R.Clapperton, Selkirk (the Mungo Park Monument and the Andersons' house); the Royal Geographical Society (the Awuru rapids); and Messrs. Aerofilms Limited (the Niger at Bussa).

Contents

———— ⚯ ————

List of Illustrations

———— ᙚᙚ ————

List of Maps

———— ∞ ————

Section of Major Rennell's Map of Africa, 1790

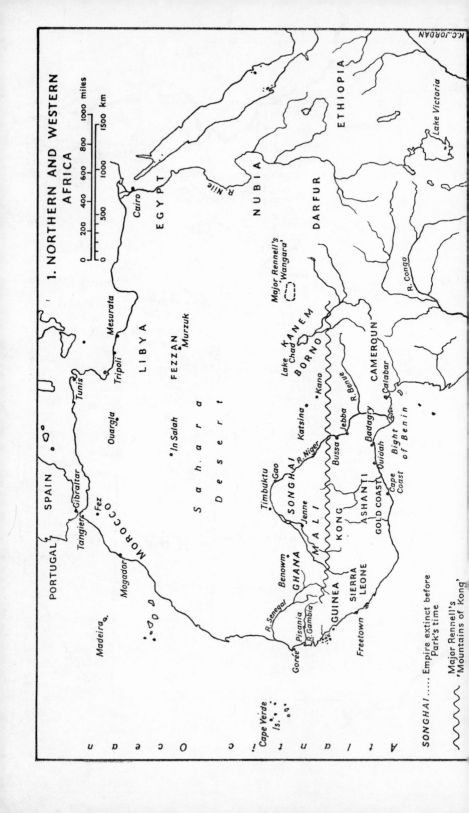

1. NORTHERN AND WESTERN AFRICA

K.C.JORDAN

SONGHAI...... Empire extinct before Park's time

〜〜〜 Major Rennell's "Mountains of Kong"

Scale: 0 200 400 600 800 1000 miles
0 500 1000 1500 km

Atlantic Ocean

PORTUGAL
SPAIN
Gibraltar
Tangiers
MOROCCO
Fez
Mogador
Madeira
Cape Verde Is.
Goree
Pisania
R. Gambia
R. Senegal
Benowm
GHANA
GUINEA
SIERRA LEONE
Freetown
MALI
KONG
ASHANTI
GOLD COAST
Cape Coast
Ouidah
Badagry
Bight of Benin
Calabar
CAMEROUN
Bussa
Jebba
R. Benue
Kano
Katsina
SONGHAI
Jenne
R. Niger
Gao
Timbuktu
In Salah
Sahara Desert
Ouargla
Tunis
Tripoli
Mesurata
LIBYA
FEZZAN
Murzuk
EGYPT
Cairo
R. Nile
NUBIA
DARFUR
ETHIOPIA
R. Congo
Lake Victoria
Lake Chad
KANEM
BORNO
Major Rennell's "Wangara"

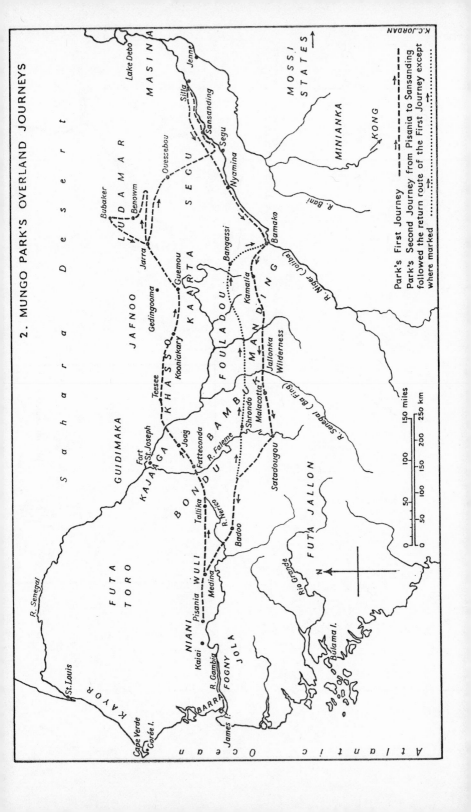

2. MUNGO PARK'S OVERLAND JOURNEYS

K.C.JORDAN

Park's First Journey --------
Park's Second Journey from Pisania to Sansanding
followed the return route of the First Journey except
where marked ....

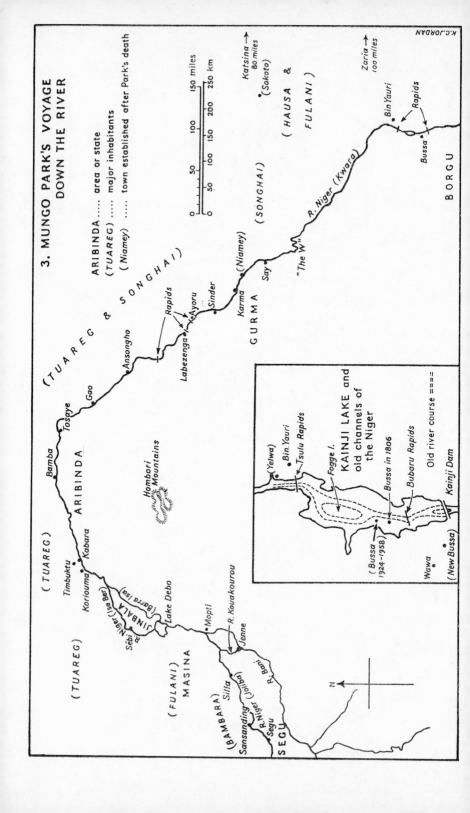

3. MUNGO PARK'S VOYAGE DOWN THE RIVER

ARIBINDA ...... area or state
(TUAREG) ...... major inhabitants
(Niamey) ...... town established after Park's death

0   50   100   150 miles
0   50 100 150 200 250 km

K.C.JORDAN

Katsina →
80 miles

Zaria →
100 miles

(Sokoto)

(HAUSA &
FULANI)

Bin Yauri

Bussa

Rapids

BORGU

R. Niger (Kwara)

(SONGHAI)

Say

"The W"

Karma (Niamey)

GURMA

Sinder

Ayoru

Labezenga

Rapids

Ansongho

Gao

Tosoye

Bamba

(TUAREG & SONGHAI)

ARIBINDA

Hombori
Mountains

(TUAREG)

Timbuktu

Koriouma

Kabara

Sébi

Niger (Isa Ber)

Barra Isa

JINBALA

Lake Debo

Mopti

R. Kouakourou

Jenne

(FULANI)

MASINA

(BAMBARA)

Silla

Sansanding

Segu

R. Niger (Joliba)

R. Bani

SEGU

N

KAINJI LAKE and old channels of the Niger

(Yelwa)

Bin.Yauri

Tsulu Rapids

Fogge I.

Bussa in 1806

Bubaru Rapids

Old river course ====

(Bussa
1924–1958)

Wawa

(New Bussa)

Kainji Dam

Glossary

—— ∽∾ ——

Note: Most of the following words are derived from Arabic

Al-Hajj	A person who has made the pilgrimage to Mecca.
Alkaid	(Gambian usage) A town or district chief.
Almami	Political and religious head of a Muslim community.
Bentang	(Mandingo) A platform used for public business in a town or village.
Bushreen	A local term for a Muslim.
Caliph	'Successor' – Commander of the faithful.
Coffle	A caravan.
Cowries	Small white shells formerly used as currency.
Dooty	(? from Mandingo and Bambara, *Dougoutigui*) Chief of a town or village.
Fama	(Bambara) King.
Harmattan	A cold, dry wind blowing southwards from the Sahara for part of the dry season.
Jihad	A Holy War for the spread of Islam.
Kafir	An unbeliever or infidel.
Kouskous	A food made from grain.
Mansa	(Mandingo) King.
Marabout	Generally, a Muslim religious leader. In Gambian usage, any fully practising Muslim.
Ramadan	The ninth month of the Muslim calendar, a month of fasting.
Ruma	Descendants of the Moroccan conquerors of Songhai, settled and married in that area.

Sahel	Borderland between desert and sown areas (literally, shore).
Saphie	A charm.
Savanna	Predominantly grass-covered land in the wide belt between the Sahel and the tropical rain-forests.
Shaikh	An elder, head of a tribe, etc.
Shari'a	The corpus of Muslim law.
Sharif	One who claims descent from the Prophet Mohammed.
Slatee	Free African merchants, trading mainly in slaves.
Sudan	Short for Bilad-as-Sudan (Arabic), the Country of the Blacks; primarily the combined savanna and Sahel belt stretching across Africa south of the Sahara Desert.

Introduction

—— riqi ——

All Mungo Park's ambitions of opening a highway into western Africa along the river Niger died with him one day early in 1806. The 34-year-old Scot, making his second major journey in Africa, arrived then, in a large canoe of unusual construction, at a point on the river Niger near Bussa in what is now Nigeria. His unexpected arrival from the north was an extraordinary event there. In the resulting confusion he and his few followers perished and the records of his long journey down the river were lost. It was another twenty-five years before the brothers Richard and John Lander triumphed by covering the last few hundred miles down river to the ocean.

Mungo Park is the outstanding name in the early European exploration of inland West Africa. His achievements have maintained his fame ever since, and his *Travels* have always been regarded as a classic of their kind. Interest has been held too by the adventurous side of his journeys, by the tragedies of the last one in particular, and by the uncertainties, never fully cleared up, surrounding the circumstances of his death.

There was a file at Bussa when I was District Officer there in 1958, recording a story about his death told by an old man in 1913, and also containing some speculations by later Administrative Officers. It presented an incomplete and unsatisfying picture of events. I set out to read the early sources and other reconstructions of what had happened, to find out whether anyone could be sure when, where, how, and why Mungo Park had died. My conclusions were set out in an article published in *Nigeria Magazine* in 1962.

It struck me at the time that his death was not an isolated event, but could only be understood in the light of what had occurred earlier in this journey, and indeed in his previous African journey. In fact, nothing less than an understanding of his whole life and its setting both in Britain and in Africa would suffice to explain his death.

Several questions came to mind – what were the problems he set out to solve, as seen by him and his contemporaries? How much or how little previous knowledge was there to go on? What were his motives and aims, and those of his sponsors? What was the significance of his achievements for Africa and for Europe? What kind of man was he, after all, and how was he seen by Europeans and Africans? Why was his last expedition beset from its inception with so many misfortunes, and why did he then behave as he did?

Mungo Park rode the crest of the first large wave of European energies to pass beyond the Atlantic coastline into West Africa. What might follow was for long unclear. There were many localized ebbs and flows, rather than a steadily growing swell, before the spring tide of imperialism gathered and swept in during the 1880s and 1890s. Most lives of Park date from the time when this tide was high, and are coloured by the assumptions of that period, including the belief that the historical culmination was necessarily implied in the beginning. This is true even of Lewis Grassic Gibbon's *Niger: The Life of Mungo Park*, published in 1934, which set out to counter the romantic and heroic portrait previously depicted.

Now the tide has gone right out; the one-way flow of energies and ideas from Europe to Africa has begun to give way to an exchange, as Africa has recovered its own voice and will. It is time for a reassessment of Mungo Park, who was there when it all began.

CHAPTER I

Mungo Park's home country

———— ⚬⚬⚬ ————

An imaginative man, if asked in 1750 to guess the birthplace of the African travellers to come, might well have selected Scotland. The Scots were already showing that activity of spirit which, besides re-animating their native land, carried many of them to England and then overseas as voyagers and settlers. When Park was born, James Bruce was in Abyssinia, the country now known as Ethiopia; after his death, Gordon Laing was the first white man to report from Tim-buktu; Hugh Clapperton was the first to visit both the great West African states of Borno and Sokoto, and to enter Bussa; later David Livingstone travelled over much of East and Central Africa; and Joseph Thomson made several journeys, on one of which he touched on Park's route at Yauri. (He published a life of Park in 1890.) It would, however, have needed more than normal imagination to select the self-contained country town of Selkirk as a point of origin, still more the isolated farmhouse of Foulshiels, four miles west of it, where Mungo Park was born.

Graceful hills surround Selkirk, straddling the border with England; not high and stark mountains like those of the wilder Highlands of the north-west of Scotland, but not inconsiderable. Foulshiels Hill rises steeply behind the house; upon it is a grave where, when Mungo Park was a young man of 19, a poor woman driven to suicide by spiteful gossip was buried. Opposite stands Fastheugh Hill, the highest in the area, 1,645 feet above sea level. Between the two runs the river Yarrow, one of several fast streams which intersect the area. Starting from the south-west, the foot of Foulshiels Hill diverts it eastwards towards Selkirk, where it joins Ettrick Water, and the combined rivers join the larger river Tweed a few miles north of the town.

For centuries the border area had known raids and wars between English and Scots, and there had been many local feuds, celebrated in ballads and legends. A monument in the town commemorates the Selkirk men who had died at Flodden Field in 1513. During the Civil War, the Battle of Philiphaugh had been fought between Selkirk and Foulshiels. Since then there had been peace, even when in 1745 Bonnie Prince Charlie's army passed nearby, in its abortive attempt to regain the British crown for the Stuarts. By then the parliaments as well as the crowns had been joined in the United Kingdom; Mungo Park's letters home were addressed to Selkirk, North Britain. As a relic of earlier, fiercer days, the substantial remains of Newark Castle still stand on the south bank of the Yarrow, right before Foulshiels, for the valley narrows here and the castle's position dominates the road running through it from Selkirk.

In the times of peace which had thus become normal long before Mungo Park was born, the border area went quietly on with the business for which it is pre-eminently fitted, and is still noted: sheep farming. Crops were grown only down in the valleys. In summer especially great numbers of white sheep, and some cattle, stand out on the green hillsides, the visible wealth of this land.

Together with England and southern Scotland as a whole, the borders were moving forward at that time into what are known as the Agrarian and Industrial Revolutions. The population was rising faster than before. The recurrent years of hunger of the previous century were now very infrequent, although there was one in 1783 when Mungo Park was a schoolboy. The new developments in industry and the growing of crops are better known, but sheep farming was not without its advances too. The gradual increase in general prosperity had meant almost a doubling of the price of woollen fleece in the years before he was born. These changes were not so far-reaching as elsewhere, however, and the sheep farmers seem to have felt less than some others the accompanying social dislocation. Foulshiels shows continuity through at least three generations of Parks spanning over a century, although strictly speaking a tenant had no inheritable right to his land.

Other social changes may also have come more slowly in these parts. For example, while most successful tenant farmers elsewhere were by then living in more elegant and exclusive accommodation, Foulshiels remained a simple and rough 'but and ben' house of a type in which all the family and often the farm servants as well lived together. In its present partly restored form it is a plain rectangle measuring about 45 feet by 12 feet, with a door on the south side, four windows, and a fireplace at the east end. It was then divided into three rooms, with a loft above.

It was certainly a small house for such a large family, and this has misled some into believing that the Parks were poor. But, however simple the conditions in which they lived, successful tenant farmers like Mungo Park's father could often be quite prosperous. Foulshiels farm was middling-sized for the area; in 1766 it carried 720 sheep and 10 cattle and had an annual rent of £74, paid to the Duke of Buccleuch, the major land-owner of the district. Mungo Park's father was sufficiently well-off to lend the Burgh Council £200 for a number of years, and Selkirk Public Library holds a receipt for £9 interest on this loan paid to him in 1772. He had the capital to set up his eldest son Archibald as tenant on another farm. Three other sons were seen through their education and into professional positions, two as surgeons and one as a 'writer' or attorney. There may not have been many luxuries in the family but, as will be seen, the father's will left substantial property when he died.

Foulshiels lay within Selkirk parish, and looked for its market and its services to Selkirk itself, a Royal Burgh created before 1366 and the headquarters of Selkirkshire. This was still only a small country town, standing on a hill overlooking the Ettrick river. The first census in the year 1800 showed a population of 2,098, of whom possibly half lived in the town itself and the remainder in the farms scattered around. Many of those in the town probably also farmed, and in 1778 the Council made an order to seize swine straying inside the town. Its manufactures were few and simple, produced by cottage industries such as spinning, weaving, tanning, and especially shoemaking, from which the local inhabitants derive their own name for themselves, the 'Souters'. In 1747 the parish church collapsed, and a new one had to be built. The poet Southey visited Selkirk in 1805 and found that the new church still had an earth floor. He described Selkirk as 'truly a dismal place . . . . The clocks here are stopped by night.'

Not that it was a town entirely buried in rural somnolence, oblivious to new opportunities. Most of the new factories went to nearby towns – to Selkirk's scenic, if not economic, benefit – but not for lack of effort on the Council's part. In 1791 the Council donated £10 towards the cost of new buildings for the University at Edinburgh, forty miles to the north. Later it was ready to subscribe £1,500 towards a railway line, twenty years before a successful line was built anywhere.

Home, its traditions, and the beauty of its surroundings, meant much to Mungo Park. However, the rising prosperity opened new opportunities for an enterprising young man beyond anything his home environment could muster. Like many young Scots of his time and many young Africans today, he was naturally led further afield to large cities, and in his case to distant countries, to fulfil his hopes and ambitions.

CHAPTER II

Family and education

—— ୨୯୧ ——

10 September 1771 has always been given as the date of Mungo Park's birth at Selkirk; he was the seventh of thirteen children. The Scottish Parish Registers, however, record the birth, or rather baptism, of only twelve children; perhaps one child died at birth unrecorded. They also show the birth date, probably correctly, as 11 September. This is just one of several small, long-accepted errors, mostly based on faulty information from his own family.

The Parks must have had some connection with Galashiels, a town later industrialized, six miles north of Selkirk; what this was nobody knows, but it was strong enough for family burials in the old church-yard there to continue into the next century, the last being of Mungo's mother. The death in 1768 of the traveller's grandfather, Archibald Park, aged 86, is known only from the gravestone, although records had been made earlier when his grandmother Jean Jerdon, or Jane Jerdane – the spelling differs – was buried in 1751, and when Walter Park, the first of the family mentioned in the registers, died in 1748 at the age of 27.

Walter was probably a son of Archibald and Jean, as was John Park, who died a few days after his nephew Mungo was born. The only known survivor in 1771 of their generation was the traveller's father, also named Mungo, born probably in 1714, who took over the tenancy of Foulshiels farm at the end of his father's life. St. Mungo is the patron saint of Glasgow, and there was a well named after him in what was then a part of Selkirk parish, but Mungo is not a common name even in Scotland. However, it became embedded in this family, and possibly a cousin of the same name was raising a family at Galashiels, also begetting yet another, short-lived Mungo out of wedlock, at the same time as Mungo Park of Foulshiels was bringing up his children.

This Mungo Park was aged 47 when, in 1761, he married his 19-year-old bride Elspeth, daughter of the tenant in Tinnes, John Hislop, and his wife Margaret Turnbull, who lived westwards up the Yarrow valley. Elspeth then embarked, as many wives did, on nearly twenty years of child-bearing. A year after the wedding a daughter was born, and called Margaret after her maternal grandmother. The next three children, John and twins Jean and Helen, died young. Then came, at two-year intervals from 1767, children who all reached adult life. By the time of young Mungo's birth there were Margaret, already 9 years old, Archibald aged 4, and Jean aged 2. After Mungo there were added, still every other year, Alexander, John, Adam, Isobel, and lastly James, born when his father was 67, but James died, aged 3, in 1784. The registers and the early biographers agree that Mungo was the seventh in the family, and if there was a thirteenth child he must have come later. Even without a thirteenth, it was indeed a family, complete with a housemaid, to fill Foulshiels cottage.

Eight days after his birth Mungo was baptized, with two of his father's farm servants as witnesses, not in the earth-floored parish church but in Selkirk's well-supported Secession Church. It was only the second baptism the Revd. Dr. George Lawson had ever conducted, and he remained always particularly interested in Mungo's education and development. Mungo Park senior had gone with those who seceded from the established Church of Scotland in 1733 over the issue of whether lay patrons should nominate Ministers. Their basic motive was to defend the pure Calvinist teaching of the seventeenth-century Covenanters. A romantic interest in the lost Stuart cause has been read into his having been prosecuted on an unknown charge in 1757, but this surmise fits poorly with his known adherence to the Secession Church.

Putting education first in the Scottish fashion but in an unusual way, Mungo Park senior hired a private tutor for some years to teach his children. This practice was more common among farmers in Cumberland across the English border.[1] Presumably the instruction included the three R's and some Bible study, possibly a beginning in Latin too. Mungo also acquired a lasting love of the ballads and stories of the old turbulent days, which perhaps first stirred a taste for adventure, and later formed a natural basis for friendship with Mr. (subsequently Sir) Walter Scott, the poet and novelist who was steeped in such lore.

The parents must have put all they had into the maintenance of the farm and home and the rearing of the family. More is known of

Archibald than of the other brothers – mainly from Sir Walter Scott –
and he appears in contrast to the introverted Mungo as a complete
extrovert: a bluff, hearty countryman intent on his farming, hunting,
and conviviality. One of Scott's anecdotes was of his winning over a
surly Highlander by taking his dirk and, with a single blow, driving
its point right through a thick wooden table.[2] Alexander, the brother
with whom Mungo kept in closest touch, made himself a substantial
position in Selkirk as a lawyer, the Procurator Fiscal for the Burgh,
and Secretary of the Farmers' Club. He also dabbled disastrously in
business. Adam became a ship's surgeon. The eldest sister, Margaret,
moves in and out of Mungo's story, but no clear picture emerges of
her or of the others, least of all when they were children together.

While still very young, it is said, Mungo remonstrated one day
with the housemaid who was sweeping up some loose pages out of a
book. She said contemptuously that they were only some pages of
'old Flavel' – a book of divinity – and he retorted, 'Ay, you, or somebody else, will one day be sweeping in my book leaves, saying they
were old Mungo Park's.' To this his mother said lightly, 'You poor
useless thing, do you think you will ever write books?' This looks like
an apocryphal story designed to show precocious ambition, but it was
said by a brother (probably John) to have been repeated by Mungo
himself when presenting his mother with a copy of his *Travels* in 1799.

After some years with the private tutor, Mungo started attending
the Grammar School in Selkirk's old churchyard. He presumably
walked four miles each way daily, to learn English, Latin, Religious
Knowledge, Mathematics, and some Geography. A printed map of
Scotland still exists with his writing on the back: 'My Map of Scotland
– M. Park.' With boyish high spirits he went on to add, 'Drawn from
the best authorities – Hurray, hurray – The emblem of Scotland,'
under which he drew a man in Highland dress.[3] From early days he is
said to have been fond of solitary country rambles, and on one of them
he inscribed his name, still visible a century later, on the inner wall of
nearby Newark Castle.[4] He soon acquired the reputation of being shy,
serious, and bookish, successful in his studies and always head of his
class. He was open with those he knew well, but unable to make
friends easily, and the most frequently used term to describe him was
'reserved'. He was sometimes rather aloof from other boys, but could
stand up for himself.

One biographer, Lewis Grassic Gibbon, has attributed his seriousness and reserve to repressions due to domination by his mother and to the grim world-picture of Calvinism, but the evidence does not support this. The only description of his mother's character is as 'a woman of great prudence and good sense', which can indeed be interpreted in any way that one wants,[5] but if she unduly dominated any of the children, it must have been John, who lived with her until she died and only married afterwards when he was forty-two. As for religion, Selkirk parish adhered to the more tolerant 'Burgher' party within the Secession Church, from which the extreme 'anti-Burghers' had subdivided. Dr. Lawson, who served at Selkirk for nearly fifty years, was an unusual man with the rare distinction, for a Minister, of rating a full-length biography: that work makes clear that Mungo would have learnt his faith in an atmosphere of personal tolerance and kindliness.[6] If some of the teachings were grim, these were not the ones which remained in his mind.

His father thought him best fitted for the church, the profession most easily entered by those of limited means. Young Mungo, however, insisted that he wanted to become a surgeon; if at first this was from a positive love of medicine, then that soon wore off. Probably he met Alexander Anderson at school, came to know and revere his doctor father, and thus decided, like Alexander, to follow the same profession.[7] Possibly too he was already looking, consciously or otherwise, for a way out into the wider world.

Mungo went to live with Dr. Thomas Anderson in 1785, when he was fourteen, not a year later, as has been supposed from a misdating of his subsequent time at university. The house in Selkirk town, still standing facing the Mungo Park monument, must have seemed palatial after Foulshiels. An apprenticeship preceded the study of medicine at that time. The apprentice would ride with the surgeon on his rounds and observe his methods, and in the surgery he would learn the compounding of drugs, which was a major item in a doctor's work. Mungo also continued attending some lessons at the Grammar School.

Dr. Anderson had moved, probably in 1775, from Earlstoun, about twelve miles to the north-east, with his wife Elizabeth and with Alexander, the first of eleven children, born on 7 February 1773. At the time of Mungo's apprenticeship there were six Anderson children living, three of them only babies. Alexander always remained Mungo's closest friend. From what we may glimpse later, he seems to have been serious, devout, and phlegmatic, and Mungo, nearly eighteen months older and with a more active and ambitious temperament, was always clearly the leader of the two. The oldest daughter, Allison, has been described as light-hearted and a tease but she was only eight years old when Mungo left, having been born on 2 February 1780.

Mungo was just seventeen when he went to Edinburgh University in the autumn of 1788, taking with him the wooden trunk still preserved in Selkirk Public Library. The fine domed Adam building on South Bridge, to which Selkirk Burgh Council had contributed, was being built when Park was there. The students lived out, and it is likely that he shared lodgings with Alexander Anderson when he joined him a year behind, and also perhaps with his own brother Alexander when he was apprenticed to the legal profession. His father could apparently meet the moderate costs of a Scottish university education. One estimate is £30 a year all in, but fifteen years earlier Dr. Samuel Johnson had been told that, in the rather down-at-heel setting of St. Andrews, under £10 a year might suffice.

The medical school had nearly one-third of the university's 1,300 students, attracted by the high standards set by distinguished teachers such as Joseph Black, Professor of Chemistry, and his own former teacher William Cullen, who died just too soon for Park to come under him in 1790. The Professor of Anatomy and Surgery, Alexander Munro, was the second of three of the same name, fathers and sons, who between them held the Chair for 123 years. That the students' fees were their main source of income is commonly held to have helped maintain the standards!

Park applied himself quietly and diligently to his studies, and he was especially interested in botany, which, like chemistry, was then studied only within the medical school. He was a fairly regular borrower from the University Library, using one book at a time. A deposit had to be paid, usually one pound or one guinea, the modern equivalent of which would seem grievous to students. The surviving record shows that he only once went outside his field of study, to borrow a life of Mary Queen of Scots by the University's Principal, William Robertson.

Outside his work, being fond of verse writing, he once came second in some society's competition for a prize poem. According to the informant – possibly not impartial himself – the vote was swayed by the personal popularity of the winner more than by the merits of his poem.[8] Park's later correspondence with Alexander Anderson suggests that any other interests he may have had were religious rather than political. Indeed there is no sign, then or later, of Park's being willingly involved in the great political issues of the day, such as the French Revolution, Parliamentary Reform, or the abolition of the slave trade.

Scotland could then boast of some of Europe's best minds: Adam Smith, most famous for his *Wealth of Nations*; the Scottish school of 'Common Sense', or realist, philosophers, then represented at Edinburgh by the eloquent Professor Dugald Stewart; and Joseph Black and other scientists. Broadly speaking, the university stood for a combination of a fairly tolerant religious orthodoxy with the positive and non-sceptical ideas of the Enlightenment. Park's subsequent history shows that he found this combination very congenial, and a more lasting influence than either Calvinist theology or the border legends.

Like many other students, Park did not enter for the final oral examinations; possibly the fees, ten guineas to the examiners and one guinea to the Secretary, were a deterrent. Completing his education in the summer of 1792 and equipped, even without the formality of a degree, for a surgeon's post, Park prepared that autumn to leave home and to take the road to London in search of opportunities.

1a. Foulshiels, from a drawing by Tom Scott for (but not used in) Thomas Craig Brown, *The History of Selkirkshire* (1886)

1b. The Park Memorial and the Andersons' house in Selkirk

2. Sir Joseph Banks, from a drawing by George Dance, 1803

CHAPTER III

'First step of the stair of ambition'

———— ↜↝ ————

Before going to London late in 1792, Park had had his first taste of travel further afield than Edinburgh when he accompanied his brother-in-law James Dickson on a tour of the Scottish Highlands. Dickson had been born of poor parents at Traquair, in the neighbouring county of Peeblesshire, only a few miles from Foulshiels over the hills. As a young man he had gone to London, and after some hard-working years as a gardener he was able to set up on his own as a seedsman in Covent Garden market. He also educated himself to become an accepted authority on botany. In 1786 he married Mungo's eldest sister Margaret at Selkirk, being then a widower and just twice her age of twenty-four.

Some say the tour took place in 1789, but 1792 is more probably correct, when Park had just completed his studies with botany in the final year. Dickson visited the Highlands in both those years, going to Ben Nevis, Britain's highest mountain, to Ben Lawers, and (at least in 1792) as far north as Inverness. Places in the Lowlands, mainly along the Firth of Forth east of Edinburgh, were also included. These were not gentle sight-seeing tours; although Dickson was then aged over 50, they climbed far up in search of new plants. As Dickson said, 'Large tracts in Scotland are still unexplored by any naturalist.'[1]

Park and Dickson had therefore both a family bond and a common interest. At that time an unknown young man needed influential friends if he was to find employment, so naturally enough Park made for the Dicksons' home in Bloomsbury, then on the northern edge of London but within easy reach of Covent Garden, and began the first of several extended stays there.

Sir Joseph Banks, who had encouraged Dickson and had allowed him the use of his extensive library, was the means of starting Park on his path to fame. Differences of class notwithstanding, Banks became their friend and patron; he shared their interests and perceived their merits. Born in 1743, Banks was educated first at Harrow, then at Eton, where he became passionately interested in botany. When he found that the Oxford Professor of Botany neither taught himself nor, as was then normal, engaged a substitute, Banks hired a tutor from Cambridge at his own expense. Falling heir at the age of eighteen to the Revesby estates in Lincolnshire, he had no need to earn a living, but his energy drove him on to pursue his many interests until old age and illness slowed him down.

In his youth he travelled on botanical expeditions in parts of England and the Scottish Isles, to Iceland, Newfoundland, and Labrador. His principal journey was with Captain Cook to Tahiti, taking a party of scientific gentlemen to observe a transit of Venus across the sun's disc. They returned via New Zealand and the east coast of Australia, which Cook charted. Banks's keen interest in botany, his share in the founding and early development of the first Australian colony of New South Wales, and his service on the Board of Longitude that sought better means of fixing geographical positions, are all relevant to Park's life.

Banks never published anything of note, but he may have been the greatest scientific entrepreneur of all time. Though he refused to take any elective public office, his expert advice on various problems was sought and valued by successive governments. As President of the Royal Society from 1788 up to his death in 1820, and as scientific adviser to the King on the development of Kew Gardens, he exercised unique opportunities to promote, guide, and partly finance journeys, mainly by botanists, to Australia, south, west, and east Africa, Iceland, and elsewhere. He arranged trial exchanges of plants between different parts of the world; for example he introduced tea to India, and had breadfruit shipped twice from Tahiti to the West Indies under Captain Bligh, the first time disastrously in the *Bounty* of the famous mutiny.

Park accordingly acquired at a stroke a most influential patron and a mentor in his own scientific interests. Lewis Grassic Gibbon says that at their first encounter Park was so tongue-tied that Banks could make nothing of him, and that he went back to Scotland, returning only when Banks found a post for him.[2] This fits Gibbon's picture of Park as a repressed Calvinist mother's boy, but the evidence for these statements is hard to discern. It is far more probable that Park's interest in botany won him Banks's approval straight away.

Two events which marked Park's definitive start in life are referred to, after a flowery introduction, in a letter he wrote on 23 January 1793 to Alexander Anderson:

'I have now got upon the first step of the stair of ambition here's a figure of it [a sketch was inserted showing a man on a step-ladder] . . . Now if I should run up the stair you see the consequence. I must either be mortified by seeing I can get no farther or by taking an airy step, knok my brains out against the large folio of some succeding author. May I use my little advantage in height [he was about six feet tall] to enable me to perform the office of watchman to the rest of mankind, and call to them, "Take care, sirs! Don't look too high, or you'll break your legs on that stool. Open your eyes; you are going straight for the fire!"

'Passed at Surgeons' Hall! Associate of the Linnean Society! I walked three or four times backwards and forwards through the hall, and had actually begun to count the panes of glass in the large window, when the bell rang, and the beadle roared out, "Mr. Park!" Macbeth's start when he beheld the dagger was a mere jest compared to mine . . .'

The Linnean Society of London was founded in 1788 to promote botanical and zoological studies. It was named after the Swedish Professor Carl Linnaeus, whose new system of classifying plants had recently set the subject on a firm scientific foundation. Nominated on 20 November 1792 by James Dickson, a founder member, Park was, there and then, elected an Associate Member and remained one until his death.

His letter was much more concerned with the fact that he had passed an oral examination at the Company of Surgeons. This, formed by dividing the Company of Barbers-Surgeons as recently as 1745, was then responsible for examining surgeons who were to practise either at home or abroad. Together with one other candidate he passed on 14 January 1793, but qualified only for the lowest grade of appointment. Banks's recommendation had found him a post, and in haste he had entered for a private examination, for which an extra fee was payable, instead of waiting for the regular bimonthly examinations.[3]

He was to go as Surgeon's Mate, or Assistant Surgeon, on the *Worcester*, an East Indiaman, and his letter to Anderson continued:

'I have purchased Stewart's Philosophy to amuse me at sea. As you are in Edinburgh, you will write to me what people say of its religious character . . .

'I have too much to say, and must therefore speak by halves. The melancholy, who complain of the shortness of human life, and the voluptuous, who think the present only their own, strive to fill up every moment with sensual enjoyment; but the man whose soul has been enlightened by his Creator, and enabled, though dimly, to discern the wonders of salvation, will look upon the joys and afflictions of this life as equally the tokens of Divine love. He will walk through the world as one travelling to a better country, looking forward with wonder to the author and finisher of his faith . . .

'p.s. – I sail in about a month.'

Shortly before sailing, on 9 February, he wrote again in similar vein to Alexander:

'. . . I have now reached that height that I can behold the tumults of the nations with indifference, confident that the reins of events are in our Father's hands. May you and I (not like the stubborn mule, but like the weaning child) obey His hand, that after all the troubles of this dark world in which we are truly strangers, we may, through the wonders of atonement, reach a far greater and exceeding weight of glory. I wish you may be able to look upon the day of your departure with the same resignation that I do on mine. My hope is now approaching to a certainty. If I be deceived, may God alone put me right, for I would rather die in the delusion than wake to all the joys of earth. May the Holy Spirit dwell in your heart, my dear friend, and if I never see my native land again, may I rather see the green sod on your grave than see you anything but a Christian.'

It seems he must, just this once, have had some interior religious experience giving him this 'hope now approaching a certainty', presumably of salvation. The language is quite unlike anything written in his later, precise, detached style, and he was indeed flying high: being watchman to the rest of mankind, beholding the tumults of the nations with indifference, and so on! For once Lewis Grassic Gibbon had a point in describing these phrases as almost the most appalling example in letters of the humourless piety of adolescence, but he was wrong in supposing, like Joseph Thomson, that they were written to Dr. Anderson. They *would* then have been quite preposterous; written as they were to his fellow-student Alexander, they are much more acceptable.[4] The second letter may be exaggerated in its expression, but it must be remembered that France had declared war on Britain on 1 February 1793, and Park's family and friends might well fear some danger for him in sailing amidst these tumults of the nations.

What is certain is that he prepared for his departure in a state of elation, and with evident ambition to make a mark for himself in some way as yet undefined, but not with a mind devoid of humour, which the first part of the earlier letter clearly shows.

CHAPTER IV

From Gravesend to the Dead Land and back

———— ಬಬ ————

Part of the confusion over the letters just quoted springs from the opening words of Park's own *Travels into the Interior of Africa*, which were: 'Soon after my return from the East Indies in 1793 . . .' Even Joseph Thomson, who saw that the letters had been written before sailing but early in 1793, did not unravel this. Like everyone else he supposed that Park had sailed in 1792 and returned in 1793. In fact this was a careless slip on Park's part, and the log of the *Worcester* shows that the voyage was one year later.

Having drawn £10 in advance, representing four months' pay, Park embarked at Gravesend, down river from London, on 18 February 1793. Although the war between Britain and revolutionary France had only just begun, it was already deemed necessary to sail in convoy, and the ship waited at Portsmouth until 5 April. Like previous eighteenth-century wars, this one was fought on a world scale, and it continued for twenty-two years, with only short breaks in 1802–3 and 1814–15. From the outset, therefore, the war formed the background to Park's career and influenced it at several points.

The *Worcester* carried ten officers, as many passengers, and a hundred crew. Mungo Park was listed as Mate to the Surgeon, Richard Lane. A ship's log does not, of course, include all the details of a voyage, but during the whole voyage it listed the deaths of only one passenger and three members of the crew, one of whom fell overboard, and only one serious injury. There were no outbreaks of scurvy or other disease. On three occasions seamen were given lashes and would have needed the surgeon's attention. He and his mate would not have been overburdened with work.

It must have been then that Park learnt something about astronomy and the methods of determining latitude and longitude. He must also have had time to read the Edinburgh Professor Dugald Stewart's first major work, *Elements of the Philosophy of the Human Mind*, Part I.

Park had asked Alexander Anderson about its 'religious character', but
reading it he would have found none. However, he probably did find
such enlightened reflection on human nature very much to his taste.

On 9 May, when in latitude 6°23' north, Park had his first experience of a tropical storm, with lightning and heavy rain. (The rains
usually come a month later in the regions where he subsequently
travelled on land, farther north, but perhaps this early experience, and
the date, remained in his mind.) Otherwise it was an uneventful
voyage out. Most of the convoy of nine East India ships and seven
naval escorts remained together until it rounded South Africa and
headed for India, when the *Worcester* and another small ship, the
Minerva, sailed on eastwards. The ship's guns were frequently exercised but never had to be used in earnest. The voyagers saw nothing
but ocean, hardly even a sail either friendly or hostile, outside the
convoy, until they sighted Christmas Island on the final northward leg
of their journey. On 22 August 1793 they reached their destination,
Bencoolen, on the south-west coast of Sumatra.

The British East India Company had occupied Bencoolen, undis-
puted by the Dutch, since 1685. There was a Lieutenant-Governor
commanding its Fort Marlborough, but essentially it was a staging-
post, unprofitable in itself, on the way to China. Its name comes from
a Malay word, *Bankalau*, meaning 'The Dead Land'. The anchorage
to which the ship soon moved, Rat Island, sounds equally insalubrious.
In 1824 Britain exchanged Bencoolen and another outpost with the
Dutch, for Singapore, Malacca, and £100,000 in cash; surely one of
the most profitable exchanges in British imperial history.

The cargo was unloaded and replaced with goods for the Company
and some for Captain John Hall personally, the latter being a recognized captain's perquisite at the time. The return cargo was mainly
pepper and cassia (senna) but it also included arrack, the oriental spirit
distilled from coco-palm sap, which Smollett's novel *Roderick Random*
shows to have been available in London taverns. Being at leisure,
Park occupied himself in seeking out and recording plants and fishes
not yet scientifically known.

After quitting Bencoolen on 14 November 1793 the party met
some dangerous squalls but then continued on its way without incident
to the small Atlantic island of St. Helena, which was occupied by the
East India Company up to 1834, and had not, by the time of Park's
visit, achieved fame by housing Napoleon in exile. In the month they

spent there the main excitement came when a runaway sailor was caught after a day and given twelve lashes. A convoy joining them again, they sailed on 18 February 1794 via Portsmouth back to Gravesend, where Captain Hall and his crew disembarked on 2 May.

A letter from Park to his brother Alexander written on 20 May tells us:

'Dear Brother – When I arrived in London it required a great effort before I could lift the knocker of Mr. Dickson's door; I felt the same sensation I suppose as a criminal feels when the verdict of the Jury is open and Death or Life hangs on the next minute. Peggy's Gown told me the secret before she opened her mouth and as I had long expected it, I was prepared. The melancholy news, and the sudden change, from the Bustle of a sea life to the stillness of the fire side, wrought so powerfully on my mind that I found no desire to do any thing. I remained a mere inactive lump and stared about me as if I had newly come into the world. It was owing to this dozing state that I have wrote only one letter since my return. I was happy to hear that you had got your present situation, fortune became freinds with you all at once and she has been pretty favourable to me by easing me of the intolerable load of £50 yet I cannot Guess how she may behave in future. The Worcester and the other three ships are to go out this season but as the same surgeons go in them, there is no preferment. I have, however, got Sir Joseph's word that if I wish to travel he will apply to the African Association and . . . I am to hire a trader to go with me to Tombuctoo and back again . . .'[1]

The anticipated but still melancholy news was of the death of his father, at the age of seventy-nine. It had occurred on 22 May 1793 before Park had even crossed the Equator on the way out. His sister Margaret was still wearing mourning clothes nearly a year later. Alexander had had the good fortune to get a position as a Writer or attorney back home in Selkirk. As Mungo's gross pay for the fourteen and a half months he had been away was £36. 5s. 0d., and after deducting the £10 advance and some other small amounts he was left with a mere £25. 6s. 2d., we cannot tell how he came to be relieved of the 'intolerable load' of £50! He was rather impatient for preferment: his brother Adam later had to wait until his third voyage before being promoted to full surgeon.[2]

The last part of his letter shows that, recovering from his 'dozing state', he lost little time in tendering his compliments to Sir Joseph Banks, together with some specimens of plants and some watercolours, with anatomical descriptions, of twenty species of fish that he had

observed at Bencoolen. The watercolours are now housed in the British
Museum of Natural History in South Kensington, London, some
bearing comments in Park's own hand, such as 'a good figure' or 'very
indifferent'. Impressed, Banks quickly saw in Park a possible African
traveller.

Having collected his pay on 20 May 1794, Park went home to see
his widowed mother at Selkirk. The members of the family were, apart
from Margaret Dickson in London, still within easy visiting distance of
each other. In 1793 Jean had married a Mr. Andrew Thomson in
the neighbouring parish of Ashkirk, leaving only the youngest sister,
Isobel, at home. With Archibald on another farm at Selkirk, Mungo
committed as either a surgeon or a traveller, and Alexander as a
Writer, it fell to the fourth son John to take over the farm and support
his mother. The youngest living brother, Adam, was just about to
begin the surgeons' course at Edinburgh, probably together with the
second Anderson boy, John (who afterwards married Isobel Park in
1807, but died two years later). Alexander Anderson had already had
a year working with his father as a qualified surgeon. Allison was
growing up, having reached the age of fourteen. Mungo was a frequent
visitor to the Revd. Dr. Lawson's Manse too, just across the street from
the Andersons' house. Cigars, of which both were fond, accompanied
their conversations about distant places.

Under Mungo's father's will, made in 1791, each of the brothers
except Archibald was to receive £400, and the sisters £150 each.
Mungo's mother was to be paid £15 every year, representing the
interest on about £300. The residue, doubtless expected to be the
largest share, was to go to Archibald, who was also the executor. It
seems, therefore, that Mungo Park senior must have estimated his
wealth at around £3,000. This was certainly not the estate of a poor
man at that date. Much of the capital must have been tied up in farm
stock; over ten years later, when making his own will, Mungo listed
among his assets: 'Due to me from my brother Archibald such money
as I have not yet received of the sum left me by my Father's Last
Will.'[3]

Even today, 'Go to Timbuktu!' is easier said than done. When
Mungo broke the news of his plans at home, the reaction was evidently
just what might be expected. This came out some years later when
James Dickson, denying that he had discussed new ideas of travelling
with Mungo, told Banks, '... when he went to Africa some of his

friends was so imprudent as to say I was the cause of him being sacrificed, for they were sure he would never return . . .'⁴ If his later behaviour may be taken as a guide, Mungo would have crossly rejected attempts to dissuade him. He might have recognized the force of the arguments; but he would not have wavered, except for a brief moment.

After only a few weeks at home, he returned to London to pursue the proposal for an African journey. The mistake in the dating of his first voyage has led to the supposition that after it he idled for a year in London, neglecting his family at home. Now it can be seen that he had barely had time to look around before he found a baited hook dangling before him. His voyage to Sumatra had pointed him in the direction most congenial to him, where he could find scope for his ambition – travel with a scientific purpose.

CHAPTER V

'Rescuing the age from a charge of ignorance'

The founding of the African Association

—— ᖹᖱᖱ ——

The African Association which now entered Park's life was initiated by twelve well-to-do gentlemen, including peers, baronets, members of Parliament, a retired general, and a bishop. The two who took the lead and became its officers were Henry Beaufoy, M.P., the Secretary, and Sir Joseph Banks, the Treasurer. Originally members of a group called the Saturdays Club, the twelve used to dine together at St. Alban's Tavern in London. The discussions were probably intellectually distinguished, six of them being Fellows of the Royal Society, but at first they showed little concern with Africa, although Banks had touched at Cape Town on his voyage with Captain Cook, and Beaufoy, as befitted the son of a Quaker wine-merchant, supported the movement to abolish the slave trade. At a meeting held on 9 June 1788, their interest in Africa passed beyond dinner-table talk to a belief that something should be done, and done by themselves. A surprising resolution was passed:

'That as no species of information is more ardently desired, or more generally useful, than that which improves the science of Geography; and as the vast Continent of Africa, notwithstanding the efforts of the Antients, and the wishes of the Moderns, is still in a great measure unexplored, the Members of this Club do form themselves into an Association for Promoting the Discovery of the Inland Parts of that Quarter of the World.'

A constitution was at once adopted. Three members were elected to form a committee together with the officers, and the annual subscription was set at five guineas. The Association's membership grew to 95 by 1790. These included some Abolitionists, with their leader William Wilberforce, but also members opposed to that cause and, coincidentally, the Park family's landlord, the Duke of Buccleuch. This growth created a sounding-board for the Association amongst the governing aristocracy.

A Plan of the Association, written by Beaufoy for publication in 1790, probably reflects the general course of the original discussions. Following Captain Cook's remarkable voyages, it said, little remained to be learnt about the oceans except the Poles, while journeys were then in progress, or had recently been made, which would open to view large areas previously unvisited in Asia, North America, southern Africa, and Ethiopia. Least known in Europe was the heart of Africa, for '. . . the map of its Interior is still but a wide extended blank, on which the Geographer, on the authority of Leo Africanus, and of the Xeriff Edrissi the Nubian Author, has traced, with a hesitating hand, a few names of unexplored rivers and of uncertain nations.' Continuing in this fine style Beaufoy pronounced, '. . . that ignorance must be considered as a degree of reproach upon the present age. Sensible of this stigma, and desirous of rescuing the age from a charge of ignorance which, in other respects, belongs so little to its character . . .' this small group had decided to take action.

The Association was not the first in this field. Ancient Carthaginians, Romans, and Greeks (or people known to them) on rare occasions possibly crossed the Sahara Desert as far as the river Niger. Then the Arab conquest of Christian North Africa interposed a barrier at least as formidable as the desert to European ingress. The Arabs themselves made contacts across the desert, largely so as to trade in slaves and gold, but also carrying their religion with them. Their writers and geographers compiled what information they could obtain on the 'Sudan', the country of the blacks, and these accounts will have a part in this story.

Quite large numbers of Europeans served in Moroccan armies that crossed to the Niger, either as *renegados* (Muslim converts) or as captive slaves; seventeenth-century Borno also had Christian slaves serving in its army. Occasionally free men, traders or priests, managed to make the crossing, like two Italian fathers who reached Katsina: they were unable to preach, and died there, early in the eighteenth century. The scanty records left by some of these individuals have been rediscovered in recent times.

In the fifteenth century Portuguese vessels followed in the Carthaginians' wake round the west coast, seeking to outflank the North African states and to find the elusive sources of the gold that came across the desert to Europe. They also wanted to find a route to India, and to see the court of Prester John, the Christian king who

was said to rule in the midst of Africa. They twice sent embassies far
inland to the Emperor of Mali and to other states, and remains of
Portuguese cannon have been found at Gao on the Niger. They may
have visited the gold-bearing country of Bambuk, between the rivers
Senegal and Faleme, probably part of the original 'Wangara', of which
more will be heard later.[1] So secretive were the Portuguese, and so
limited are the writings they have left, that, although they must have
learnt much about the interior, including the river Niger, only the
barest facts about their efforts are known.

The coastal forests and the mountains of Sierra Leone and Guinea
were found to pose obstacles from the south, but these obstacles were
not so intimidating as fevers and other diseases that took a terrible toll
of European lives, worse than in other tropical areas. On the west
coast only two usable rivers of any length were found, the Senegal and
the Gambia. Their use came to be monopolized by the French and the
British respectively; these slowly ousted the Portugusee, who then
concentrated on southern Africa. Finding no rich and easily accessible
gold and silver to match Peru's or Mexico's, and no wealth of spices
comparable to those of the Indies, the Europeans fell back on trading
along the coasts and rivers. From the Senegambia, as the region
around the two rivers became known, they conducted the notorious
slave trade, an average of 2,000 slaves a year being exported for most
of the eighteenth century, in addition to a much larger number bought
farther south. Gold was bought from the Gold Coast (the modern
Republic of Ghana); and gum, ivory, beeswax, and lesser articles came
from the Senegambia. In return the Europeans sold iron bars, cloth,
salt, tobacco, guns, alcohol, beads, trinkets, and a variety of other
things. None of this trade entailed travelling inland, and it did not
support a body approaching the East India Company in wealth and
influence. A succession of companies set up under the aegis of the
British and French governments flourished briefly, had long periods
of stagnation, and were eventually abolished and replaced.

Securely ensconced as middlemen were the coastal peoples, who discouraged all European inquisitiveness about the interior. They kept
their secrets, such as the sources of their gold, as they had kept them
from the Arabs. The European traders in the Niger delta had no idea
that beyond its tangled creeks their goods, and some knowledge of
their language, had preceded them inland into a great river basin (as
the Lander brothers were to discover in 1830). Ignorance and dread

discouraged European penetration inland, and without such penetration, the ignorance was invincible.

Curiosity and the lure of wealth did occasionally incite attempts. In 1621 Captain Richard Jobson led a small boat party well over 300 miles up the Gambia into its shallow reaches. Proudly he sought not slaves but gold, purchasing some in exchange for salt. He heard exciting tales of the golden trade of the Moors inland, where there was 'a great Towne above, the houses whereof are covered onely with gold', four months' return journey away. Perhaps the London merchants found his profit account less fascinating than his narrative account, for they did nothing more. Cornelius Hodges, from the river Gambia in 1689, and the French from the river Senegal several times in the early eighteenth century, actually saw the gold workings in Bambuk, but had to withdraw because of famine and local hostility. Between Bambuk and the Gambia lay Bondu, made known by the high-born freed slave Job ben Solomon, as he was called when being fêted in England in 1733–4. On ben Solomon's return home, publicized in 1738 by Francis Moore in a good description of the Gambia region, an English trader accompanied him to Bondu. Over some years there were further visits to Bondu and probably to Bambuk as well, but these contacts gradually lapsed. A solitary and unknown Englishman spent nearly two years in Bambuk not long before Park's time, but of organized action there was none.[2]

Similarly, the French traded along, and described, the lower Senegal up to its junction with the river Faleme in the country of Galam or Kajaaga, in which they established their Fort St. Joseph soon after 1700. They were familiar with Bambuk, and they knew a little by hearsay of Khasso. Beyond that, there were merely vague reports of the existence of cities like Jenne and of a state called Bambara, both near a river perhaps flowing eastwards.[3] Only the French published anything on Galam and Bambuk, but English translations became available, and an increasing sale for such travel books in the second half of the eighteenth century reflected popular interest.

Official and commercial interests in the Senegambia were at their lowest ebb in the last decade of the century. The British Company of Merchants Trading to Africa had by then abandoned the Gambia, withdrawing from its only fort on a tiny sandbank called James Island near the river's mouth, the scene of numerous miniature battles earlier in the century. There remained a few individual traders working on their own account, and existing on the sufferance of the African rulers. The slave trade there was less than a quarter of what it had been,[4] and the traders were lucky if they saw more than three small British ships in a year, while their combined turnover averaged only £20,000. The new British possession of Freetown in Sierra Leone, purchased in 1791 as a settlement for freed slaves and governed by a company, could not then exert much influence. The bulk of the slave trade having moved permanently to a zone stretching southwards from the Niger delta, trade had diminished on the Gold Coast and in neighbouring areas as well. These areas had earlier attracted the literary talents of men of several nationalities, who had described the countries accessible from the coast, but written little on the interior. In the period we are concerned with, the men of the Company of Merchants seem to have looked hardly at all beyond their castle walls.

By 1790 the French in Senegambia were a shade more strongly placed than the British. True, they had lost the Senegal to Britain in 1758, and the British had then combined the few posts they chose to occupy, and their own Gambian hamlets, into the largely fictive Crown Colony of Senegambia, equipped with a Governor and his panoply. Later, in 1779, when they were helping the rebellious American colonists to defeat Britain, the French recovered the Senegal, but did not trouble to re-occupy permanently Fort St. Joseph and other stations up-river. They did, however, re-enter a single post on the Gambia, also the fortified isle of St. Louis in the mouth of the Senegal and, midway between the two rivers, the rocky offshore island and fortress of Gorée. This stands at the entrance to what is now Dakar harbour, and it had been French since 1677, apart from two short British occupations, the most recent having been from 1779 to 1783. The superiority of the French position was, however, very modest. The long-continued fights over the external trade of this area had, in the event, nearly killed that trade for both countries, and neither of them seemed likely to make further attempts to move inland.

Where the capitalists with their narrow concentration on slaves and gold had failed, aristocratic intellectuals were to prove more successful. The merchants had looked for a quick, certain, and accountable return on their outlay; the members of the African Association were prepared to back a broader and more speculative venture, in line with the new ideas sweeping through Europe and overflowing beyond it. On one commodity they sought for its own sake, knowledge, a handsome return was almost certain if any of their travellers survived to tell his tale, but knowledge was expected to open new commercial opportunities as well. This is shown by the resolution setting up the Association, and also by a provision in its constitution, that the Committee need only disclose even to the other members such information as might, 'without endangering the object of their Association, be made public'.

Banks was not immune to the interest in gold, as will be seen later. Another Committee member, Sir John Sinclair, is on record as writing of Timbuktu, '... gold is there so plentiful as to adorn even the slaves ... If we could get our manufactures into that country we should soon have gold enough.'[5] Their ambition was, however, more national than personal, and it is doubtful whether any member of the Association ever profited by its activities. The botanist Banks was also interested in the natural products growing, or capable of being introduced and grown, in the 'tropical exuberance' of African vegetation, and he had already some slight contacts with botanical work in various parts of Africa. Thoughts were beginning to surface that a trade in such products might be of mutual benefit to Europe and Africa, and be preferable to transporting Africa's manpower across the Atlantic to work plantations. The Association never involved itself either way in the Abolition issue, or with the impulse of evangelization in Africa just beginning to stir, but its interests were broadly benelovent.

Thus Beaufoy in 1790, after surveying what had so far been learnt, and making an optimistic forecast of the trade possibilities, ended by declaring that:

'... while the contemplation of national interests, and of the still more extended interests of philosophy, directs their [the Association's] efforts and animates their hopes, they cannot be indifferent to the reflection, that in the pursuit of these advantages, and by means as peaceable as the purposes are just, the conveniences of civil life, the benefits of the mechanic and manufacturing arts, the attainments of science, the energies of the cultivated mind, and the elevation of the human character, may in some degree be imparted to nations hitherto consigned to hopeless barbarism and uniform contempt.'

There was one other reason why the Association felt freer to move than the commercial interests. The latter had sent out relatively large and costly expeditions to explore inland. The Association's novel plan was to send one man travelling light, for, as a matter of policy, 'the Committee are persuaded, that in such an Undertaking Poverty is a better protection than Wealth', and the individual traveller would not be expected to earn his keep. Combining this with the belief in all things working together for good, with no divergence between the pursuits of knowledge, ethics, and mutual benefit, and fortified by the sense of cultural superiority then felt by even the most liberal minds in Britain, the Association was therefore enabled to take a new view of the possible advantages of exploration inland, as against the costs and obstacles. It remains to see how far they had advanced before they found in Mungo Park a supreme optimist, with scientific interests attuned to their own.

CHAPTER VI

'Using materials of so coarse a kind'

The early years of the African Association

——— ∞ ———

'Naturally anxious for the speedy attainment of the important object thus recommended,' Beaufoy said, '. . . the Managers proceeded with the utmost ardour to the immediate execution of the Plan.' Only four days after being formed in June 1788, the Committee approached its first traveller, Mr. Simon Lucas, the Oriental Interpreter to the British Government. He had previously spent three years in Morocco as a slave and, after his liberation, another sixteen years as British Vice-Consul. His experience and his knowledge of Arabic fitted him for an attempt from the north coast of Africa. As Park and others were to find, Muslim sensitivities dating back over a thousand years of conflicts with the Christians, of invasions and counter-invasions, could easily be aroused by pressure on an old sore. Traders and pilgrims carried news of such happenings even to remote corners of the Muslim world. For much of the time, however, relations between them were characterized by what we would call 'peaceful co-existence'. At that time there were friendly relations with the Karamanli dynasty ruling Tripoli, and it was hoped that this would prove a satisfactory starting-point. Lucas set off in August 1788.

Already another traveller had been despatched. He was an American, John Ledyard, who had spent some years with the American Indians, then had sailed round the world under Captain Cook. He had just journeyed on foot in winter from Sweden through Finland into Russia, then right across Siberia, meaning to sail to America and be the first to cross that continent. The Empress's long reach had had him brought back, in winter again, and ejected from Russia's western frontier in a penniless state. Knowing Banks, he was able to borrow small sums in his name to get back to England. Banks promptly suggested that he might like to travel in Africa, and Ledyard replied that he had had just that in mind for his next journey. Beaufoy asked him when he would be ready to go, and he said, 'Tomorrow morning.'

He set off on 30 June 1788, to go to Egypt, then south to Nubia, and westwards across Africa.

From Cairo he was able to send back some information about trade routes southwards and westwards as far as Timbuktu, gathered from enquiries made in the slave market and elsewhere. He got no further, for he gave himself an overdose of acid of vitriol to treat a bilious complaint, followed by a strong tartar emetic, and died in agony. Had this impetuous and courageous man survived, there might have been no cause for Mungo Park's journeys.

In Tripoli Lucas obtained the Bashaw's goodwill, but this was of little help for reaching the interior. His journey with a caravan took him along the coast only as far as Mesurata, from where he turned back because of troubles inland. He never left the coast, but at Mesurata he heard from an elderly Sharif called Imhammed a detailed account of Fezzan in southern Libya, of Borno and 'Cashna' (Katsina) beyond the desert, with a more general description of other Negro countries south of the Niger.

When presenting a report to the Association in 1790 Beaufoy was fortified by apparent confirmation from other sources. He cited a Moroccan called Ben Ali who was in London in 1788 but who had disappeared the next year. Ben Ali's briefer accounts of Katsina and Borno tallied with Imhammed's. The Government had also obtained and published reports from its consuls in Tangier and Tunis, and Consul Magra in Tunis wrote to Beaufoy too. They gave details of trade routes from Morocco to Timbuktu, and from Tunis through Katsina right down to the Bight of Benin.

Progress was being made but still only a few names of unexplored rivers and uncertain nations could be traced on a blank map. Even on the coastal outline, it was only just becoming possible to situate places accurately. The main problems were made clear in a *Construction of the Map of Africa* included in the 1790 Report. The writer, Major James Rennell, drew heavily on Herodotus, the Greek author of the fifth century B.C., about whom he had written a book, and on other classical Greek and Roman authors. It was partly the ancients' superior knowledge of north Africa which made Rennell's contemporaries feel the 'stigma' which the Association sought to remove.

Rennell had studied African geography after an injury forced his premature retirement from the post of Surveyor-General of Bengal, which he had obtained at the age of twenty-two and had held for thirteen years, producing the best map of India to date. Accepted as the leading British authority on Africa, he was made an honorary member of the African Association. In this capacity, though he often went badly astray in his attempts to construct an African geography, he usually gave very sane advice, which was not invariably followed.

Almost the only contribution of the ancients to a knowledge of Africa south of the Sahara was to describe a great river flowing from the west across the continent until it joined the Nile. Some Romans gave it the name 'Nigir', thought possibly to derive from a Berber word, *N-ger-n-gereo*, 'river of rivers'. After them, Rennell had largely to rely on imperfect texts of the two mediaeval Arabic writers whom Beaufoy had cited as 'Leo Africanus and the Xeriff Edrissi'. The more informative Ibn Battuta and al-Sadi of Timbuktu were not yet known in Europe.

Interpreting their descriptions was difficult. They reckoned distances in numbers of days of travelling, and their indications of direction were often vague. It was hard to know whether or not apparently similar names were really the same. The task was more like that of an expert decipherer, trying to crack a difficult code from limited clues, than scientific geography. Rennell was also misled by his almost total ignorance of the rise and fall of three great empires in the space of over six centuries since Idrisi had written.

The Ghana Empire, lying between the upper Niger and the desert (far to the north of the present Republic of Ghana), was already in decline when the Sharif al-Idrisi wrote his compilation of African geography, from other people's accounts, for the Norman King Roger II of Sicily in 1154. Within a hundred years it had been absorbed into the much larger Empire of Mali, roughly corresponding to the modern republic of that name. Tales of the pilgrimage of its fourteenth-century ruler Mansa Musa, disbursing fabulous quantities of gold in Cairo on the way, led to its appearing on European maps, usually as Melle. Its territory included the new city of Timbuktu, and for a time it stretched further down-river to Gao.

Leo Africanus, a Moor born in Granada about the time it fell to Ferdinand and Isabella of Spain in 1492, visited Timbuktu when Mali was already being eclipsed by a new empire, known to us as the Songhai Empire. This had arisen from Gao and had quickly captured Timbuktu and much of northern Mali. He wrote about West Africa in 1526 for his patron Pope Leo X, after he had been captured by

Christian pirates and converted. Songhai in its turn came to an abrupt
end in 1591, when it was shattered by a Moroccan invasion across
the desert, led by a young Spanish eunuch, with many of his compatriots in his army. The invaders' descendants by local marriages,
soon ruling independently of Morocco, managed to hold only a much
more limited territory for a few hundred miles along the river on
either side of Timbuktu, and even that gradually shrank, while Mali
continued to suffer a protracted disintegration.

Leo said he had also visited a group of states further to the east, including Kano and Katsina, which are in the north of present-day
Nigeria. What really threw out the European geographers of the eighteenth century, first the Frenchmen Delisle and d'Anville, and then
Rennell, was that Leo had mysteriously included in this group a state
called Wangara, producing gold, near Kano and, as his text indicated,
on its eastern side. Wangara had been marked as the main gold-
producing area ever since Idrisi had written, placing it just east of
Ghana. The temptation was therefore strong to equate Idrisi's Ghana
with Leo's Kano, especially as Idrisi's estimates of distance from the
upper Nile seemed to locate Ghana nearly half-way across Africa
from west to east, just about where Leo placed Kano. They were in
reality a thousand miles apart. Both d'Anville and Rennell fell for this
temptation. To clinch matters, Lucas's informant identified as the same
kingdom under alternative names Idrisi's Kanem and Leo's Borno,*
which both writers had placed to the east of Wangara.

This informant, the Sharif Imhammed, had described Borno as
lying east of south from Tripoli, with Katsina to its west. He was
corroborated in essentials by Ben Ali, interviewed in London, and by
the consuls' reports. That he had some genuine knowledge is shown
by his reciting numerals and some other words which recognizably
belong to these countries' respective languages. Borno was a prosperous
agricultural country, its black inhabitants being well governed under
a rule of law, with regular trade connections to north Africa, and substantial armed forces. Katsina was similar but, he said, less prosperous.
Optimistically, Beaufoy envisaged a population of a hundred millions
there.

The main effect of Rennell's construction was to shift all the prin-

---

* Kanem, the original part of the empire before its centre moved westwards about
A.D. 1400, was by 1790 only loosely attached to it.

cipal states and the centre of interest far to the east. So much so that in his 1790 essay and on his map he made not the least use of the information that had been gathered in Senegambia, beyond showing the country that the French called Galam half-way up the Senegal. To the west of Timbuktu none of the other countries that Park would traverse, and no single town that he would visit, featured even as a name, rightly or wrongly placed. It was a wide blank indeed! In the whole interior of West Africa only one town, the elusive Timbuktu, was nearly correctly situated, as bearings on it could be obtained along several routes. Perhaps, to be charitable, we should allow that Kano and Katsina were also not excessively displaced to the north-east; as Rennell said, '. . . in using materials of so coarse a kind, trifles must not be regarded'! There was no place on his map for Mali, and Gao appeared only as a vaguely marked country, Gagoo, south of the Niger.

This eastward shift of interest was heightened when another Moroccan, called Shabeni, volunteered information in London soon after Rennell had written in 1790. He introduced to Europe a new name, 'Housa', which he said was a thriving empire, five easy days' travelling along the river to the south-east of Timbuktu. Soon the consuls' reports were confirming its existence. It was later learnt that Hausa is basically the name of a language and of the people who speak it, who inhabit a group of states including Kano, Katsina, and Zaria, but Leo Africanus had never used the word. In 1790 it seemed to be a separate state in uncertain relation to them.

The rest of what Shabeni said was a farrago of second-hand titbits and, not to put too fine a point on it, nonsense. A Muslim Arab who had lived years in these places could not truthfully report that Timbuktu had no mosques or regular worship, that it produced some of the ploughs it used, that the river journey from there to 'Housa' was short, placid, and busy with traffic, that neither place used the Arabic script, or that 'Housa' bordered on countries now known to be all to the west and south of Timbuktu. The Association could not of course check this at the time, and anyway the one item 'Housa' was genuine enough and important.

There was another way in which Idrisi and Leo had combined to confuse issues. Both said that the river Niger came from the east. Idrisi said it rose from the same Mountains of the Moon as contained the source of the Nile, and Leo said it came from a lake in the desert. Leo even said he had travelled for hundreds of miles down it going

west on his way to Mali! At its western end it flowed into the Atlantic
Ocean. European maps up to about 1750 generally showed it emerging
as the Senegal or the Gambia, or dividing between them. After that
date maps were influenced by d'Anville, who, using rather confused
information from the French on the Senegal, had concluded that the
rivers were separate, the Niger starting near the source of the Senegal,
south-west of Timbuktu, but flowing *eastwards* past that city to end
somewhere in the desert.

Had the manuscripts of Ibn Battuta's travels been known then, it
would have been seen that he described the Niger as flowing east. This
great traveller, who had visited, amongst many other countries, East
Africa, India, and China, made his last journey in 1352 to the western
Sudan, a hundred and fifty years before Leo Africanus. He had been
to the capital of Mali on the Niger, and although he travelled by land
to Timbuktu and Gao before returning northwards across the desert
to his home at Tangier, he described the river's course that far correctly
– unlike Leo – even though he was mistaken in believing that further
east it became the Nile. However, not only was he unknown in
Europe until the 1820s, but his view had not prevailed even in the
Arabic world. Leo Africanus did not seem to know of his account of
the area, although he did refer to some other earlier writers. The
Sharif Imhammed and Ben Ali in 1789 both maintained that the river
flowed westwards. In the face of this testimony, Rennell was reduced
to showing the Niger on his map following d'Anville's conjectured
course but in the opposite direction, from east to west, beginning and
ending nowhere in particular.

It was obvious that only by tracing this river could the puzzle be
made to fall into place. There was reason to think, moreover, that the
river's course would lead to the main centres of population. Even less
was known of the peoples of the interior than of their countries. Wild
speculations based on the slenderest facts ranged from idealistic hopes
nursed by the Swedenborgians of finding a new light for the world
inside Africa, to the slavers' belief that, in the conditions there, 'the
Africans ought to be thankful that they had been carried safe into the
British colonies'.[1]

It is surprising that the Association allowed its next expedition into
the interior to set off from the Gambia, to make its way *up-stream*
along the Niger, when all the main interest was focused beyond Timbuktu, and the Association's instructions laid emphasis on finding 'a

considerable Empire, distinguished by the name of *Houssa*'. The choice was presumably dictated by the previous experience of the new volunteer, Major Daniel Houghton. He had been on an official mission to Morocco in 1772, and from 1779 to 1783 he was Fort Major on Gorée, learning something of local languages. After that he had unsuccessfully offered his services to the Government for exploration beyond the Gambia, and now he renewed his offer, this time to the Association.

He sailed from Plymouth in October 1790. At Jonkakonda on the Gambia he overheard African traders' wives talk of a plot on his life. Hastily escaping up-river, he made the acquaintance of a trader called Dr. John Laidley, and went on to Medina, the capital of a kingdom named Woolli (Wuli) north of the river. The hospitable king wanted him to build a trading fort at Fattetenda on the Gambia. The impoverished Houghton would have liked to settle there; it was a pleasant spot where one could live for £10 a year, and where a Captain Littleton had saved enough in four years to retire. He had to go on, however, after losing much of his gear in a fire at Medina and more with an absconding interpreter. Bondu was not interested in going beyond its existing trade with the Gambia, and he got a cold reception there. In Bambuk, on the other hand, which had just lost a stretch of territory to Bondu, there was an eagerness for trade, especially in arms.

While there he met a Sharif from Timbuktu whom he had known in Morocco. From him he learnt that '. . . in the river I am going to explore, *they have decked vessels, with masts, with which they carry on trade from Tombuctoo* eastward, *to the centre of Africa*. I mean to embark in one of them from Genne in Bambara to Tombuctoo.' This was the most important item of information sent back by Houghton, but he also learnt the bare names of some places on both a northern and a southern route from Bambuk to Timbuktu. The latter included Bamacoo (could this be the same as Bambuk, Rennell wondered?), Segu and Yamina, then Genne 'the capital of Bambara', after which the river went north to Timbuktu and then turned eastwards.

Rennell produced a new *Elucidations of the African Geography* in 1793, reconciling Houghton's information with that of d'Anville and the consuls' reports, and rightly leaving Shabeni's account on one side. Of course he had to reverse his idea of which way the Niger flowed, and he admitted to being still in the dark how it ended. Rennell discounted the belief, originally stated by Herodotus and shared by

Houghton, that it joined the Nile. All one could say was that Housa seemed to be a country, or a city, or both, near the river a few days' journey south or south-east of Timbuktu. After that, who knew?

The last brief note received from Houghton, dated 1 September 1791, came from a place called Simbing beyond Bambuk: 'Major Houghton's compliments to Dr. Laidley, is in good health on his way to Tombuctoo, robbed of all his goods by Fenda Bucar's son.' Later Laidley received reports of his death, unclear as to the location or the circumstances. The Association held back any announcement, but the continued silence inevitably eroded the euphoria with which Houghton's earlier reports had been received. Another brave man had died; again, if this one had been successful, Park might never have travelled in Africa.

The early euphoria had led the Association's General Meeting in 1792 to empower the Committee to ask the Government to take steps to follow up Houghton's discoveries. By the following May a young man, James Willis, had been found who was keen to be appointed Consul in that area. The Association then voted more explicitly:

'That as there is reason to believe that an extensive and lucrative Trade from Great Britain may be opened by the way of the Gambia and the Niger ... [which] would equally promote the Interests of the Public and facilitate the Geographical Improvements that are the peculiar objects of this Association. The Committee be requested ...' to propose to the Government '... at least the Experimental and Temporary Appointment of a Consul to Senegambia.'

This proposal was accepted, and Willis was appointed Consul-General in April 1794. He would be based, with a garrison of fifty troops and a small armed ship, at Fattetenda, which had delighted Houghton so much. He was to open communications to the Niger, by then reckoned to be only 350 miles from the upper Gambia, and mistakenly believed to be bordered by Bambuk. In taking this novel decision the Government presumably saw an opportunity to outflank the Senegal interests of France, by then at war with Britain.

By invoking Government action the African Association was raising its activities to a new plane. It had managed, even on the basis of its partial early successes, in which two men had died and one had been unable to leave the coastline, to break through previous indifference.

All the same, an enormous ignorance about the interior remained, which Willis, tied to his consular base, could tackle only in part. Only an eyewitness could resolve the confusion still persisting over the course and the termination of the Niger, and if another suitable candidate appeared who was willing to take the risks involved, the Association still had much for him to do. It was therefore a superb although unplanned piece of timing that Mungo Park should have returned from Bencoolen just when matters had reached this point and, on hearing from Banks what was afoot, offered his services to the Association.

CHAPTER VII

'It is a short expedition'

Park's departure

——— ഇ ———

Park's offer of his services was especially timely, for the 1794 General Meeting of the African Association was to be held on 31 May. Beaufoy was therefore able to announce the offer less than a month after Park's return from Bencoolen. No definite commitment was made at that stage, but the Committee was authorized to proceed.

The reasons for his interest come out at the end of the letter to his brother Alexander, partly quoted in Chapter IV:

'I have, however, got Sir Joseph's word that if I wish to travel he will apply to the African Association and I shall go out with thier Consul to Fort St. Joseph on the river Gambia where I am to hire a trader to go with me to Tombuctoo and back again. The Association pays for every thing and they will allow *200* Guineas to the trader, who goes as my guide and interpreter, when we return to Fort St. Joseph. I shall write more particularly in my next but as it is a short expedition and will give me an opportunity of coming to Scotland before I set off, besides the hopes of Distinguishing myself, for if I succeed I shall acquire a greater name than any (man?) ever did! and at present I see no reasonable objection against accepting it . . .'

Not only was his prose rather tangled, but his facts were awry: it was of course the Government's Consul, not the Association's, and Fort St. Joseph lay up the Senegal, while James Island Fort was in the Gambia.

Banks did not conceal from him the hazards of the journey and the fears that Houghton was dead, but Park's reaction was given in his *Travels*:

'But this intelligence, instead of deterring me from my purpose, animated me to persist in the offer of my services with the greater solicitude. I had a passionate desire to examine into the productions of a country so little known; and to become experimentally acquainted with the modes of life, and character of the natives. I knew that I was able to bear fatigue; and I relied on my youth, and the strength of my constitution, to preserve me from the effects of the climate. The salary which the Committee allowed was sufficiently large, and I made no stipulation for future reward. If I should perish in my journey, I was willing that my hopes and expectations should perish with me; and if I should succeed in rendering the geography of Africa more familiar to my countrymen, and in opening to their ambition and industry new sources of wealth, and new channels of commerce, I knew that I was in the hands of men of honour, who would not fail to bestow that remuneration which my successful services should appear to them to merit.'

Seized by this passion for travel with a scientific and commercial objective, he set aside any thoughts of practising as a surgeon. For himself he sought not wealth but fame, a fame which he was prepared to earn by arduous achievement and at the risk of his life. He must have been more impressed by how far Houghton had got than by his unfortunate end. It was presumably in relation to other travellers such as Houghton or James Bruce (whose account of his travels in Ethiopia had been published in 1790) that he made the extraordinary statement about gaining 'a greater name than any man ever did', not thinking of, for example, Caesar, Shakespeare, or other great names in unrelated fields. What is most surprising is the casual statement, 'It is a short expedition'! It was already known to be over a thousand miles from the Gambia each way. His unusually deep and innate optimism, then first glimpsed, was to enable him to go on when others would have given up hope and turned back or collapsed.

After returning to London from Scotland he was interviewed on 23 July by Banks and Beaufoy. Although he had neither the African experience of Lucas and Houghton nor Ledyard's record of tough travelling, his strength of will must have shown through the mild exterior: '. . . the Committee, finding him sufficiently instructed in the use of Hadley's quadrant to make the necessary observations; geographer enough to trace out his path through the Wilderness, and not unacquainted with natural history, accepted his offer.'

He was to go with Consul-General Willis to Fattetenda, beginning in September or October 1794. For the first time the Association offered to pay a traveller; he was to have 7s. 6d. a day from 1 August until he left the Gambia for the interior, and then double pay for up to two years in Africa, with £200 allotted for outfit. This was a distinct rise on the 50s. a month he had received as Surgeon's Mate, but he could not be considered overpaid for what he was taking on.

October came and went, and still Willis was not ready. He had put the recruitment of soldiers to escort him, and some money, in the hands of a Captain Barbauld, who proved to be readier with excuses than results. When Beaufoy eventually persuaded Willis to take over recruitment himself things began to move, but then Willis decided he needed a second ship, and further delays ensued.

While waiting, Park prepared and read to the Linnean Society on 4 November a paper about eight of the species of fish he had observed in Sumatra, including some new species of perch and mackerel. The opening paragraph described when and where he had made his observations, and said modestly, '. . . being my first attempt, the descriptions may in many places be inaccurate'. The rest consisted entirely of anatomical descriptions in the approved Latin. This was another small step up the stair of ambition, but by the time it appeared in print three years later he was about to produce a more notable work.[1]

He also occupied himself in obtaining some 'valuable Instructions' from Major Rennell. For the early stages of his journey, he could learn from the writings of Richard Jobson and Francis Moore on the Gambia, and of French writers on Galam or Kajaaga. He would expect, as a result, to find both banks of the Gambia lined by small kingdoms peopled mainly by Mandingoes, who originated from inland Manding, bringing the royal title Mansa from the Mali Empire. Francis Moore had described how the kingship in most states rotated between lineages of 'Lords of the Soil', deriving their rights of control over land and trade from the first settlements. Most Mandingoes still followed their traditional religion but many had become Muslims, living in separate houses or even towns, and marrying only amongst themselves. Using a term limited in north Africa to religious teachers, all Muslims here were called 'marabouts', a word Jobson had heard as 'Mary-buckes'. Abstaining entirely from alcohol – an abstention which distinguished Muslims from others – they lived soberly under the rules of their faith. Their knowledge of writing, law, and medicine had given them influence, but not power. Their medicine, as Park found, combined the use of drugs with that of charms, used not only against bodily ailments, but also to procure good fortune or to ward off bad luck. The charms normally consisted of Koranic writings, either worn permanently wrapped in leather amulets, or washed off a writing-board and drunk, by Muslim and pagan alike. The word Park learnt for such charms was 'saphie', whereas for Jobson it had been 'gregories', or *grisgris*.

Jobson had described also 'the wandering Fulbie', a tawny-skinned people with long black hair, who 'live in great subjection to the Mandingo, under which they seeme to groane, for he cannot at any time kill a beefe but if they know it, the black-men will have the greatest share . . .' Some lived in towns but most spent their lives wandering with their cattle in a way familiar to Jobson but now long extinct, '. . . which but few yeares since was the Irish Kernes true course of life; but with cleanlinesse your Irish woman hath no acquaintance . . .' Their ultimate origin is still obscure, but they can be traced back to an area north of the Gambia, from which they have migrated over several centuries with their cattle far across West Africa to Nigeria and Cameroun. They are known variously as Peuls, Fulbe, Fellata, or, in Nigeria, as Fulani. Many converted to Islam and some became especially devoted scholars, but most remained nomadic and many pagan. A good deal more besides could have been gleaned from the vivid if often naïve prose of Jobson, and from the pens of others.

At the Association's General Meeting in May 1795 the Secretary reported, 'That early in the present year, he [Park] complained of being tired of leading what he called a Life useless to his Employers'. Only in April was he able to book a passage in a vessel ready to sail for the Gambia, 'Immediately on the Embargo being taken off the Ships in the River Thames'; this embargo was presumably caused by the war. On 17 April the Committee sanctioned his departure, and four days later it issued his formal instructions. In his *Travels* Park said of them:

'My instructions were very plain and concise. I was directed, on my arrival in Africa, "to pass on to the river Niger, either by way of Bambouk, or by such other route as should be found most convenient. That I should ascertain the course, and, if possible, the rise and termination of that river. That I should use my utmost exertions to visit the principal towns or cities in its neighbourhood, particularly Tombuctoo and Houssa; and that I should be afterwards at liberty to return to Europe, either by way of the Gambia, or by such other route, as, under all the then existing circumstances of my situation and prospects, should appear to me to be most advisable".'

In fact this was the brief statement of the purposes of his engagement given to him the previous July. The full instructions, almost identical to Houghton's, elaborated on it considerably and included fifty-four 'Queries to those who have visited Houssa'. Due to some hostility shown towards Houghton there was one small omission, of a paragraph about travelling with a trader, as mentioned in Park's letter to his brother. Oddly, no mention was made of Consul Willis, nor did the Government's instructions eventually issued to the latter say anything about Park. Willis was supposed to be preparing to sail in September, ready to catch the dry season.

It cannot have taken Park long to pack his bags. He took a few changes of clothes, a cloak and a blanket for the nights, an umbrella, a pocket sextant, two compasses, a thermometer, and two fowling-pieces or shotguns. No concessions were made to the tropical climate in the style of clothing then thought suitable, although lighter materials were used. Some later travellers went in a kind of African dress – it looked more Turkish, to judge by the pictures – and even at that time some thought Park should have done so. But, instead of adopting the dress he found common wherever he travelled (for men a long garment like a surplice, and trousers reaching half-way down the leg, both made of local cotton), he preferred to appear quite openly as the stranger he was. He went off in the same kind of clothes as he wore in Scotland: on his head his wide, thick hat; and on his body a shirt, waistcoat, and long, heavy coat with brass buttons, above nankeen breeches.

On 9 May Park wrote to his brother Alexander that he would sail soon and he expected to be back in less than two years, a more realistic appraisal than his earlier one of the likely length of the journey. His letter ended with a prayer which was fulfilled in its essentials: 'I hope that He who has blessed me with tranquillity of mind will likewise smooth my way, will give me Phylosophy enough to overcome every obstacle and strength sufficient to surmount every danger.'[2]

He sailed from Portsmouth on 22 May in the small brig *Endeavour*. On 4 June he could see the mountains above Mogador in southern Morocco. It was his first sight of Africa, although he had sailed round much of it. He set foot on the continent for the first time at Jillifree (near present-day Jufureh) on 21 June 1795. This town, now totally vanished but for some ruined stone walls lost among shrubs and grass, was in the kingdom of Barra on the north bank of the Gambia, oppo-site James Island. Two days later he crossed to Vintain (now Vintang) in the kingdom of Fogny. Here he took the trouble to learn the numerals of the Feloops – actually the Jola, misnamed from their common word of greeting![3] He noted how Mandingoes, supposed to be their trading agents, in fact colluded with Europeans to quote one price to the Jola while using another between themselves, and pocketed the difference, 'very truly called the *cheating money*'. More generally, he said, '. . . the white trader has infinitely the advantage over the African, whom, therefore, it is difficult to satisfy; for, conscious of his own ignorance, he naturally becomes exceedingly suspicious and wavering . . .' This touches on the unequal relationship which has been the most constant feature of Europe's contact with Africa from the earliest Portuguese voyages down to today's aspirations for 'technology transfer'.

The Mandingoes had earlier pressed the Jola back from the south bank and had continued to harry them. It is therefore hardly surprising that, as Park heard, the Jola were supposed to be gloomy and unforgiving, keeping as far as they could to themselves, although strictly honest in the dealings they had with outsiders. 'How greatly it is to be wished', he said, 'that the minds of a people so determined and faithful, could be softened and civilized by the mild and benevolent spirit of Christianity!' His age believed in 'uplift' without the obliteration of existing cultures, unlike later periods with more racist attitudes.

As they went up-river from Vintang, low tides made them stop at intervals, leaving them a dreary view of exposed mudbanks and impenetrable mangrove thickets. More interestingly, he saw much life in the river itself: sharks near the sea, many other fish, and, higher up, hippopotami and crocodiles. A message from Jonkakonda, whence Houghton had fled, soon brought Dr. John Laidley to him. Beaufoy and Laidley had earlier corresponded, and Park brought a letter of introduction. Neither he nor Laidley knew then that Beaufoy had died just five days before Park had sailed. Warmly welcomed by Laidley, Park was in his house at Pisania by 5 July, and his real preparation for his inland journey could begin.

CHAPTER VIII

'Like a child of the family'

At Pisania

———— ເ∞ ————

Pisania, in Niani kingdom, was occupied only by Laidley, two brothers Ainsley, and their dependants. It was an empty ruin by 1818, and has since completely disappeared but for a nearby monument recalling the start of Park's two African journeys. There were, however, other villages around, and Park found it a good base for learning Mandingo, which Laidley spoke fluently.

Pisania existed to carry on the slave trade. It had no other trade to attract Europeans. If no ship was available when a slave caravan reached the coast, the unfortunates were distributed among neighbouring villages to wait, fettered together in pairs, and employed in the fields. 'I am sorry to add,' Park said, '(they) are very scantily fed, as well as harshly treated.' Such was Dr. Laidley's mainstay, and it is strange to think that a doctor who was likable and kindly in his private life could engage in this loathsome business. He was highly regarded by his African neighbours, who were, of course, dealers with him, not his victims. As Major Rennell said, 'He received Mr. Park into his house, and treated him more like a child of the family than a stranger.'

Five months were spent at Pisania, first waiting for the rains to end. Park went down with a heavy dose of fever at the end of July, having imprudently exposed himself to the night dew when observing a lunar eclipse. A hundred years before the discovery of the virulent mosquito-borne malaria parasite, fevers were then attributed to such climatic causes. The White Man's Grave could equally have been called the Black Child's Grave; for both, early attacks by these parasites led either to death or to acquiring a partial immunity, as Park now did, a process which the whites called 'seasoning' because of their mistaken ideas on the causes of fever. During August he slowly recovered, but in September he had a relapse. He found it very trying, watching the pouring rain in the suffocating heat, while sleep was hindered by the croaking of innumerable frogs, the cries of jackal and

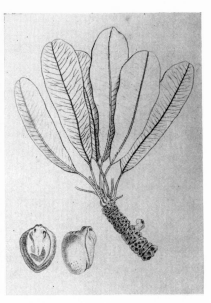

3a. James Dickson, aged 83, from a
watercolour by Thomas Charles
Wageman, 1821

3b. The shea tree, as illustrated in
Park's own drawing reproduced
in his *Travels in the Interior
Districts of Africa* (1799)

3c. Fish observed and painted by Park at Bencoolen in Sumatra, from a
watercolour, c. 1793

4. Ali's tent at the camp of Benowm, from an engraving based on Park's own drawing reproduced in his *Travels*

hyena, and tremendous thunderstorms. Dr. Laidley's company and conversation were a great boon to him at that time, and to pass the time he drew botanical sketches. Some of these may now be found amongst a set of fifty-four drawings by Park in the Library at the Royal Botanic Gardens, Edinburgh.

When the dry season came and his health returned, he tried gathering information from the slatees, or traders who came from the interior with slaves and other merchandise. Quickly, however, he dropped an initial idea of travelling inland with a caravan, on realizing how suspicious they were and how reluctant to give any reliable information, and also how uncertain it was when they would depart.

It is at once apparent on starting to read Park's *Travels* that he had found the métier for which his interests and ambitions had been searching. From his first arrival at Jillifree he set to work enquiring, observing with directness and zest, and recording (although material for his early chapters was drawn from his later experience as well). All aspects of the country and its people came under his observation: its physical condition – no longer mangrove swamps at Pisania, but flat, wooded, and fertile land – and the different peoples, their appearance, dress, foods, languages, customs, states, forms of government, social systems, laws, and beliefs. He showed an ability to observe precisely and in detail, and to set down what he had seen in clear and simple terms. Although handicapped by the brevity of his encounter with local peoples, by his lack of historical background, and by the fact that there were not yet tools shaped for the study of unfamiliar societies, he could none the less make these societies come to life in the imaginations of his readers.

Among the peoples he saw in the Gambia area were the Jola, already mentioned but with whom he had no further contact. To the north was the country of the Jaloffs (Wolof) but they too lay off his route and he saw little of them. They were described to him as an 'active, powerful, and warlike race', but they were not the aggressors in the fighting he later heard of with Futa Toro, on their inland side, already turned into an Islamic state by revolution from within. In the Gambia basin there were also numbers of Jobson's 'wandering Fulbie', many of whom had migrated over the years from the south, where a second Islamic state of Futa Jallon had been established. Park probably left England too soon to hear of the first, friendly visit paid to it in 1794 by Watt and Winterbottom from Sierra Leone, nor does he seem to have heard of it while in Africa. In the vicinity of Pisania the Fulbe or Fulani appear to have been few, and he became better acquainted with them only when he went inland.

The dominant Mandingoes in the Gambia he reckoned to be 'of a mild, sociable, and obliging disposition'. They were ruled by kings whose powers were limited by the need to act with the consent of councils of their principal men. There were Alkaids, or chief magistrates, in each town, who administered local affairs, again with the advice of councils of elders. Park observed that Islam had advanced although the majority were still pagan. Frequented mosques were in all the towns; Arabic titles like Alkaid were used; pork was avoided even by the non-Muslims; and kouskous was a staple food, named and made as in the Arab lands to the north. There was some separation, but as yet no visible strain, between the Muslims and the traditionalists.

It was sixty years before strains grew into civil wars that tore apart most of these Gambia Mandingo states, and replaced them with unstable Muslim states which, in their turn, were divided between the French in Senegal and the British on the Gambia. As we shall see, Park later found other societies further advanced in the transition from being ruled under traditional beliefs, with Islam alongside but not overcoming them, into stable societies dominated by Islam's sacred law, intent on rooting out paganism and injustice. This was to be the real substance and drama of their history until very late in the nineteenth century, when European penetration further inland first became a significant force for change. Park detected signs and symptoms of this process, but their full meaning is only evident with hindsight.

Park's reactions to the Africans he met were basically a friendly interest, and a readiness to see the same human needs and concerns as in his own country. He was not blinded by preconceptions brought from Europe. For example, he rejected the idea that Africa lived in a lawless state, and observed how lawsuits were conducted, '. . . with sufficient solemnity. Both sides of a question are freely canvassed, witnesses are publicly examined . . . the general rule of decision is an appeal to *ancient custom* . . .' The setting must have appeared at first exotic, with cases heard in the open air and audience reactions freely expressed. But the spread of the written Islamic law was also giving rise to a class of professional advocates, to Park's expressed surprise. Showing the very dry and nearly always friendly humour which spiced much of his *Travels*, he added, 'I believe that in the forensic qualifications of procrastination and cavil, and the arts of confounding and perplexing a cause, they are not always surpassed by the ablest pleaders in Europe.'

Only where his religious beliefs were involved was he unprepared to place himself in others' shoes and see life from their angle; the Europe of the Enlightenment had little more sympathy for Islam than had the Europe of the high Middle Ages. Nor did it yet have much understanding of how traditional 'pagan' beliefs made sense to agrarian peoples of their lives and relationships and sanctified the authorities in society. However, though unsympathetic, he did report clearly enough what he saw, and he showed that respect for persons of character and good will of any faith, without which one cannot be a good Christian. It was not defect of sympathy but lack of the rare gift of foresight that prevented him from reading the signs of change.

As to how the Africans saw him, we are unfortunately almost entirely dependent on his own account, but there is so little vainglory shown in it that we can accept it as probably near the mark, although of course he must sometimes have failed to interpret their motives and their thoughts correctly.

His plan had been to wait at Pisania for Consul Willis unless a favourable opportunity presented itself for his earlier departure alone. Impatient to be on his way, he was not going to wait indefinitely. His *Travels* give the impression that he was deprived of Willis's support by the cancellation of the latter's appointment. This is not strictly correct, as the cancellation came in February 1796 when Park was already well inland. Willis had had instructions issued to him by the Government, but he had been required to submit his accounts for examination by the African Association. They revealed no impropriety, but they did show an expenditure mounting far beyond what the Government had envisaged. This, with the late date in the dry season when the examination was completed, and the presence of French privateers in the Gambia, led to the postponement of his expedition and the annulment of his appointment. Thus Willis faded out from the scene for good, apart from some minor correspondence.

It was these privateers whose attentions prevented most of Park's letters home arriving on the *Endeavour*, in which he had sailed, or on another ship. The only letter to reach England was sent the day before he left Pisania, covering his illness, the arrangements for departure, and his obligations to Dr. Laidley for his kindness. It also gave details, based on enquiries he had been making, of points of call on the way to Segu and the route beyond to Jenne, Timbuktu, and 'Houssa', down the river Niger flowing to the east. This made Major Rennell check over his previous work, which he found not too inaccurate, but he was puzzled by the location of 'Houssa' as described by Park, because he still believed it to be nearer Timbuktu than it is.

The final arrangements for departure owed much to Laidley's help. He provided two servants to accompany Park. Johnson, who came as his interpreter in Mandingo, had been taken as a slave to Jamaica but later freed, and after seven years' residence in England he had now returned to his home country. He was to be paid ten bars a month, and during his absence his wife was to receive five bars monthly. Park explained to his readers that the 'bar' was a measure of value used in barter trade. It was originally based on iron bars, and in his time taken on the Gambia to be equal to two shillings. The other attendant was a sprightly youth called Demba, who was a domestic slave of Laidley's, and he was to receive his freedom on his return, if he behaved well on the journey. Besides Mandingo he spoke the language of the 'Serawoollies' (Serahuli) whose area on the banks of the Senegal they would traverse. For the first part of the journey Park was also to travel with three Serahuli merchants and a blacksmith called Tami, all Muslims, but they were not in his employment.

Also from Laidley, Park bought a small but hardy horse with accoutrements, asses for Johnson and Demba, two pistols, and an iron pot. In addition he purchased trade goods, in place of some he had expected Willis to bring out, for use as presents to chiefs and to buy what he would need himself. It was a small quantity to last him to Timbuktu and back: six pieces of cloth, 36¼ ounces of amber, 90 pounds of tobacco, and 20 pounds of beads. But the Association discouraged him from taking very much, thinking that Houghton had probably excited the desires of thieves with what he had carried. In all, Park incurred a debt to Laidley before his departure of only £44. 14s. 9d., and with purchases in England his outfit cost just about £100. Compared to most later European expeditions into Africa, including his own second journey, these were very modest loads he took with him. Not least important in his equipment was his beaver hat with its capacious crown, possibly the only item with which he managed to return, for this was the brief-case in which he carried all his notes.

He started with two days' provisions, but little or nothing from England, and he was prepared to eat whatever was available. In these areas this meant mainly foods like kouskous, made from corn or rice, cousins to his native porridge. He carried no tent or bedding other than his blanket and cloak, and he was going to sleep on mats or, if he were very lucky sometimes, a bed made of canes or thick corn-stalks tied together and raised above the floor of a simple thatched hut, the walls of which generally reached a height of about four feet from the ground.

So equipped and supported, without any map that could really help, and with the usefulness of Rennell's 'valuable Instructions' already largely exhausted, he was set for departure. He was to enter the 'wide extended blank' before him, choosing the paths that appeared best suited to his purpose as they led between towns and villages, and relying on his intelligence and common sense to deal with the unforeseeable problems that would arise. On 2 December 1795 all was ready, and Park's journey into the interior of Africa started at last.

CHAPTER IX

'Before me a boundless forest'

From Pisania to Kajaaga

———— ʊʊ ————

It began like a pleasant outing in the Yarrow valley at home, with Laidley and the Ainsley brothers joining Park to start him on his way. Late that first day they rested at the house of an African woman who had been the *chère amie* of a white trader and who was distinguished by the title Seniora Camilla, a rare trace of the old Portuguese influence in the Gambia. An amusing evening was passed at a neighbouring village, smoking and listening to Mandingo tales, whilst a late meal was prepared. Early next afternoon Park parted from Laidley and the Ainsleys and rode slowly into the woods to begin in earnest, 'and, I believe,' he said, 'they secretly thought they should never see me afterwards'.

On his side, finding himself more dependent on his own mental resources than ever before in his twenty-four years, at first he naturally conjured up the more lurid European conceptions of Africa:

'I had now before me a boundless forest, and a country, the inhabitants of which were strangers to civilized life, and to most of whom a white man was the object of curiosity or plunder. I reflected that I had parted from the last European I might probably behold, and perhaps quitted for ever the comforts of Christian society. Thoughts like these would necessarily cast a gloom over the mind, and I rode musing along for about three miles . . .'

Gloom never lasted long for Park, and this time he was brought to by a group of people demanding that he go with them some distance to the King of Walli, or else pay customs. Properly, Walli was a district of the kingdom of Niani. Its becoming almost independent was one of the earliest signs of the decay of the traditional powers. Park's arguments that he was no trader, required to pay customs, did not move them, and so, as always on this journey, he paid in order to be allowed to go on. Next day took him out of Walli, and the day after brought him to Medina, the capital of Wuli, or Woolli as he called it.

This clay-walled town with its Arabic name struck him as considerable, with 800 to 1,000 houses – which were indeed twice as many as Selkirk had. Today it is only a small village, and many other places he visited have also declined or changed their names or even disappeared. These countries had then a much smaller population than now, and even now it is not dense. Much of his route lay across the savanna vegetation zone; thick woodlands covered gentle slopes separating the clearings where lay towns and villages, with their surrounding fields. The valleys were fertile but the low ridges between, formed of red ironstone, the laterite so common in West Africa, were barren and bore only stunted shrubs. In December, after harvest, the country, except in valleys or swampy places, would have appeared dry with bare earth or corn stalks where cultivated, and dried grass between the trees elsewhere.

The young white man was led before the venerable King or Mansa Jatta who was seated on his mat amongst his attendants. The king was spared the embarrassment of being offered Park's hand to shake, as one of his relatives, with whom Park lodged, had warned him this would not be proper. The young man seemed quite respectful, and explained his journey sufficiently, so the Mansa was pleased to give him permission to travel through his country with a guide, adding that he would pray for his safety. When this benevolence caused one of Park's companions to roar out in praise an Arabic song the Mansa, ready to pray with anybody, and all those with him chorused 'Amen!' at regular intervals. Like most of his subjects, the Mansa adhered to traditional beliefs, which were a bulwark of his kingly authority, but he had no objection to any of his subjects following the Muslim creed. Such Muslims, or Bushreens in the local term, were often useful as advisers, as long as they did not aspire to power. Later on, Wuli was the one Mandingo Gambian state that managed to survive the wave of Muslim revolt, possibly because it had a single ruling family, as Park noted, unlike the other states; it therefore avoided internecine disputes.

Before Park returned the next morning the Mansa had been reflecting on the strange new propensity of the Europeans not to rest content with trading on the Gambia but to want to travel inland. He saw no harm in it, but the previous traveller, Houghton, had come to grief, and he feared Park would as well. He therefore tried hard to dissuade him from travelling into countries less accustomed to dealing with white men but, alas, this young man was too determined. In the

end the Mansa could only shake his head sadly and repeat his offer of
a guide. If all the rulers proved as gracious and civil, Park would have
little to fear.

At Kolor, not far beyond Medina, he first encountered a practice
associated with the traditional beliefs, then found in all Mandingo
towns, and still known although more as a memory. When women's
quarrels became excessive in the polygamous households, a man completely covered in a masquerade costume would appear at night, an-
nouncing himself by loud and dismal screams in the woods outside the
village. The women were never allowed to know anything about the
cult or the wearer of the costume. However unwillingly, they had to
dance and sing, with every woman wondering who was to be punished,
until around midnight the masquerader seized and stripped his victim,
tied her to a post and beat her with a rod. During this humiliation all
the assembly, both men and women, jeered at her, until daylight put
an end to an 'indecent and unmanly revel'. Park saw clearly enough
that the whole point was to enforce subjection on the women, and his
distaste for the custom and his unsympathetic account of it have made
its name, Mumbo Jumbo, better known as a synonym for meaningless
mystification than it had become from the earlier but less publicized
work of Francis Moore.

By contrast, at Koojar, where, although many had seen white men
at the coast, he was looked upon with a mixture of curiosity and
reverence, he enjoyed an evening's entertainment of wrestling and
dancing, improved with a strong beer as good as was brewed back
home. At the end of his first ten days, as he left Wuli, he felt appre-
ciative of the hearty welcome he had received everywhere. Quickly
getting over the absence of the food and comforts he was used to, he
said, '. . . the African mode of living was at first unpleasant to me, yet
I found, at length, that custom surmounted trifling inconveniences,
and made every thing palatable and easy.'

One man engaged as a guide for the next stage absconded, with his
wages paid in advance, whereupon Park determined to set off before
two others could follow suit. They entered a wilderness, a wooded
no-man's-land between Wuli and Bondu, in the barren eastern part
of the modern state of Senegal. It took more than a full day's hard
travelling to cross it, with only one satisfactory watering-point reached
after dark, and with his companions in constant fear of brigands lurking
in the woods.

On his approach to Tallika in fertile Bondu he found that most of the inhabitants were settled Fulani, farming extensively as well as tending cattle. They had excellent milk and butter, but to Park's surprise never made cheese, explaining that this was because of the heat, the scarcity of salt, and the length of the process involved (but cheese is known in Africa: the Hausa have a word for it). The country also prospered by standing on major trade routes between the coast and the interior, considerable duties being levied on goods in transit. Mandingoes and Serahuli, a mixing of peoples by no means uncommon in the areas Park visited, conducted most of this trade. Bondu's population was growing, as it served as a refuge from troubled areas around. It had risen from small beginnings to some local strength, although it paid tribute to Kaarta to the north-east. Arms were not lacking to this strategically situated state; when Houghton had passed through, it will be recalled, it had just conquered from Bambuk the eastern bank of the river Faleme.

From Tallika, Park wrote to Laidley, but the letter never arrived, although Laidley did hear rumours of his early progress from traders. Nor did a letter from Willis which he promised to forward ever get to Park, who was entirely cut off from outside communication.[1]

As they went along one day a violent quarrel broke out between the blacksmith and one of the traders in the party, intensified by their breaking what Park found to be a cardinal tenet of Africa: 'Strike me, but do not curse my mother.' The quarrel was about to develop into a cutlass attack on the blacksmith, and Park felt impelled to intervene. He threatened that if this happened another time he would regard the assailant as a robber and shoot him. It was in sullen silence that the party marched on, but in the evening an exchange of presents and a good meal restored amity. They enjoyed some stories and music from an itinerant 'singing man', a kind who still 'sing extempore songs, in honour of their chief men, or any other persons who are willing to give "solid pudding for empty praise" ', as Park put it.

The party soon dividing up, Park went on with one trader and the blacksmith to Koorkarany, crossing on the way the river Nerico, which had been the limit of earlier expeditions up the Gambia. In this Muslim town Park enjoyed a talk with the Marabout, or local religious leader, who showed him some Arabic manuscripts, while Park in return showed an Arabic grammar he carried but had not got far with as yet. He misunderstood 'Al Sharra', the Shari'a, to be the name

of a particular book, whereas it is the whole body of Muslim law,
which was widely observed in Bondu.

He also saw little schools everywhere, in which the children of
pagan as well as Muslim parents were keenly learning the text of the
Koran and some Arabic, and becoming adherents of the faith. (He
might be surprised to find such schools even more widespread today,
a supplement rather than a rival to the primary schools.) Park was
impressed by the desire for education, as were his readers subsequently.
In fact it has been estimated that 60 per cent of the population of
Bondu were literate in Arabic script, a higher proportion of literates
than in England at the same period.[2] Nevertheless, he 'heartily wished
thay had had better instructors, and a purer religion'. In spite of this
lack of sympathy he was well on the mark in observing, 'Religious
persecution is not known among them, nor is it necessary; for the
system of Mahomet is made to extend itself by means abundantly
more efficacious.' To a large degree Islam spread peacefully through
the schools.

Throughout his journey he found one standard kind of women's
dress, only the headdress varying. The clothes were made of cotton
grown locally and consisted of an ankle-length skirt, gathered up and
tied at the waist, and another cloth slung loosely upwards from the
waist to hang over the shoulders. Some women he met beyond Koorkarany were exceptional; they were clad in a light French gauze,
'well calculated to display the shape of their persons . . . The manners
of these females, however, did not correspond with their dress; for they
were rude and troublesome in the highest degree.' Normally he was not
especially bashful towards women, but these strenuous souvenir-
hunters had torn his cloak and cut buttons from young Demba's
clothes, '. . . and were proceeding to other outrages, when I mounted
my horse and rode off, followed for half a mile by a body of these
harpies'.

Passing through more hilly country, he came to the banks of the
fast and rocky Faleme, the Senegal's main tributary, and turned northwards along it. Quantities of fish were being caught both in basket
traps and nets, to be pounded and dried for sale far to the north. He
met an old man who had seen Houghton further on, near where he
had died. Not far beyond the river lay Fatteconda, the capital of Bondu.
Following local custom, Park waited at the 'bentang', a shaded platform
which was the public meeting-place in every town, until a slatee or

trader invited him to his house. In the absence of public inns such hospitality was traditional in Africa, and rarely did Park find himself refused it.

In Bondu the ruler used the Muslim title Almami. He was then almost alone among the leading men in clinging to traditional ways, but some years later he found it politic to be converted. Park had not been long in Fatteconda when he was summoned to meet the Almami, whose name (unrecorded by Park) was Amadi Isata. Mindful of Houghton's poor reception, Park was apprehensive, especially when led right out of the town to meet the Almami under a secluded tree, but his presents were well received, especially his one umbrella, which he offered. The only snag was that the Almami took a fancy to his best blue coat, which he had put on lest it be stolen if left at the lodging, and Park found himself obliged to hand it over with the best grace he could muster! In return the Almami gave him ample provisions and a little gold to buy more supplies on the road.

The Almami was at first suspicious, not believing that anyone could undertake so dangerous a journey merely out of curiosity to see the country and its people. He seems to have suspected that Park was trying to conceal being a trader in order to avoid paying duties, and when he was convinced otherwise he became very friendly. On one visit the Almami said he was sick and asked for some blood to be let, but the sight of Park's lancet soon cured him. It has been said that Park did not in general use his medical skills to render himself acceptable, but he often lacked the means to do so. His own training involved the use of drugs derived from vegetable sources, and was much closer to traditional African practice than modern European medicine. He described African medical practices sympathetically, especially minor surgical treatments, such as those for fractures, dislocations, abscesses, and inflammation. The diseases he encountered, especially fevers, dysentery, guinea worm, and leprosy, remain all too evident today.

At the Almami's request he visited the prettily dressed ladies of the court, and he was content to let the joke be on him in the banter that ensued:

'They were ten or twelve in number, most of them young and handsome, and wearing on their heads ornaments of gold, and beads of amber. They rallied me with a good deal of gaiety on different subjects; particularly on the whiteness of my skin, and the prominency of my nose. They insisted that both were artificial. The first, they said, was produced when I was an infant, by dipping me in milk; and they insisted that my nose had been pinched every day, till it had acquired its present unsightly and unnatural conformation. On my part, without disputing my own deformity, I paid them many compliments on African beauty. I praised the glossy jet of their skins, and the lovely depression of their noses; but they said that flattery, or (as they emphatically termed it) *honey-mouth*, was not esteemed in Bondou. In return, however, for my company or my compliments (to which, by the way, they seemed not so insensible as they affected to be), they presented me with a jar of honey and some fish . . .'

In all, it was a pleasant stay that Park had had in Bondu, the eastern frontier of which was close to Fatteconda. His route so far had been rather north of east, so he missed the gold-bearing country of Bambuk – old 'Wangara' – and instead entered Kajaaga by another night march through a wilderness, emerging into a fertile country, watered by rivers large and small.

He had spent a week crossing Bondu, but took only two days to travel through Kajaaga, inhabited by the Serahuli (or, as the French would say, Galam inhabited by the Serakolets). Active trading had carried their language from the Gambia on one side to northern Bambara on the other. Park did not meet King Batcheri, but heard he was 'sufficiently powerful'. In fact 'Batcheri' was a title, not a personal name, as Park supposed, and he was one of the chiefs in a small confederacy of chiefdoms. Most of Kajaaga's history had been spent as a tributary of an empire or a powerful neighbour; then, however, it was independent and was preparing for a war with Khasso, to the east (called Kasson by Park). His first seriously unpleasant experience came on Christmas Day, when he was resting at the bentang in the walled frontier town of Joag. He found himself surrounded by twenty horsemen, muskets in hand, who had newly arrived in town. One tugged at Park's musket while he was lying down, but desisted when he found him awake. They accused him of entering the town without first paying duties, so that not only his belongings but also all his people were forfeit to the Batcheri. To the terror of Tami, the blacksmith, who was a native of Khasso and visualized himself losing all his savings and being enslaved into the bargain, Park at first feigned readiness to comply, but he seized an opportunity to consult his host, who advised him against going to the Batcheri if he could avoid it. He therefore offered the horsemen as a present for the Batcheri the gold given him by the Almami of Bondu. They agreed and went, but not before searching his baggage and removing all that they fancied, up to half his belongings – apart from some articles he had concealed, as he seems to have made a practice of doing. His servant Johnson was reduced to misery; the last trader from Pisania still with him urged him to turn back; whilst the poor blacksmith tried to make himself invisible and dumb. As for Park himself, he always behaved as if he had made up his mind from the start to lose all his property if need be, as long as he had his life and freedom to proceed. This business lasted all day up to dark, and an indifferent supper concluded it.

Next day they were afraid to produce any articles with which they could buy food, in case this led to further robbery, and they fasted all day. In the evening, as they sat dejectedly on the bentang, an old slave woman passed by. Hearing that they had nothing to eat, she presented them with some handfuls of groundnuts. 'Experience had taught her that hunger was painful, and her own distresses made her commiserate those of others.'

Immediately afterwards a higher-ranking visitor came. He was called Demba Sego, described as a nephew of the King of Khasso, on whose behalf he had come on an unsuccessful attempt to improve relations with Kajaaga. His offer of protection and guidance on the journey to Khasso was gladly accepted, and on 27 December they set off with a large retinue. On the way Johnson insisted on sacrificing a chicken on a tree, and Park was amused to find him wanting to do this after so long a residence in England. 'I laughed at his folly, but could not condemn the piety of his motives.'

The boundary between Kajaaga and Khasso was formed by the Senegal, a beautiful but shallow river between steep banks. The party crossed it at Kayee (now Kayes) near a fair-sized cataract, the horses being forced down the bank and across the river. With baggage to carry too it was late evening before they finished. Demba Sego had given them a wetting, upsetting their fragile canoe in what was fortunately shallow water, whilst trying to put his hand into Park's tin box!

CHAPTER X

'For fear some accident should befal me'

In Khasso and Kaarta

———— ∞ ————

Park entered Khasso on 28 December 1795. In under four weeks he had come, by his own reckoning, 335 standard English miles. Up to this point he had been in areas visited by Europeans. From here on, he had been preceded only by Houghton, and nothing had come back from the latter but one short note.

Demba Sego wasted no time in telling Park that he expected due recompense for his help. Park felt aggrieved, since Demba Sego knew how he had been plundered at Joag, but he gave him a small present which contented him for the time being. Late the next day they reached Teesee where Demba's father, Tiggity Sego, was chief. He was described as the brother of the King or Mansa of Khasso, but in fact was apparently his nephew, making Demba a great-nephew. Tiggity Sego was an old man who had never seen any white man save Houghton, and he studied Park's appearance closely. He was friendly, but he seemed to doubt the explanation Park gave for his journey.

Park was at Teesee until 10 January 1796. Demba Sego twice borrowed his horse, once to catch a runaway slave and the second time to visit Gedumah (Guidimaka) to the north, from which some Moors had stolen three horses in a raid. During the second absence, which lasted over a week, Park wandered round the town, finding the inhabitants curious to see him but always kind and generous with provisions.

'On a very extraordinary occasion' he attended a court case, reminiscent of some of Chaucer's tales. A young pagan, recently married, had obtained some 'saphies' or charms from a very devout Muslim, a close friend, to protect him in war. This Muslim, or Bushreen, had ordered him to make the saphies more effective by abstaining from intercourse with his wife for six weeks, and the young man had complied. 'In the mean time it began to be whispered at Teesee, that the Bushreen, who always performed his evening devotions at the door of the Kafir's hut, was more intimate with the young wife than he ought to be.' It took a month before the husband could credit these rumours against his good friend, but then he found them to be true, and complained. The court sentenced the Bushreen to be sold into slavery, but at the intercession of the complainant this was commuted to thirty-nine strokes with a black rod, executed to great popular amusement.

Dangers then threatened the state of Khasso. It was expected that the Moors of Guidimaka would raid the country during the coming war with Kajaaga, and Park saw great stores of provisions being brought into Teesee for safety, on Tiggity Sego's orders. Next an embassy came from Almami Abdulkadir, of Futa Toro to the west, pursuing his policy of trying to extend Islam by war or diplomacy as occasion offered. A demand was made that Khasso should adopt the Muslim religion and say public prayers, or else Futa Toro would support Kajaaga. Although humiliated by this demand, compliance was found expedient for the time being, whilst plans for the war with Kajaaga went ahead. (It is not clear how this relates to a story of a similar demand said to have been made in the same period by a Fulani from *Futa Jallon* much to the south, under threat of invasion, which led the Mansa of Khasso to a sincere conversion that earned him the title of Almami.)

Much later in his journey Park heard how Abdulkadir had come to grief in neighbouring Kayor, a Wolof state near the coast, after threatening the ruling Damel with death if he did not embrace the faith. Defeated, Abdulkadir was led in as a prisoner expecting death himself, but the Damel showed amazing clemency and even restored him to his throne before long. Some years after Park's journey was over Abdulkadir received his due when, again the aggressor, this time against Bondu allied with Kaarta, he lost support and was put to death.

These alarms made Park anxious to get away, but first he would have to pay duties and it was hinted that he should also make a present to the chief for his kindness. Demba Sego spurned the seven bars of amber and five of tobacco which Park offered. Instead he helped himself to everything he wanted, not omitting the tin box he had earlier coveted. Having lost half his belongings at Joag, Park reckoned they had now been halved again. 'There was, however, no remedy; and having been under some obligation to Demba Sego for his attention towards me in the journey from Joag, I did not reproach him for his rapacity, but determined to quit Teesee at all events the next morning.'

The next day the party set out and came to Jumbo, the native town of Tami the blacksmith. He had been away four years working for Dr. Laidley, and his reception was like that of the prodigal son returning. Many of the townspeople jumped for joy and sang lustily, and the arriving party fired a musket salute as they dismounted. The most tender and happy welcome was from his aged, blind mother, who caressed him and lengthily expressed her delight at hearing the music of his voice again. This scene moved Park to write:

'. . . whatever difference there is between the Negro and European in the conformation of the nose and the colour of the skin, there is none in the genuine sympathies and characteristic feelings of our common nature.'

He himself sat almost unnoticed while all this was going on until Tami, nearing the end of a detailed account of all that had happened to him since he left home, referred in affectionate terms to Park and exclaimed, 'See him sitting there.' Only then did everybody register the presence of a man of such uncommon appearance, and for some time mothers scampered off with their young children whenever he moved or even happened to look at them, but before long, reassured by Tami, they accepted him without fear. Then there was feasting and rejoicing, with dancing to the ubiquitous African drums. Additional accompaniments were provided on such occasions by various kinds of harps, flutes, guitars, fiddles, bells, and rich-sounding horns of ivory. (Down to the present, out of earshot of amplified urban music, such instruments continue in use, maintaining themselves against the transistor radio.)

After two days of this revelry, the blacksmith accompanied him on his way to Koniakary, the capital of Khasso. A little short of it they stopped to visit Salim Daucari, a noted trader to the Gambia, who owed Dr. Laidley the value of five slaves, for which Park carried an order upon him. They had little time to talk of this before he was summoned to the court by the Mansa's second son, Sambo Sego. The three of them reached Koniakary late in the evening, and deferred visiting the Mansa until next morning.

Mansa Demba Sego Jalla, the first effective king of a former congeries of small chiefdoms, was aged about sixty in Park's estimation. He was all pleasantness, accepting the explanation of the journey and promising every assistance in his power. He said he had given Hough-ton a white horse before he crossed into Kaarta and lost his life, the Mansa knew not how. As in most of Park's interviews discussion seems to have remained on this personal level, and never entered into any question of future relations with the whites. Khasso had some trading relations with the French on the Senegal, although at rather long range since Fort St. Joseph had been vacated. Before he left the Mansa Park made a small present, which was accepted, and in his turn was given a bullock, considered particularly well-favoured by his attendants as it was a white one.

Afterwards Salim Daucari arranged to pay him the value of three slaves, about £60. This transaction demonstrates the efficiency and honesty of a credit system working at long range in the interior of Africa. On hearing of it, Sambo Sego came and demanded half for the Mansa and more for himself and his followers. Park was ready to sub-mit again, when Salim Daucari vigorously interposed on his behalf, and reduced the claim to about £2 worth of goods in payment of every demand that could be made upon him. This left Park well provided for – if he could manage to keep what he had.

He went up into neighbouring hills and looked over a wide and well-populated plain. Holes in the rocks concealed hyenas and 'wolves' by day. He often mentioned wolves and, since he knew of jackal and hyena already, it seems he must have meant the wild hunting dog, as there are no true wolves in Africa. These vicious animals roam in packs like wolves and will tear flesh from their living quarry. On this occasion they had killed five cattle and maimed others.

The Mansa had frankly explained to Park the problems he faced. On the west and north Khasso expected war with Kajaaga and the Moors of Guidimaka. Its eastern neighbour, Kaarta, was daily expecting an invasion from Segu to the south. Park asked if he could miss Kaarta and go south direct into Segu, and the Mansa replied that this was feasible but in that case he could not provide a guide, as he had an agreement to send all travellers on through Kaarta. (This friendship was something new between these two states, each being then pre-occupied in other directions.) Rather than travel without a guide Park decided to risk entering Kaarta. Accordingly, on 3 February he parted from his excellent friends Tami and Salim Daucari, and went on his way with two guides.

On 9 February he entered Kaarta, and at his first stop his host exhibited those characteristics of the nominal Muslim which so incensed reformers. 'He was one of those Negroes who, together with the cere-monial part of the Mahomedan religion, retain all their ancient super-stitions, and even drink strong liquors.' Kaarta itself was a new kind of countryside to Park, a level and sandy plain, in the dry, less wooded area known as the Sahel. It was subject to periodical drought, as in the early 1970s. Then, however, the threat of war was evident. Already in Khasso territory he had seen groups of refugees fleeing from Kaarta, and now inside the country he passed whole villages deserted by their inhabitants.

Many people in Kaarta had never seen a white man. Houghton was the only one to have passed that way. Park met two horsemen who were horror-struck at sight of him. By the time they met his attendants a mile behind him, their fears had dressed him in the flowing robes of a tremendous spirit, and one of them declared that the appari-tion had been accompanied by a cold blast of wind pouring down from the sky! This was no more absurd, of course, than some European beliefs about Africans.

The capital, Kemmoo (Guemou), had not been established many years in the territory of the Diawara people – Park called them the Jower – formerly Kaarta's allies, but now her subjects. It was set in an open plain, all the wood for two miles around having been cleared. The Fama, or King, provided a lodging and a man to keep off the mob, but so curious were the people that they pressed in, staring and quietly asking questions, then making room for others: a process repeated thir-teen times. In the evening Park was summoned to meet the Fama, whom he found seated on a leopard skin upon a raised bank of earth amongst a large retinue. Park gives his name as Daisy Koorabarri, but it is now generally written less picturesquely as Desse Koulibali. He was satisfied with Park's reasons for his presence, and very friendly, as indeed most of the rulers up to now had been: Park's troubles had come mainly from chief's sons or their followers, possibly 'over-mighty subjects'. However, Desse was quite frank about his limited power to help.

He said that in view of the invasion already on its way from the south, Park could hardly go that way for fear of plunder or being mis-taken for a spy. If there had been peace he would have been welcome to stay, but as it was, '. . . he did not wish me to continue in Kaarta, for fear some accident should befal me, in which case my countrymen

might say, that he had murdered a white man'. (Here he took a prescient view of what did happen later in some parts of Africa.) 'He
would therefore advise me to return into Kasson, and remain there
until the war should terminate, which would probably happen in the
course of three or four months . . . This advice was certainly well
meant on the part of the king; and perhaps I was to blame in not
following it . . .' Desse's accurate forecast of the duration of the war
was based on the limitation of campaigning to the dry season, and his
advice was indeed reasonable. Park was anxious, however, neither to
turn back nor to spend the rainy season in the centre of Africa, and he
pressed for an alternative. Cautiously Desse admitted that there was
one other possible course, not without danger, through the Moorish
kingdom of Ludamar.

As they were talking a messenger arrived post-haste with news that
the Segu army was approaching, and the interview was abruptly ter-
minated. Next morning Park sent his horse-pistols and holsters as a
gift, asking for a guide, and soon the Fama sent eight horsemen to
conduct him north-eastwards to Jarra. Three of Desse's sons and two
hundred more horsemen also provided a friendly and honourable escort
for some way.

He had little chance on this fleeting visit to delve into history, but
he did appreciate that the theft of some cattle from Segu land, and
their retention and sale in Kaarta, were only pretexts for war seized
by Mansong, Fama of Segu. In fact there had been continual troubles
ever since 1670 when these two rival military Bambara states had
emerged and subsequently grown at the expense of their neighbours.
Their rivalry was a major contribution to the instability of the area
which no longer came under the defunct Mali Empire, nor under
conquered Songhai, nor the new rulers of Timbuktu. Other factors
included the pressure of Futa Toro from the west and of the Moors
from the north. Their disputes continued almost up to the conquest of
Kaarta in 1855 by Al-Hajj Umar from Futa Toro, Segu following
in 1861, and Khasso being finally crushed between him and the French
in the same period. Park observed that nearly half Desse's troops were
Muslims, who thronged the mosques as the Segu army drew near, but
both Bambara states successfully kept their Muslims from achieving
power, despite allowing them some influence, until they were conquered from outside.

There are different versions of what the relationship was between the kings Desse and Mansong, depending on who was doing the telling, but all accounts agree that there was an underlying dispute as to which was the suzerain of all the Bambara. In one account Mansong, with macabre humour, sent to Desse to choose between a hoe – symbolizing peace and the abandonment of mutual claims – and shackles – needing no explanation – or a jaw – outright war. It was the jaw that Desse chose. What Park heard was that, after the cattle incident, Mansong sent a message to Desse that he was coming to Guemou on a visit with nine thousand men, and Desse should set his slaves to sweep out his accommodation. This insult was accompanied by a present of iron sandals to speed Desse's flight. Kaarta was at a disadvantage, with a much smaller Bambara population and with the Diawara and others disaffected. Park observed them leaving Kaarta with Desse's permission as war approached, but not all obeyed his injunction to be neutral if they wanted to return.

As Park heard, Desse evacuated his capital without a fight and retired to a mountain stronghold, Gedingooma, where he held out. Mansong devastated and looted much of the country, but, after unsuccessfully summoning his ostensible ally Ludamar to his aid, he raised the siege of Gedingooma and marched against Ludamar instead. The ever-mobile Moors simply went north towards the desert, and in May Mansong returned to Segu with great booty but having been only partly successful strategically. In the aftermath, Desse had to contend with rebellious Diawara and other subjects, and with a new attack from Khasso, where the Mansa so recently seen by Park had died and had been succeeded by his rapacious son Sambo Sego.

It was not a very opportune time that Park had chosen for travelling. He was robbed during the first night on the way, and further on from a vantage-point on a flat roof he actually witnessed Moors raiding a village and stealing cattle. A young herdsman who tried to resist was brought in after the raid, badly wounded in the leg and losing much blood. His mother was beside herself with grief, telling over and over his good qualities and endlessly repeating as the greatest of them, 'He never told a lie; no, never.' To Thomson in 1890 this seemed 'a phenomenal occurrence in a continent where lying is a virtue', but to Park it had been plain, simple truth. Asked to help, Park could only advise that the leg be amputated above the knee, but this was rejected with horror. So the unfortunate young man sank slowly to his death, being persuaded at the end to accept the Muslim faith.

After this, although there were still fears of Moors on the road, the party travelled on uneventfully by night. The temperature dropped as low as 68 °F. (20 °C.) and his companions could not sleep for the cold. This temperature would be astonishingly warm in Europe in February, but anyone who has experienced the harmattan season preceding the hot weather will know what Park meant. The temperatures in fact often fall substantially lower, occasionally into the 40s Fahrenheit, and the intensely dry and dusty wind from the desert removes all skin moisture, exaggerating the feeling of coldness.

On 18 February he left Kaarta behind and entered Ludamar at the frontier village of Simbing. He reckoned this to be 560 miles from Pisania, whence he had travelled in two and a half months. It was from Simbing that Houghton had written his last pencilled note to Laidley. The last word that Laidley had of Park while he was in the interior came from this same area. On 1 August Laidley wrote to Willis that he had heard that Park had 'reached the residence of an Arabian king, situated to the northward, and considerably to the eastward of Sego' – the eastward being incorrect. Evidently he had no idea what took place at the Arabian king's residence.

CHAPTER XI

'A lonely captive, perishing of thirst'

In Ludamar

———— ⟨⟩ ————

A few miles beyond Simbing lay Jarra, a considerable town at the foot of some rocky hills, north-east of present-day Nioro, near Mali's frontier with Mauritania. There Park lodged with Daman Jumma, a leading trader. Like Salim Daucari, Daman Jumma readily acknowledged a debt to Dr. Laidley, incurred five years earlier. He owed the value of six slaves, but could not pay the whole amount at once, and the value of only one slave, £20, appears in Park's final accounts. He also helped Park to change some goods into the more readily concealed gold. By this time Park must have had some £70 to £80 worth of gold, and some trade goods were left too, enough, with luck, to carry him through his journey. Daman Jumma sent a messenger on his behalf to Ali, King of Ludamar, and a fortnight later one of Ali's slaves arrived, ostensibly to guide him on his way to Segu.

Ali was nearing the end of a long reign, lasting from 1762 to 1800, over certain 'Moors', properly called the Oulad-Mbareck. Ludamar was a corruption of the name of the ruling family's clan, the Ahl-ould-Amar. The baffling usage of the word 'Moor' at that time seems to have embraced both desert-fringe tribes and Moroccans. They all professed Islam and spoke Arabic, and were of mainly Arab and Berber descent, sometimes mingled with black African blood, but the tribes had little in common with the comfortable merchants and scholars of Fez. Living a hard, nomadic life in country barely able to maintain their cattle and camels, they mulcted support from the black farmers in more fertile southern areas, and treated them with contempt. Periodically their needs or desires brought them into conflict with Kaarta or Bambara (Segu). They had a terrifying reputation for plundering both sedentary peoples and travellers.

Park accepted the plea of Johnson, frightened by the Moors' reputation, to be allowed to return to the Gambia, carrying his papers. He retained a duplicate he had made, but left some superfluous goods with Daman to reduce the temptation to the Moors. Johnson had planned to get Park himself to turn back, by suborning Demba also into refusing to continue but, seeing his master's determination to go on, Demba agreed faithfully to follow him.

Houghton had set out from Jarra, Park learned, together with some Moorish merchants who promised to guide him across the desert towards Timbuktu, but after two days he had suspected treachery and tried to turn back. The Moors took everything he had, and he returned on foot to a watering-place, where some other Moors refused him any food. Whether he died of hunger or was murdered Park could not find out, but after leaving Jarra himself on 27 February he was shown the woods where Houghton's body had been dragged and left.

Park's spirits must therefore have sunk low when at the town of Deena a body of Moors surrounded his lodging:

'. . . they hissed, shouted, and abused me; they even spit in my face, with a view to irritate me, and afford them a pretext for seizing my baggage. But finding such insults had not the desired effect, they had recourse to the final and decisive argument, that I was a Christian, and of course that my property was lawful plunder to the followers of Mahomet. They accordingly opened my bundles and robbed me of every thing they fancied. My attendants finding that every body could rob me with impunity, insisted on returning to Jarra.'

Not giving up, he set off alone by moonlight, but soon Demba came running after him, and fetched Daman's slave who had been with them; Ali's slave had gone off. For several days they toiled through sandy country in the true Sahel, which lay beyond the limit of regular cultivation, and was the home of the nomadic pastoral Moors. Once they saw the foliage of a tree being devoured by locusts. They got to within two days' journey of Segu territory and were amongst hospitable non-Moorish people, where for once Park's host felt it an honour to entertain a white man. Then his dreams of soon reaching the Niger were abruptly shattered by the arrival on 7 March of a party of Moors who announced that they had come to take him to Ali's camp at Benowm, peaceably if he did not resist. The reason given was that Ali's wife Fatima was anxious to see a Christian. Seeing that resistance was hopeless he agreed to go with them, also taking Demba. Daman's slave had vanished.

They returned first to Deena. There Park went to pay his respects to one of Ali's sons who, without any ceremony, thrust a double-barrelled gun at him and ordered him to repair it. With difficulty Park persuaded him he knew nothing of such things. Ali's son then demanded instead some knives and scissors. Demba interpreted to him Park's reply that he had none, whereupon Ali's son snatched up a musket, cocked it, and, putting the muzzle close to the boy's ear, would have shot him dead had not the other Moors seized the gun and motioned them to retire. Demba was of course terrified and would have escaped in the night but for the vigilance of the escorting Moors.

Still unnerved by this reception, they travelled northwards a day's journey to Benowm, through country ever barer and drier. It was now the hot season, and Ramadan, the month when Muslims take neither food nor drink from sunrise to sunset, had started. Whilst on the journey his captors did not forbid him the use of such water as he could get, or even refuse a drink themselves, but water was scarce. In Benowm no such liberties were permitted.

Benowm proved to be a camp of many tents around some wells, with a small black community living nearby. On arrival Park was immediately surrounded by inquisitive people examining and handling his outlandish clothes, and the same curiosity was displayed inside Ali's tent. The latter looked sullen and said nothing after ascertaining that Park could not speak Arabic, but to show his contempt for the Christian he had a hog brought in and told him it was his food. This Park wisely declined, knowing the Muslim abhorrence of pig meat. They then untied it, expecting it to run at him, but in fact it showed no discrimination in its attacks, and ended up under the couch on which Ali was sitting! Next morning he found the same animal assigned to share what would otherwise have been quite a pleasant hut, and as some small boys took pleasure in goading it, it was not a friendly companion. During the night it caused further disturbance when Park rose to deal with an intruder who fell over it in trying to escape, whereupon the hog bit him and his screams brought Ali and many others, thinking Park was trying to escape.

The long period of confinement that then began was a misery to him. Time dragged interminably, waiting for Queen Fatima (the Moors themselves would probably have simply said, Ali's wife) who was away somewhere in the north. In such bare country and during Ramadan, his lack of food and water may be largely explained, but he also had to endure insults and humiliations. Until the novelty wore off people came continuously demanding to see him take off and put back on his unfamiliar socks and coat, the first day as a non-stop performance from noon until eight o'clock. Whilst the spectators enjoyed themselves they taunted Park, and the small boys continued rousing the hog. At night he was closely watched by guards. He concluded that the Moors studied mischief as a science, and exulted in the miseries of their fellow creatures.

Even then he could take a partly objective view of his situation:

'I was a *stranger*, I was *unprotected*, and I was a *Christian*; each of these circumstances is sufficient to drive every spark of humanity from the heart of a Moor; but when all of them, as in my case, were combined in the same person, and a suspicion prevailed withal, that I had come as a *spy* into the country, the reader will easily imagine that, in such a situation, I had every thing to fear. Anxious, however, to conciliate favour, and if possible, to afford the Moors no pretence for ill treating me, I readily complied with every command, and patiently bore every insult; but never did any period of my life pass away so heavily: from sunrise to sunset, was I obliged to suffer, with an unruffled countenance, the insults of the rudest savages on earth.'

This is the first time that the suggestion of Park's being a spy had come up. It is possible, though unlikely, that the Moors even then feared white men crossing the hundreds of miles of territory which shielded them from the coast in order to take their inhospitable land – as of course did eventually happen. It is more probable, however, that their suspicion had local roots; he had come from Kaarta, against which Ali had an alliance (that he had no intention of keeping) with Segu, towards which Park was heading. Ali was by nature a suspicious man, constantly afraid of being poisoned and never letting even his domestic slaves know where he would sleep each night.

The Moors tried to put Park to work as a barber, but that soon ended with his first exhibition in the royal presence, when he accidentally made a small cut on the head of a young prince of Ludamar. So he was left to idle away the days, which suited him, for, he said, 'I had laid it down as a rule, to make myself as useless and insignificant as possible, as the only means of recovering my liberty.'

Soon Johnson was brought from Jarra where he had been seized, together with the clothes Park had left there, but Johnson had managed to leave his papers with one of Daman's wives. Ali found this a convenient opportunity to have all Park's belongings, even his spare clothes, removed to his own tent, supposedly to protect them from theft. The same excuse could hardly cover having Park himself thoroughly searched. That was the last he saw of all his gold and amber, his watch and other instruments, but Ali returned to him his compass, which he looked upon with fascinated awe. Puzzled how to explain its pointing north however it was turned, Park eventually said it always indicated where his mother was!

He heard through various informants about a council of chief men which had debated what to do with him, whether to kill him, cut off his right hand, or, as Ali favoured, put out his eyes which, they said, resembled those of a cat – but this was not to be done until Fatima had seen him. This last plan was told to him, with great concern, by a young son of Ali himself. Park went to beg Ali to let him return to Jarra, but Ali said he must wait for Fatima, then he could go.

When sick with fever he was roughly treated by some Moors, and when he sought rest in the shade of some trees he was accused of trying to escape. He pleaded to be left alone to rest but one of the Moors pulled out a pistol and snapped it at him twice and seemed to be intent on shooting him. This made him agree to go with them to Ali, who repeated the threat to shoot him if he went outside the camp again. Nature added to his miseries with intense heat and with occasional sandstorms, and he had no change of clothes in the hot weather. Once Ali took him round the camp, after solving an initial problem of how to cover his tight breeches for respectability, to show him off to groups of ladies. There was mirth, but at him, not with him.

It was, however, the ladies who, as so often in his travels, provided more relaxed moments. Once a group of them came to his hut and clearly indicated that they wanted to see for themselves whether Christians were circumcised. Deciding to treat the business jocularly, 'I observed to them, that it was not customary in my country to give ocular demonstration in such cases, before so many beautiful women; but that if all of them would retire, except the young lady to whom I pointed (selecting the youngest and handsomest), I would satisfy her curiosity.' Everybody enjoyed the jest and he was sent some meal and milk by the young lady referred to. A few days later an old lady attending a wedding celebration just after the end of Ramadan came and dashed in his face what he described as 'the same sort of holy water, with which, among the Hottentots, a priest is said to sprinkle a new married couple'. Lewis Grassic Gibbon deciphered this obscure description as meaning urine! Before he could take offence, she seriously assured and convinced him that it was a nuptial benediction from the bride's own person!

He occupied some of the time in learning to write a little Arabic, and using this to divert the attention of some of those who came intent on mischief. In late April, after Ali had gone northwards leaving him at Benowm, he had two travelling Arabs stay some time with him in his hut, one after the other. They were friendly and gave him information about the desert routes to Timbuktu to the south-east and Morocco to the north-west. The first warned him against going to Timbuktu, as 'Christians were looked upon there as the devil's children, and enemies to the Prophet'. The second had spent some time at Gibraltar and spoke some English. These visitors cheered life for Park, but on the other hand, with Ali away, the slaves often neglected to provide him with food. Demba managed sometimes to beg a few handfuls of groundnuts at the nearby Negro village, but all three of them, Demba, Johnson, and Park himself, spent long periods lying in the languor of extreme hunger.

On 29 April there was a sudden alarm when news came of Mansong's army approaching to avenge Ali's failure to supply his promised aid against Kaarta. Everyone hastily packed and went north to Bubaker where Ali was with his wife Fatima. This was in even barer sandy country, with only scattered trees and thorn bushes. For the only time, Park said, Ali was pleased to see him and shook hands with him. Then he was introduced to Fatima who, after an initial shock at being so near to a Christian, was pleasant and presented him with a bowl of milk. She was enormously fat, but he found this was the ideal of feminine beauty amongst the Moors; mothers forced reluctant daughters to eat quantities of kouskous and milk to fatten them up. Another fashion in Ludamar, as in Kaarta also, was astonishingly similar to the almost contemporary mode in Europe: the use of a pad to raise the hair to great height.

Nearly all of May was spent at Bubaker where water was scarce, and the weather became more unbearably hot whilst the limited rains were awaited. Occasionally Ali or Fatima sent some water, but mostly Demba had to go begging until the poor lad could stand no more of the ill-treatment he received. Then Park went begging too – he had more freedom of movement than he had been allowed at Benowm – but with little success although he was persistent. Often he could not sleep

for thirst, and his imagination carried him home to the banks of Yarrow, '. . . but alas! disappointment awakened me; and I found myself
a lonely captive, perishing of thirst amidst the wilds of Africa!' Once
on his begging round, after various failures, he found an old man at a
well prepared to give him water, but at the last moment, fearing that
his bucket would be polluted by Christian lips, he dashed the water
into the cattle-trough and motioned Park to drink there. Desperate
with thirst, Park knelt down and thrust his head between two cows,
drinking with pleasure until it was all gone.

It may be surmised that Ali was not merely callous; he was reluctant to let Park go until the Segu army withdrew. When it had done
so, Ali decided to return to Jarra to treat with some of the Kaartan
refugees, who wanted two hundred Moorish horsemen to attack and
finish off their Fama Desse. Through Fatima's intercession Park was
allowed to go with him, and his emaciated horse and a few of his
clothes were restored to him. They set off on 26 May. He was greatly
shocked two days later to be told that Ali was keeping Demba as his
slave. For the only time in Ludamar, indeed in the whole journey,
Park lost his temper and stormed up to Ali, arguing furiously that this
was the height of cruelty and injustice. Ali's only answer was that if
he did not mount his horse immediately he would be sent back with
Demba. Thus these two, Park and Demba, had to part, in tears both
of them. Park was told he could keep 'the old fool', meaning Johnson.

Back at Jarra on 1 June he lodged again with Daman Jumma, and
was able to make a conditional arrangement for Demba to be redeemed
by Daman after he had left, but what actually became of the poor boy
is not known. Ali soon completed his business with the Kaartans, exacting a large price for his help, half of it paid by a forced loan from
the people of Jarra. On 8 June he went back north, completely
neglecting his side of the bargain. To Park's joy, he was allowed to
stay at Jarra, and observe a Muslim festival. Soon rejoicing turned to
sorrow. Desse had been far from finished by the Segu invasion of
Kaarta, and as soon as it was over he set about restoring his power.
First he counter-attacked Khasso, where many Jarra people were
caught in the slaughter; then, turning towards his rebellious subjects
in Jarra who were plotting his downfall, he caught them completely
by surprise by powerful, swift moves. Lacking Ali's promised support,
they broke. By 27 June Desse was hourly expected to arrive in the
town with his army, and the people fled in panic. Park had no fear of

Desse himself, but he was afraid of his army, and he therefore went with Daman and Johnson to the east.

On 1 July, resting at Queira and preparing to go on into Bambara, he was alarmed when Ali's chief slave and four other Moors appeared. Sending two boys to eavesdrop, Johnson soon found out that they had come to take Park back to Ali, but they made no immediate move, and Park decided to make a get-away in the night. Johnson would not go on, but wanted to return to the Gambia, taking Park's papers with him. Neither what he had been through nor his state of destitution would, however, deter Park from going ahead; he was not going to return to England with relatively little achieved.

Just before daybreak Johnson whispered to him that the Moors were at last asleep, and they said a very quiet farewell, Park giving him messages for his friends on the Gambia. Then, with a cold sweat on his forehead, and knowing that the next day must decide his fate one way or another, he stole quietly out of town with his horse. Once he was hooted and pelted with stones by some Moorish shepherds, but they did not stop him. All seemed to be going well until three Moors on horseback rode up to him, brandishing guns and saying he must go back to Ali. After the anxieties he had been through, he said, 'it affords a sort of gloomy relief to know the worst that can possibly happen'. Fatalistically he turned to follow them, but soon it became apparent that what they were really after was theft. All they found worth taking was his cloak, which had protected him from the occasional early rains and the mosquitoes; his appeals for its return were ignored. Then they rode off and, clutching his little bundle of clothes, he was free to turn east again, thankful to have his life and his liberty.

We cannot help wondering whether, when Ali left him at Jarra, he had lost interest in him. Did Ali really send his men to Queira with the special object of fetching him back? If so how, we might ask, did they explain away their failure to recapture this conspicuous white man six feet tall, with flowing beard and hair, in European clothes, making his way slowly and alone on his scraggy horse?

With this escape, after four months in Ludamar, Park left behind the miseries of Benowm and Bubaker. He had suffered hunger and torturing thirst, insults, humiliations, some nasty threats, and the theft of almost all his belongings, and above all of his faithful Demba. Nevertheless he was apparently never assaulted or physically maltreated.

It might indeed be thought, after reading Park's account, that what he actually suffered did not quite suffice to support his general condemnation of 'the hostility and savagery' of these Moors towards Christians, but for three things. First, the record of other desert-fringe peoples in their conduct towards their settled neighbours and travellers mostly bears him out. In Ludamar, partly isolated and with most rudimentary education, a crude and bigoted outlook and a contempt for all outsiders did but reflect the harsh setting of life. Secondly, this unusually tough and resilient man still sometimes awoke from nightmares years after his return home, seeing himself again a captive in Ali's camp.

Finally, we know that his *Travels* do not relate all that happened to him. In 1804 he told his friend Walter Scott about various incidents omitted from the book. He explained these omissions by saying that he had only communicated information 'which he thought of importance to the public . . . but that he would not shock their credulity, or render his travels more marvellous, by introducing circumstances which, however true, were of little or no moment, as they related solely to his own personal adventures and escapes'. Some of these circumstances almost certainly relate to Ludamar. When preparing the Biographical Memoir which was published in 1815, John Whishaw twice tried to extract from Scott details of these episodes, but Scott, whilst sure of the general tenor of what Park had told him, pleaded inability to relate with sufficient accuracy years later these anecdotes 'communicated near the close of an evening of conviviality'.[1]

CHAPTER XII

'The great object of my mission'

From Ludamar to Silla

———— ঙ্গ ————

When Park escaped, he was completely devoid of his gold and every-thing else he had relied on for meeting expenses and making presents, down to the last bead. His only instrument was the compass which Ali had feared to possess. In a small leather bag he carried his last two ragged changes of clothing. He was parted from his attendants and his horse was in poor shape. Altogether his situation was, as he said, 'very deplorable', but still his only thought was to travel towards the Niger. As soon as he found himself free his spirits rose. 'It is impossible to describe the joy that arose in my mind, when I looked around and concluded that I was out of danger. I felt like one recovered from sickness: I breathed freer; I found unusual lightness in my limbs; even the Desert looked pleasant . . .'

He set a course east-south-east, to the south of the line he had first travelled across Ludamar before being caught. The sun's burning heat from above was redoubled by its reflection from the sand, and distant hills shimmered like an unsettled sea. It was vain to climb a tree and search for signs of human life; nothing was to be seen but thick under-wood and hillocks of white sand. When he did meet two Moorish boys with a herd of goats, they demonstrated with empty water-skins why they were heading west towards Deena. In the great heat thirst became a torment.

By sunset, having been constantly on the move, both he and his horse were exhausted. Turning his horse loose to graze on the dried grass and survive if it could, he fell down on the sand thinking that the hour of death was fast approaching. He soon rallied, however, and pressed on. Once his hopes of rain were dashed when a wind blew only sand in his face, but finally it did rain for an hour, and he spread clothes on the ground and then sucked water from them. Pressing on through the night, after skirting a Moorish camp and nearly being caught, he found a pool where both he and his horse could drink, beating back numbers of frogs with a stick.

At the first village he came to he was refused all help by the Dooty, or village head, but an old woman kindly fed him and his horse. The best return he could make was one of his two pocket handkerchiefs. 'Overcome with joy at so unexpected a deliverance, I lifted up my eyes to heaven, and whilst my heart swelled with gratitude, I returned thanks to that gracious and bountiful Being whose power had supported me under so many dangers, and had now spread for me a table in the Wilderness.' Thus could a bowl of kouskous left over from the previous night appear to one in his position. He hurried on when he overheard some Fulani discussing the possibility of seizing him and taking him back to Ali. That night, having had only two hours' rest in two days, he was able to sleep for the night, as well as the mosquitoes and wild beasts permitted. Next morning a hospitable Fulani shepherd fed him and sold him corn for the price of some brass buttons from his coat, although the shepherd's family cried and fled from the tiny tent, just high enough to sit in, when they realized he was a Christian.

By the following day he was finally out of Ludamar and into greener Segu territory. Having travelled some seventy-five or eighty miles in three days, he reached a town called Wawra. A good sleep there was disturbed by a loud general argument outside as to whether he were an Arab or a Moor. Finally the Dooty, who had visited the Gambia, silenced it firmly by declaring that he was a European, but clearly a very poor one. He was no longer in danger of pursuit, and some women even entreated him to enquire after their captive sons at Segu, especially one woman who made a point of assuring him that her son was no heathen, but prayed regularly. Beyond Wawra some towns were Muslim, others not, but in both he usually found hospitality. At one his landlord diffidently begged a lock of his long hair to make a saphie to bring him all the knowledge of the white men, a simple mode of instant education that startled Park. Once begun on the haircut, his thirst for learning was so strong that Park had to stop him by clapping his hat on his head and saying that he must 'reserve some of this precious merchandize for a future occasion'.

The rains had now begun, and in this area, he was told, hunger was never known. At Ouessebou (Park's Wasiboo) he helped the family who lodged him to plant corn. Then as now the farmer's first concern was to provide his family's food, and only after that to grow produce for sale. Park noted that the people took their weapons to the fields in case of Moorish raids. The master of the house marked out with his spear parts of the fields, each to be worked by a group with three domestic slaves, the general practice being for slaves to work alongside their masters. Mostly, slaves lived tolerably well as dependants of the family, custom setting limits to any ill-treatment. Their sale was prohibited unless they were convicted of an offence, except in times of famine or if their master became insolvent. This was a far cry from the West Indian conditions then often alleged to be superior! Park reckoned that a surprisingly high proportion, three-quarters of the population, were slaves, but a strict definition of slavery would probably regard many of them as in some less onerous condition of dependence; reliable information on this subject is still scarce.[1] Seventy years later Park's stay of four days at Ouessebou was recalled to the French Lieutenant Mage by Djolo, a Bambara who was about ten at the time.[2] Park soon found he could understand the Bambara language, which he described as a 'corruption' of Mandingo.

He frequently had company on the road, fugitive Kaartans wanting to offer their services at Segu, or people going there to trade, but rain now often made the paths slippery and he could not always keep up. His horse was too weak to be ridden, and Park often plodded along barefoot, carrying his boots to conserve them. For the first time he encountered a slave coffle or caravan, seventy in number, tied together in groups of seven with thongs round their necks. With them was the servant of one of the Arabs who had visited him at Benowm. He learnt that they were to go all the way to Morocco through Ludamar and the desert. Soon afterwards, meeting some of the Moorish owners, he found them inquisitive but less rude than in their own country. The Arab he had known was not with the party.

To the local people the shabby state of his clothes and his horse became increasingly a subject for jokes at his expense, and he believed that even the slaves were ashamed to be seen in his company. His spirits rose sharply, however, at a little village marked on his map, with good cause, as 'Lions', where he was told that he should see the Niger the next day. It was called in that country the Joliba or 'the great water'. He could not sleep that night for excitement, and was up and ready to go long before the gates in the village stockade were opened. As soon as they were open he set off, accompanied by many people going for market-day in Segu. On this most important day for him his dating is confused, and although he said it was 20 July 1796, in fact it seems it must have been 21 July.

For that last day on the way to his longed-for goal he rejoined the fugitive Kaartans. It was one of them who, as they were coming into low, marshy ground, and he was eagerly looking ahead, called out to him:

'*Geo affili* (see the water); and looking forwards, I saw with infinite pleasure the great object of my mission; the long sought for majestic Niger, glittering to the morning sun, as broad as the Thames at Westminster, and flowing slowly *to the eastward*. I hastened to the brink, and, having drank of the water, lifted up my fervent thanks in prayer, to the Great Ruler of all things, for having thus far crowned my endeavours with success.'

Park had earned his moment of triumph by his perseverance through distance, discouragement, and privations. What he saw was of course common knowledge to the peoples living far and wide in West and even North Africa and had, indeed, been *seen* by Europeans as well as Arabs. What he had heard many times, he said, prepared him to see the great river flowing towards the rising sun, as Houghton too had heard. Ibn Battuta had preceded Park by over four hundred years, but his true account was not effectively fed into a developing world geography until after Park's death. Had he been known of in Europe in 1796, he would still have seemed to be contradicted by the later 'authority' of Leo Africanus. To have settled once and for all, and in a way that could lead to further advances in geography, even this one important fact was a legitimate cause for triumph and thankfulness on Park's part, something that had not previously been achieved.

From the river bank he could see that Segu consisted of four separate towns, two on each side of the river. One on the south bank was the royal capital, to which he wanted to cross. Three ferries, formed by joining two hollowed-out tree-trunks end to end, were constantly passing to and fro, but he could only join the large number of people waiting for their turns. He noted with concern the number of Moors amongst those crossing. He could pick out mosques in every quarter of the city, even though the Bambara themselves have always been resistant to Islam. Each town had a high mud wall round it; the houses were built in clay, square-shaped and flat-roofed, some of two storeys, and many with whitewashed walls. He gathered that there were about thirty thousand inhabitants. The whole view impressed him strongly:

'The view of this extensive city; the numerous canoes upon the river; the crowded population and the cultivated state of the surrounding country, formed altogether a prospect of civilization and magnificence, which I little expected to find in the bosom of Africa.'

This exterior view of Segu was all he was ever to get. After two hours one of Mansong's chief men came across and told him he must await the permission of the king, or Fama, before presuming to cross the river. He should therefore retire some distance and lodge at a village there. He found the villagers afraid to feed or lodge him, and he was preparing for what promised to be a stormy, wet, and hungry night up a tree for protection from wild animals, when once again a woman took compassion on him. She took him to her hut, spread a mat and broiled a very fine fish for his supper. As he lay down afterwards her daughters continued spinning cotton much of the night and singing. One song was a sweet and plaintive air with a verse composed for the occasion;

'The winds roared, and the rains fell –
The poor white man, faint and weary, came and sat under our tree –
He has no mother to bring him milk; no wife to grind his corn.
    Chorus – Let us pity the white man; no mother has he, etc.'

Touched by this unexpected kindness sleep fled from his eyes. In the morning he made the only recompense left to him, two of the last four brass buttons from his waistcoat.

Three days he had to wait in this little village, with discouraging rumours coming across from Segu of how the Moors and slatees were pouring out their suspicions of him to the Fama. Once a messenger came to ask if he had any present for the Fama, but he could only reply that he had been robbed of everything by the Moors. At last on 23 July (Park's dating) Mansong's verdict came. Park was to leave the neighbourhood at once, but if he wished to go to Jenne the messenger was to take him down river as far as Sansanding. To offset the expulsion Mansong sent him a bag of 5,000 cowries, the small shells used as currency all over West Africa. Park reckoned them to be worth about £1, which, in this area of plentiful supplies, could feed him and his horse for fifty days.

Chatting with the guide on the way, he learnt that Mansong had feared he could not adequately protect him from the Moors in Segu; they were apprehensive of European competition with their trade. Park saw that the circumstances of his arrival could generate suspicion:

as the guide argued, '. . . when he was told, that I had come a great distance, and through many dangers, to behold the Joliba river, [he] naturally inquired, if there were no rivers in my own country, and whether one river was not like another'. Mansong must have thought the same, yet, '. . . in spite of the jealous machinations of the Moors, this benevolent prince thought it sufficient, that a white man was found in his dominions, in a condition of extreme wretchedness; and that no other plea was necessary to entitle the sufferer to his bounty'. Indeed not once in either of his journeys did Park suffer any molestation or theft in Mansong's secure and peaceful kingdom.

This guide was with him for a little over a day, travelling through country richly studded with shea trees. The people were collecting fruits (or nuts) from the trees to make shea butter, which Park reckoned to be better both in keeping qualities and in flavour than butter made from cow's milk. After passing several fishing villages they parted at Sansanding, a town with eight to ten thousand people, frequented by Moors trading from the Mediterranean coast and by people speaking a variety of languages he could not understand. Nowadays it is the site of a barrage built across the river by the French to provide irrigation down-stream, where the Niger used to flood uncontrolled.

Here he came the nearest to being molested in Segu country, for the Moors spotted him. They assembled and harangued him, telling him he must say the Muslim prayers just as some wretched Jews there did, a remnant of many ancient Jewish settlements in the Sahara. As the 'king's stranger' he was protected from being physically swept off to the mosque by Counti Mamadi, the Dooty of Sansanding, but he was nevertheless obliged to sit, until it was too dark to see, on a high seat near the mosque whilst everyone gazed at him – like the spectators at an execution, he said. Even when he was taken to the Dooty's house people pushed in, demanding to see him eat raw eggs, believing that this was the main diet of Europeans. Nearly sixty years later Dr. Barth had this practice charged against him as an insult near Timbuktu and he could only surmise that tales of Frenchmen eating eggs had been carried inland from the Senegal, with this curious addition of the eggs being raw! On Park's explaining, however, Counti Mamadi gave him mutton to eat, and eventually by midnight he was left in peace. Before he retired to rest, his host earnestly asked him for a saphie, stronger than the Moors', and to provide the strongest he could, Park wrote out for him the Lord's Prayer. Rising early before the Moors were up and about, he continued on his way.

Possibly amongst the crowd of Moors the previous day, or maybe only in the general area at the time, there was one Al-Hajj Mohammed Sharif. In April 1803, a Mr. Cahill, British trader at Rabat in Morocco, passed on to Banks the Sharif's recollection of seeing Park at Sansanding, and his description of 'Mr. Park's horse, his dress, his misery and sufferings; and (of) the king of Bambarra's having sent him cowries at Sego, at the same time refusing him permission to enter the town . . .' What sharply conflicts with Park's account is the Sharif's claim to have 'offered to conduct and protect him to, and at, Tombuctoo, and [he] asserts, that he might have gone without risk, and have then proceeded to Tasslet and Fez'. It is hard to believe that if such an offer was clearly and convincingly made to him, Park would not have jumped at it, and nothing else in his record suggests either a coward or a liar. Cahill's letter was communicated to the African Association's Annual Meeting in May 1804 by Sir William Young, then Secretary, but all he told Park in a letter was, 'he saw you at Sansanding, and confirms your account of Sego'.[3] Accordingly, no comment by Park on the Sharif's story is extant.

After leaving Sansanding he had several guides in a few days. One of them called out as they passed some bushes, '*Wara billi billi*' – a very large lion – and signed to Park to ride away, but his horse was so tired he could only plod on, seeing nothing himself and hoping it was a false alarm. Again the guide called out, 'God preserve us!' and to Park's amazement he saw a great red lion lying only a few yards away with its head between its paws. A spring was to be feared at any moment and Park prepared to jump leaving his horse to shield him, but the lion seemed to have no appetite and let them jog slowly past. Not until they were far beyond it could he take his eyes away from this sovereign beast, and after that he and his guide took care to avoid any comparable clump of bushes where a lion could be hiding.

At a small village called Modiboo he had a wonderful view of the river for miles in both directions, and its great breadth there and its green islands made 'the situation one of the most enchanting in the world'. Not so its mosquitoes, which prevented all sleep. The next day his poor, worn-out horse fell on the path and could not be raised and, with sorrow, and wondering whether he himself would not soon be in a similar state, he had to leave it behind, taking off the saddle and bridle. Soon afterwards he got a lift in a fishing canoe, and at the end of the day he reached Silla, the only place he visited on the south bank, by his estimation some seventy-five miles east of Segu.

Between the evening and the early morning he talked much with traders and local inhabitants, supplementing earlier information. (Or did he spend a whole day at Silla, and get his dates wrong again?) He learnt that Jenne was two days to the eastward, and that beyond it the Niger passed through a large lake called Dibbie (properly Debo) then issued out in many streams that coalesced into two main branches, enclosing a large island called Jinbala. The Niger then reunited near Kabara, the river port south of Timbuktu, twelve days' journey from Jenne. Slightly less far again, the river passed two days' journey south of 'Houssa'; beyond that, people only said that it '*runs to the world's end*'.

He heard too of the Fulani kingdom of Masina, north-east of Silla, which was tributary to Segu; of Gotto or Mossi to the south, which had once beaten Segu in war; and of Baedoo and Maniana west of Mossi. Unlike many later travellers in Africa, he treated accounts of the Maniana being cannibals with great caution, but he heard them so often of that country alone, that he supposed they must be true.* In the circumstances what he learnt was remarkably accurate, although the Hausa states are further away than indicated; Jenne is not on the Niger itself, and Park had a confused picture of the Mossi states, taking 'Moosee' to be a king's name.

In a damp hut at Silla he passed a feverish and sleepless night in thought. 'Worn down by sickness, exhausted with hunger and fatigue; half naked, and without any article of value . . . I was now convinced by painful experience, that the obstacles to my further progress were insurmountable.' The rains would soon make travelling impossible except by river, and he had no means to pay for that. Above all, everything he heard convinced him that to go on would be increasingly to place himself within the power of 'those merciless fanatics', the Moors. 'I was apprehensive, that, in attempting to reach even Jenne (unless under the protection of some man of consequence amongst them, which I had no means of obtaining), I should sacrifice my life to no

---

*In 1912 Delafosse wrote that the neighbours of the *Minianka*, part of the Senoufo in present-day Upper Volta and Ivory Coast, said they were previously cannibals, but he found no trace then (*Haut-Niger-Sénégal*, Vol.I, p.301). 'Baedoo' has not been identified.

purpose; for my discoveries would perish with me.' There is no suggestion here of an approach by Al-Hajj Mohammed Sharif. The prospect of returning to the Gambia was his cheerless alternative. In his *Travels* he pleaded with his readers to accept his decision, and how many of them would have come as far?* But he probably always had difficulty reconciling *himself* to this most uncharacteristic action, despite overwhelming reasons for it.

His decision taken, by 8 o'clock in the morning of 30 July 1796, less than a month after his final escape from the Moors, Park stepped into a canoe to cross the river and begin a wearisome journey back.

* James Jackson, a trader at Mogador, wrote to Banks in 1798 that he believed Park could have reached Timbuktu safely but for 'some jealousy of trading people that represented to him as much danger as possible in order to dissuade him from proceeding' (D.T.C., Vol.XI, pp.21–3). To Willis in 1800 he expressed surprise at Park's dress and ignorance of Arabic. Once a prospective traveller to Timbuktu himself, his remarks have some flavour of sour grapes.

CHAPTER XIII

'Still under the protecting eye of Providence'

From Silla to Kamalia

———— ෴ ————

The rains ruling out travel on the south bank, which he would have preferred, Park could only return by the way he had come. Six days had taken him from Segu to Silla but the return needed a fortnight, so much had the route been flooded. For three days of ceaseless rain he was held up in an inhospitable village. Back at Modiboo he was pleasantly surprised to be reunited with his horse, somewhat recovered from its fatigue, though it was not of much benefit to him in such rain-sodden country.

As he went he heard increasingly that word had gone out from Segu that he was a spy, and he was naturally a less welcome visitor than before. Counti Mamadi at Sansanding accommodated him again but said brusquely that he must leave next day; at night, however, he came privately and warned Park in a friendly manner to avoid Segu, as Mansong had despatched men to capture him. Closer to Segu he was firmly refused entry to two villages.

Al-Hajj Mohammed Sharif said that Mansong was 'under the strong impression that he was a spy, sent by some Christian power to take plans of the country with a view to conquering it; or that he was a magician, who by his charms might cause the death and be the ruin of his people'. In fact, reading between the lines, we can surely see Mansong, here as later on, as an extremely shrewd politician, balancing two irreconcilables. The Moors and their local trading partners wanted Park imprisoned, if nothing more, to discourage other Europeans from coming. To assuage them Mansong sent Park away, and later despatched men down-river to follow him. But his turning a blind eye when Park came back and circuited only a mile or two outside Segu, of which Mansong could hardly have been unaware, points to a decision not to shut the door on the small chance that further contacts with the Europeans might prove beneficial.

Of course the Africans had difficulties in assessing the intentions and capabilities of the Europeans. In later travellers' experience, the same conflict, with hospitality and hope of benefit on the one hand, and suspicion or fear on the other, continued throughout the century in varying forms, sometimes mixed up with the idea that Europeans might take sides in local disputes. As late as 1894, when large expeditions of three rival European nationalities had been marching around what became Nigeria, signing treaties and asking for concessions, '. . . they were not seen as being sufficiently powerful to constitute an obvious insurmountable danger'.[1]

Park himself could see why he should be suspected, although he was evidently clear in his conscience of the charge of spying. Travelling openly and undisguised, with his own and his sponsors' interests being to gain geographical knowledge and the opening of peaceful trade, he was not looking for information to be used *against* these countries. Nevertheless, had those who suspected him known what would be meditated in Europe within a few years, they would have seen their suspicions as being justified, even if there was to be a long interval before overt action against them followed. Park did not go out to spy, but his work was used as if he had done so.

Once Park moved on west of Segu the alarms quickly died away. He decided to continue that way, instead of crossing the river and heading due south to Cape Coast, through country and peoples completely unknown to him. His pleas to be allowed into a stockaded village were long refused, although a lion could be clearly heard prowling around. At midnight the inhabitants at last let him in, convinced, because he had not cursed them, that he could not be, as they had earlier supposed, a Moor!

Beyond Segu the rains delayed him less but he and his horse had to swim across several streams. The rain kept his clothes almost constantly wet and muddy, and a swim was a way of washing them, with his precious notes secured above water in the crown of his hat. It was probably in this period that he learnt the trick of judging the depth of a stream by throwing in pebbles and seeing how long it took for bubbles to surface. Years later, Walter Scott found him doing this in the river Yarrow near Selkirk, and Park told him he had learnt it in Africa.

He heard that Yamina (Nyamina) and neighbouring villages had been plundered by Kaarta only four years previously. This attack had happened when Mansong was struggling with his half-brother for the throne, though Park did not know this. Clearly it had prompted Mansong's attack on Kaarta in 1796, but there was in any case enduring hostility between the two Bambara states.

It was a populous and well-cultivated country, although food was then scarce as the harvest was not yet in. Often Park had to be content with some raw corn in water. His first good meal for a long while was earned on 20 August, by saphie-writing again. His host, a freed slave and Muslim convert, not being content with washing off the writing from the board and drinking the draught – a standard procedure – licked the board itself dry so as to lose no part of the charm's efficacy.

Park was clearly unaware that at Nyamina he had passed near the reputed site of a major city in the last remnants of the Mali Empire only a century and a half before. Even if then recalled, this was unlikely to be the subject of conversation with a destitute stranger on a one-night stop. Beyond Nyamina he re-entered Mandingo-speaking country, still under Segu. Bamako, which he reached on 23 August, and of which Houghton had heard, is now the capital of the Republic of Mali. Park was disappointed by its small size although it was prosperous. For once, he had civil conversations with some Moorish traders there. He was told that he would have to change direction, for soon the route crossed to the other side of the river and the local ferries could not take his horse. Indeed everyone shook their heads at the thought of his travelling anywhere at that season, but eventually he found that if he left the river he could still follow one difficult road.

He was given a guide, a 'singing man', who promptly lost the way, gave some vague directions, and sprang up a hillside where it was impossible for a horse to follow. Retracing his steps, Park picked up the correct path, which he followed, usually alone, through hilly country peopled only by a few shepherds and dwellers in isolated hamlets. He had been suffering from fever since the rains set in, and this journey was most tiring to him. From one hilltop he caught sight of some very distant mountains to the south-east, which he was told were situated in a large and powerful country called Kong.* This glimpse subsequently played an unfortunate part in European conceptions of African geography.

---

*René Caillié (*Travels*, Vol.I, p.362) wrongly supposed Park had mistaken the Mandingo word for hill ('*konko*' in Park's published vocabulary) but there was a state called Kong, beyond the low mountains he had seen.

For the last time he was robbed, this time by men who were brigands pure and simple. After trying to bluff his way past he offered no resistance, which would obviously have been fatal. They stripped him naked and even carefully examined his boots, one of which was tied to his foot with a broken bridle rein. They debated whether to leave him stark naked but had the humanity to return the worse of his two shirts and trousers and finally, after nearly going off with it, his hat holding his notes; they took his horse and the rest of his clothes.

Then, reflecting on his parlous state so far from the Gambia, he felt his end had come and lay down ready to perish. As always, however, the despair soon lifted:

'The influence of religion, however, aided and supported me ... I was still under the protecting eye of that Providence who has condescended to call himself the stranger's friend. At this moment, painful as my reflections were, the extraordinary beauty of a small moss in fructification, irresistibly caught my eye ... Can that Being (thought I), who planted, watered, and brought to perfection, in this obscure part of the world, a thing which appears of so small importance, look with unconcern upon the situation and sufferings of creatures formed after his own image? – surely not! Reflections like these, would not allow me to despair ...'

Park's religious faith lay deep but its imagery and approach to God lay through nature rather than through a Calvinism based on Biblical revelation. The latter might recognize the name 'Providence', but hardly 'that Being', or the earlier 'bountiful Being' who had spread a table for him in the wilderness, or 'the Great Ruler of all things'. Being a botanist, not a physicist, he saw God not like Paley's Great Watchmaker, but as a Gardener, tending plants and men alike.

So restored, he went on his way. At Sibidooloo the Mansa, regarding him as 'Mansong's stranger', and having no hint of his being a wanted man, received him well. He soon recovered the horse and all the stolen goods, and sent them on to Park at his next stop; only his pocket compass had been broken beyond repair. Having to stay ten days at Wonda miserably with fever, Park felt less welcome every day, in the hungry season before harvest. The Mansa there, who was also the village schoolmaster, was kindly; yet he owned children sold to him by desperate, starving mothers in return for forty days' provisions to feed the rest of their families. Before he left, Park presented him with his horse; it had been rescued in Wonda when the surround of a well caved in under it, but was now too far gone to be of further use to him. To the Mansa of Sibidooloo – in Manding, the heartland once of the Empire of Mali, each village had become independent with its own Mansa – he sent back his saddle and bridle in return for the recovery of the stolen goods.

Still suffering from fever, Park pressed on over hills that exhausted him, and expected to have to plod on until he dropped in his tracks. On the contrary, when he arrived at Kamalia on 16 September he was received with the greatest kindness by a Bushreen, or Muslim, called Karfa Taura. As Park arrived with a skin yellowed by fever, a long beard, and ragged clothing, in a state of extreme poverty, Karfa and his companions did not at first believe he was a European. Karfa knew Europeans only by repute. His doubts cleared when Park proved able to read a little book obtained from the coast. It was the Anglican *Book of Common Prayer*, and was to be a great source of comfort to the Presbyterian Park over the coming months. His host advised him to stay until the dry season, when Karfa could take him to the Gambia, along with slaves for sale, and he could make what return he thought proper. Park's offer of the value of one slave was readily accepted.

Lewis Grassic Gibbon scoffs at Park's description of his slave-trading host as 'benevolent', but during most of human history benevolence would not have seemed incompatible with the ownership of slaves. Karfa visited him regularly in the clean hut he had provided, together with ample food, water, and firewood. Park's spirits rose, and the fever which at first kept him indoors gradually abated. The efforts of visiting slatees and Moors to turn Karfa against Park had no effect. Nor was he the only recipient of Karfa's kindness: one day a slave in transit begged Park for food and reminded him that only a few months before he had given Park milk when hungry in Kaarta but, he added with a sigh, 'The irons were not then on my legs!' Park approached Karfa, who gave him some groundnuts for the man.

The rains ended with heavy storms; then came the dry season in November, which would continue until the following June. Soon the dry harmattan wind came down from the north-east, taking the humidity from the air and bringing a coolness which reinvigorated him. The next month Karfa set out to buy slaves at markets on the Niger. With his strength returning, Park was able to wander in and around Kamalia, a town divided into separate Muslim and pagan quarters. Through the dust-laden haze he saw, as one can still in sparsely populated areas, spectacular and often dangerous grass fires. These evoked one of his best scenic descriptions, an aspect in which he was generally rather weak:

'The burning the grass in Manding exhibits a scene of terrific grandeur. In the middle of the night, I could see the plains and mountains, as far as the eye could reach, variegated with lines of fire; and the light reflected on the sky, made the heavens appear in a blaze. In the day time, pillars of smoke were seen in every direction; while the birds of prey were observed hovering round the conflagration, and pouncing down upon the snakes, lizards, and other reptiles, which attempted to escape from the flames. This annual burning is soon followed by a fresh and sweet verdure, and the country is thereby rendered more healthful and pleasant.'

With time on his hands, he watched the farmers at work up to harvest, and then he dried and pressed specimens of the crops and other plants in readiness for his return journey. The land was, he learnt, a communal possession, not usually purchased but allocated by the chiefs to those needing it. (This is still often the case.) He probably over-estimated the capacity of traditional agriculture to support a denser population, believing that it needed only proper example and instruction to make fruitful the well-watered countryside, then in a 'savage and neglected state'. The absence of sugar-cane, coffee, cocoa, pineapple, and citrus fruits that he noted has since been made good, especially near the coasts.

After harvest, with little to do on the farms, the men turned their attention to hunting, fishing, or crafts. He saw ivory obtained near Kamalia. The Africans could not understand what use was made of it, but it brought them profit. The hunters bravely fired crude guns from close quarters, then followed the wounded elephant until it dropped. (The same method was used to kill three beasts, one legally, in Borgu Division of Nigeria in 1958.) Outside the Game Reserves elephant are now, of course, very much rarer than in his day.

At an iron-smelter's in the town near his lodging – this craft has almost been killed now by industrial products – he was allowed to observe the processes used. The picture of Kamalia in his *Travels* shows the scene, with Park himself in the right foreground. At an appointed day, after the floods had receded and the streams dried up, the people of Kamalia, but mainly the women, went out *en masse* led by the Mansa, followed by Park watching them, to pan for gold-dust in the stream-beds or to dig it from pits. It seemed to him that up in the hills from which it was washed down there must be much more, and some readers at home later took his evidence to point to a real bonanza. Rennell took a more realistic view, although, like Park himself, he did not realize that this was part of 'Wangara', depleted by many centuries of working.

Women were also to be seen engaged on the domestic crafts of spinning, weaving, and dyeing cloth with indigo; Park reckoned its quality to be equal to that of the best Indian or European cloth. Some of the men worked leather into sandals, sheaths, amulets, and other objects; others were the smiths, forging implements with hammer, anvil, and bellows. Park might have been describing the village crafts of today, though these are becoming scarcer as modern manufactures undercut them. Within the limits of local population, resources, and markets the Mandingoes kept themselves busy, and Park strongly denied the common European belief, much put about by the pro-slavery party, that Africans were lazy and would only work if forced.

During Karfa Taura's absence, Park was left in the care of Fankooma who, as village schoolmaster, was a key man in the locality. Three times Park visited the school on 'graduation days'. Seeing the avidity for education and the pride taken in it, even when it meant non-Muslim parents losing their children to the Muslim faith, Park lamented the lack of effort made to spread Christianity in Africa. The white traders, he said, always performed their devotions in private (he might have added, if at all!). As a result, '. . . even the poor Africans, whom we affect to consider as barbarians, look upon us, I fear, as little better than a race of formidable but ignorant heathens'. He would have liked to see an easy introduction to Christianity printed in Arabic, in what would, no doubt, have been a vain hope, had it ever been seriously tried, of its finding its way into the village schools.

In polygamous households the children, weaned late by European standards, were close to, and learned from, their mothers. 'One of the first lessons in which the Mandingo women instruct their children, is *the practice of truth*,' he said; this was too much for Thomson to quote in 1890. A little later the children were inducted by their parents, the girls into domestic tasks and the boys into farming. Their growth was punctuated by ceremonies. Fankooma was much in demand for naming ceremonies on the eighth day after birth – like Park's own – which he witnessed four times. At puberty all boys, not only Muslims, were circumcised. How easily recognized, even today, are his descriptions, also those of marriages, the ills that flesh is heir to, and burials! But women now have a freedom then lacking, when refusal of the parents' choice of husband could lead to either perpetual spinsterhood, or enslavement to the rejected suitor. Park recognized that bride-price was a recompense to the bride's kin for losing her services, not a purchase of her person; the latter interpretation has been a common mistake.

Park became friends with Fankooma, an excellent man. Each was surprised at the other's knowledge of such Old Testament figures as Moses and Isaiah and the Psalms of David, available to Fankooma in Arabic, and they discussed their faiths tolerantly. Although he derided the Africans' knowledge of geography and astronomy as puerile, in the end Park was quite respectful of their traditional religions. Everywhere, he perceived, there was a belief in a Supreme Being and an after-life, although God was remote and the worshipper dealt with lesser spirits. To the outsider, the only ceremony visible was a prayer muttered to the new moon, and people were reluctant to discuss religion, taking it so much for granted. That African traditional religions are profound and not merely a superstitious worship of idols and fetishes, has again been appreciated by modern studies.

Many things have of course changed, with very different state structures, much greater urbanization, faster communications, and the rest. Yet the underlying similarities and the continuity of African cultures are such that Park's detailed descriptions are easily recognizable even today and in areas far from those he visited. For an untrained observer he made a perceptive and valuable contribution to human understanding.[2]

Wandering round making and recording his observations, clarifying his recollections of what he had seen earlier, drawing a map of that part of the Niger which he had followed, and, we may suppose, poring over the notes from the crown of his hat, occupied his time until Karfa's return on 24 January 1797, bringing with him thirteen slaves and a young girl as his fourth wife. Karfa kindly gave Park a garment and trousers in the local style, for which he was most grateful, as his own clothes were by then worn so thin he was almost ashamed to appear out of doors. With Karfa's return, Park hoped they would soon get away towards the Gambia, but he was disappointed to find he would for some time yet have to possess his soul in as much patience as, in his anxiety to return home, he could then muster.

CHAPTER XIV

'Long numbered with the dead!'

The return home

———— ౭౭ ————

The experience of travelling in a large coffle or caravan made a considerable impact on Park's future thinking by showing him there was safety in numbers, but he found the business of assembling it very tiresome. The slatees who were to join Karfa continued to find other business they had to settle first. Park grumbled to himself that time seemed to be an object of no importance. He was particularly worried because the slatees and visiting Moors continued to speak against him to Karfa, but his fears that they might succeed were unjustified.

Assembling the slaves and the trade goods and food that they would carry was the main cause of delay. All this time the slaves were kept in irons, but by day they were allowed to sit outside in the shade, and partly successful efforts were made to cheer them up by playing games and singing. Many sat all day dejected and melancholy, understandably, because the general belief, which Park tried to counter, was that the white men bought them for eating, or to sell to others who would eat them.

All of Karfa Taura's slaves had been captured in Mansong's wars. Park found that eleven of the thirteen had been in domestic slavery all their lives, for like the common soldiers of medieval Europe they had less chance of escape from capture or of subsequent ransom than their superiors. Slaves also might have been sold during famines, like the children back in Wonda, or because of insolvency, both often connected with wars, or, lastly, following conviction for murder, adultery, or witchcraft, but Park never heard of an actual case of the latter.

Being of course more prone to escape than domestic slaves, such captured or bought slaves were commonly sold in relays until they were far from home, or to the Europeans or Arabs. They became strangers without rights, and unloved, like a slave boy whose body Park had earlier seen being unceremoniously pitched into a shallow grave, his master all the while lamenting only his loss of money. As emancipation was uncommon, even for domestic slaves, escape was the main route to freedom, but when one of Karfa's slaves managed to open his fetters at night with a knife, he refused to stop to help the others.

When March came Park hoped they would set off on their way, but it was decided to wait until mid-April, when Ramadan would have come and gone. He joined voluntarily in the first three days of fasting, and so made a good impression, but then he desisted whilst the Muslims continued to fast and to meet daily for prayers, the women doing so separately from the men. At last, when the new moon signalled the end of the fast, they set off on 19 April, after saying lengthy prayers, leaving barely enough time to reach the Gambia before the rains began. In this period he heard of the French capture of a British convoy in the Mediterranean eighteen months earlier, the news having filtered slowly down trade routes from the north.

The caravan numbered seventy-three, nearly half of them slaves for sale, roped together at the neck, and secured in irons at night. Karfa was the overall leader, and there were four other slatees with him. The remainder was made up of other free men, including six singing men to jolly the caravan along, wives, domestic slaves who were not roped, Park himself, and Fankooma, the schoolmaster, with a few of his pupils.

The journey involved a trek of about five hundred miles, much of it through thickly wooded hills separated by numerous rivers and small streams. Even today there is no motor road on the route east of the river Senegal. It took them five days to cross the Jallonka (or Dialonka) wilderness, and Park reckoned they had travelled at least a hundred miles without seeing any habitation. The long marches in the hot season, one of thirty miles, were terribly fatiguing for the slaves, especially as their limbs were stiff from long confinement in irons. Some villages could offer them no food, being near to starvation themselves. Having no corn, they were existing on bamboo seeds and a paste extracted from the pods of the locust bean tree, a kind of mimosa, called locally the *nitta*.

In this wilderness a woman slave called Nealee, belonging to Karfa, became exhausted and sulkily refused to eat. Her load was removed but she lagged behind, complaining dreadfully of pains in her legs. Then a swarm of bees attacked the party, and as she was not able to escape she was badly stung. Treatment was given to her, but when

she declared she would rather die than walk another step the slatees
began instead to whip her; she tried to run off, but quickly collapsed.
Karfa had her placed on an ass but she could not sit upright, so she
was carried on a litter. The next day she was unable to stand, let alone
walk, and the slatees had her tied over an ass's back, but the unruly
animal kept throwing her off. At this stage, said Park:

'Every attempt to carry her forward being thus found ineffectual, the general
cry of the coffle was, *kang-tegi, kang-tegi*, "cut her throat, cut her throat;"
an operation I did not wish to see performed, and therefore marched onwards with the foremost of the coffle. I had not walked above a mile when
one of Karfa's domestic slaves came up to me, with poor Nealee's garment
upon the end of his bow, and exclaimed *Nealee affeeleeta* (Nealee is lost). I
asked him whether the Slatees had given him the garment as a reward for
cutting her throat; he replied, that Karfa and the schoolmaster would not
consent to that measure, but had left her on the road; where undoubtedly
she soon perished, and was probably devoured by wild beasts.

'The sad fate of this wretched woman, notwithstanding the outcry before
mentioned, made a strong impression on the minds of the whole coffle, and
the schoolmaster fasted the whole of the ensuing day, in consequence of it.
We proceeded in deep silence . . .'

Just possibly Park remonstrated with his friend Karfa at some stage
of these proceedings. It would have been in character for him not to
mention it if he did, but certainly he does not hint at it. Karfa seems
to have let the other slatees take charge although Nealee was his slave.
If Park had protested to them they would no doubt have told him to
mind his own business, but he could have tried to induce Karfa to
find some other solution.

Travelling far almost due west, at one stage after crossing the Ba
Fing or Black River, the main stream of the Senegal, they had to dodge
a band rumoured to be intent on plundering them. Then they came to
Malacotta, the schoolmaster's home town. There they spent three
days resting and feasting before they parted from Fankooma and his
pupils. Veering a little north, they crossed the river Faleme at Satadoo
(Satadougou). A day's journey beyond, at Baniserile, one of the slatees
who lived there elected to remain, the news being that there was then
little sale for slaves on the Gambia.

Slowly converging upon the upper Gambia, they took two days to
cross the wilderness of Tenda. Shortly afterwards Karfa told Park
they were reaching the limit of the country where the shea tree grew,

and Park therefore replaced some bedraggled specimens he had carried all the way. As soon as they crossed the river Nerico on 28 May the singing men gave voice to celebrate their safe arrival in 'the land of the setting sun'. The next day they stood again on the banks of the Gambia itself and he could feel, to his great joy, that he was nearly home again, and would soon be back in the familiar kingdom of Wuli.

At Medina he was unable to see the old Mansa who had been so kind to him before, as he was dangerously ill. Instead Park sent word that his prayers for a safe return had been answered. One day more brought them to Jindey, where he had parted from Dr. Laidley at the beginning of his journey. At Park's suggestion, Karfa left his slaves there until there should be an opportunity to sell them. During the journey Park seems to have got on better with these unfortunates than with their owners. Even amidst their infinitely greater sufferings they had sympathized with his, and often they had brought him water to drink or collected branches and made his bed. Now they were to part, and Park felt deeply for these men who had nothing to look forward to but a life of bondage in a strange land. Their parting was marked by mutual regrets and blessings.

Karfa declared that he himself would not leave Park until he quitted Africa, and they went on together. The next day he was able to converse once more in English, with Seniora Camilla, at whose house they stayed overnight. She did not at first recognize in this bearded, long-haired, haggard figure in African dress the young Scot who had passed that way, and who was believed to have been murdered in Ludamar like Houghton. While they conversed in this incomprehensible language, Karfa feasted his eyes on the unfamiliar furnishings in the room.

Robert Ainsley came out from Pisania to welcome Park on hearing of his return, and they moved on to Pisania together on 10 June 1797, just over eighteen months after Park had set out. Karfa was delighted when Park changed into the English clothes he had left at Laidley's house, but he was dismayed when the flowing beard was shaved off, immediately converting Park from a man into a boy! Ainsley's schooner held Karfa fascinated all day, puzzling over its construction and the uses of the sail and rigging, and amazed that wind power could move such a large body forward. His astonishment made him keep saying, 'Black men are nothing,' and asking Park whatever made him, when he was no trader, explore so miserable a country as Africa. It was the white man's command of material goods, as Park appreciated, that evoked these comments – and indeed Pisania was hardly the place in which a white man could claim any moral superiority.

Since Park's departure Laidley had moved a short distance down-river to Kaiai, Park's Kayee, but luckily that day he returned from a trading trip. He welcomed Park, 'as one risen from the dead'. He also befriended Karfa on hearing what he had done for Park, and the agreed payment was doubled to £40, a generosity which quite over-whelmed Karfa. A present worth £10 was also sent to Fankooma, the old schoolmaster. Park left with Laidley £80 for Johnson's wages, and £20 to redeem Demba if possible, although he had already heard from the Seniora that no shred of news had come concerning either of them. With the settlement of the moneys he had received from Laidley's debtors in Khasso and at Jarra, and various other items, this all came to £330. 10s. 0d., for which Park could only give a bill drawn on the African Association.[1]

Park persuaded Karfa to return on 14 June to Jindey, believing they would have plenty of opportunity to see each other again before he could sail. His final comment on this man, who had saved his life and shown him true kindness, has a cold and patronizing ring, which was surely not intended:

'I have preserved these little traits of character in this worthy Negro, not only from regard to the man, but also because they appear to me to demonstrate that he possessed a mind *above his condition*: and to such of my readers as love to contemplate human nature in all its varieties, and to trace its progress from rudeness to refinement, I hope the account I have given of this poor African will not be unacceptable.'

Looking over his shoulder to his British readers, and something in his subconscious perhaps awakened by his benefactor's flattering view of his countrymen, Park here found strangely inadequate words to sum up his debt. These words are much at variance with the attitudes his writings had displayed elsewhere, and particularly with his earlier des-scription of his dealings with Karfa.

As it happened, he was not to see Karfa again for over eight years. The very next day an American ship, the *Charlestown*, arrived at Kaiai, and was able to exchange its rum and tobacco for a waiting cargo of slaves within two days. Ships came very infrequently, and Park there-fore hastened to wind up his affairs in order to embark. This done, he thanked Dr. Laidley for all his kindness, and sailed on 17 June.

After a tedious and, for many, sickly or even fatal voyage down the river, they were delayed at Gorée until October for lack of the provisions needed for the Atlantic crossing. Gorée was a French fort, and France was at war with Britain, but nobody seems to have wanted to detain this Briton, perhaps because he was a civilian on a neutral American ship. Park volunteered to act as ship's surgeon for the voyage, as the surgeon had died from fever in the Gambia. He felt his ministrations were the more appreciated because he could talk with many of the slaves in their own language, and some had actually seen him inland. Indeed they needed his services for, although he saw no wanton cruelty, they suffered much from their severe conditions, which he thought worse on American than on British slave vessels. Over twenty of the one hundred and thirty embarked at Kaiai died on the voyage. This was a higher than average rate of loss, but not exceptional.

The ship should have gone to South Carolina, as its name suggested, but the vessel was so rickety that water leaked in faster than, even by the greatest exertions, it could be pumped out. At the insistence of the crew, the reluctant captain had to make for Antigua in the West Indies, barely limping into the harbour after striking rocks just off the island. This coffin-ship was later condemned and the slaves sold in Antigua.

It had taken five weeks to reach Antigua from Gorée, but after only another ten days Park was lucky enough to get a passage to England in the *Chesterfield Packet*, for £40. Perhaps as a precaution he wrote to Banks from there; the letter could not get to England any faster than he did.[2] In fact nothing worse than some storms happened on the way, and after another five-week voyage, he arrived at Falmouth in Devon on 22 December 1797, having been absent from England two years and seven months. Seeing the land he had barely hoped to see again, he laid his head on his hands and wept with gratitude to God.[3]

A coach took him up to London in two days. He arrived whilst it was still dark on Christmas morning. He walked about in the cold air to kill time until he could decently go to James Dickson's house, and wandered into the gardens of the British Museum nearby. The Biographical Memoir describes what took place:

'It happened that Mr. Dickson, who had the care of those gardens, went there early that morning upon some trifling business. What must have been his emotions on beholding at that extraordinary time and place, the vision, as it must at first have appeared, of his long-lost friend, the object of so many anxious reflections, and whom he had long numbered with the dead!'

Dickson was seventy-seven when he told Whishaw about this joyous reunion. Relating it many times over to his friends, he had probably come to believe it had happened just like that. It is a pity to spoil a good story, but while the happy meeting at that hour was no doubt unexpected, it can hardly have been *quite* so astonishing to Dickson. His old friend Sir Joseph Banks would surely never have kept from him the glad tidings he had received from Africa over two months earlier, and passed on to Major Rennell and another friend, that Park was indeed alive and was on his way home via America.[4]

CHAPTER XV

'The warmest approbation of this Association'

———— ❧ ————

Sir Joseph Banks had double reason to welcome Park back: pleasure that his young friend was safe, and triumph that the African Association had at last an undoubted success. Park was the first of its travellers to return alive from far inland. Soon presenting himself to Banks, Park had much to tell him, and they enjoyed examining together the botanical specimens he had brought back from Africa.

Banks saw to it that the event did not pass unnoticed. On 4 January 1798 material from a single contributor appeared in two papers, the *London Chronicle* and *St. James' Chronicle or British Evening Post*, mentioning Park's return after travelling much farther into Africa than any of his predecessors. On 29 January *The True Briton* gave a fuller description of his discoveries. On the same day *The Times*, not for the last time, carried a very inaccurate account. It implied that Park had been to the City of Houssa, on the great river near Tombuctoo, twice as large as London, and had found a welcome for specimens of English manufactures! At a time when the war, and Court and Parliamentary proceedings, dominated the press, and other people were normally only reported if they went bankrupt or committed an unusually shocking crime, even these short paragraphs signified that Park had become newsworthy.

For some months Park was entertained in London society, but he found such recognition of his fame embarrassing and difficult to cope with, while society found him aloof and awkward. One hostess, Lady Holland, recorded tartly in her Journal, 'A person who was sent about two years ago to explore the interior parts of Africa is just returned. He is a Scotchman of the name of M.Park, very much protected by Sir Joseph Banks, and esteemed a man of veracity. He has neither fancy or genius, and if he does fib it is dully.' His simplicity and straightforwardness were almost painful. Another description of him, more kindly, was that he had 'the manners and dignities of his Niger kings'. So diffident was he in strange and inquisitive company that his progress as a lion of society soon came to an end.[1]

He was too busy to go to Scotland for several months. The earliest press reports said he was working on an account of his travels. It quickly became apparent that, inexperienced as he was in writing, he alone could not complete the account in time for the African Association's meeting in May. He was therefore put in touch with Major Rennell, who was to write up the geographical side, and with Bryan Edwards, Beaufoy's successor as Secretary, to write a short version of the travels.

Born in England in 1743, Edwards had spent about twenty-five years in the West Indies, returning home twice to stand for Parliament. On the second occasion, in 1796, he was elected and was soon regarded as a leading spokesman for the 'West Indian interest' and as an opponent of the Abolitionist movement. He had, however, more genuine interest in Africa than most of his kind, and he had also written an accomplished *History of the British West Indies*, leading to his becoming a Fellow of the Royal Society.

Both Rennell and Edwards worked from memoranda written by Park himself. They worked hard and quickly; Park went to Southampton where Edwards lived and had established a bank, and he probably also visited Rennell at Brighton. By early February Edwards had his work sketched out and by the end of the month his final draft only awaited the approval of Park and Banks. On 31 March the Committee of the Association was able to approve the printing of both works.[2]

At the same meeting, Park's accounts were approved, covering his bills to Dr. Laidley and the cost of his passage home. The Committee agreed to two suggestions which Park made, that a fowling piece and a scarlet coat be sent to Karfa Taura, and that a piece of plate be presented to Dr. Laidley.[3] It seems that neither gift reached its intended destination. On his second journey Park met a member of the caravan with which he had travelled back to the Gambia, who told him that Karfa Taura was well, but that he had not received the gun. Dr. Laidley left Africa late in 1797 to return to England via the West Indies, but he died in Barbados, perhaps falling victim to one of the diseases of the middle passage which had previously felled many of both the slaves he sold and those who transported them.

By the time of the Association's meeting on 26 May 1798, both Edwards's and Rennell's works were ready for circulation to members.

The former was entitled *Abstract from the Travels into the Interior of Africa*. It was well-written and readable, describing some incidents in full in almost the same words as those finally used in the *Travels*, but skipping over considerable stretches. It also included some very brief general observations on the countries and peoples encountered, which Park later developed much more fully. Edwards had wanted to whet his readers' appetites for the work yet to come, not to satisfy them.

Rennell's *Geographical Illustrations of Mr. Park's Journey* in fact covered a good deal more than the title suggested. Starting from Park's revelations, he tried to reconstruct the geography of all northern and western Africa, on a more ambitious scale than before. Park had confirmed that a great river, long called 'the Niger' by outsiders, really did exist. For the first time it was possible to produce a map showing it and the Gambia and Senegal correctly related to each other, with the Niger's course roughly traced as far east as Timbuktu. The importance of cities like Segu and Jenne with their radiating trade routes had been made clear. The main features of Khasso, Kaarta, Ludamar, Segu, and Manding had been ascertained, together with vaguer notions of surrounding countries. The dividing line between the desert and the inhabited areas could be more confidently drawn.

Naturally some imperfections qualified this considerable achievement. Park had found latitudes fairly exactly up to Jarra, but then Ali had taken all his instruments except his compass, and even that was broken before he reached Kamalia. He had lost many papers, but he did manage to keep either his records of compass bearings or his estimates of position during most of the journey. The position Rennell worked out for Segu was some 90 miles too far east of Pisania (itself misplaced 60 miles eastwards by navigators' miscalculations) and 40 miles too far north. The errors for Timbuktu were only half as large. To have overestimated his distance to Segu by only 100 miles, or one-tenth of the total, with his exiguous resources, was no mean feat.

The trouble was that, having learnt no more of the vanished empires, Park had been unable to correct the wrong identification of Ghana with Kano. Studying Leo Africanus more closely, Rennell added a third term to the equation, Leo's 'Gheneoa, Genni or Ghinea'. Logic now compounded error; from Leo's account Mali must be south-west of Kano, although Rennell had read translations of Cadamosto and de Barros, who showed that Mali was accessible from the

Senegambia, as well as the Gold Coast. South of Mali, Leo had said, there were mountains. Albufeda, another Arabic writer known to Rennell, of the fourteenth century, had described a range of mountains stretching from the west coast to the source of the Egyptian Nile. Sharif Imhammed had told Lucas of mountains 'of stupendous height' south of the Niger. Now Park had glimpsed from near Bamako some mountains to the south-east, said to lie in Kong. Once more the pieces seemed to fall into place, and 'the mountains of Kong' are lined up on Rennell's map accompanying the *Travels*, with peak after peak stretching across Africa!

Therefore it seemed that the Niger could not turn southwards to the Atlantic Ocean, and it would be pointless to look for a way in from that coast. Rennell was rightly certain that the river lay too low above sea-level for it to cross Africa and join the Nile. His final deduction, which convinced many, although it did not wholly convince Park, was that the Niger must end, a thousand miles east of Timbuktu, in Wangara. This country like an island between two rivers, subject to seasonal flooding, as described by Idrisi long ago, became a great swampy lake where the Niger ended, and was never connected with the Bambuk-Manding area touched on by Park, lying between the Senegal and the Faleme rivers. Rennell came tantalizingly near to making the other necessary connection, of Leo's Genni with Jenne instead of with Ghana, Leo having been right in setting it to the west of Timbuktu, and wrong only in saying it was down-stream from there. Had he made the right connection, Rennell would have had to recast all his deductions, identifying the mountains south of Mali with those of modern Sierra Leone and Guinea, and clearing away his Mountains of Kong, so that the Niger might reach the ocean after all. Then Park's subsequent history might have been very different.

Such were the accounts of Park's journey and of the conclusions drawn from it, which were presented to the General Meeting of the African Association on 26 May 1798. Park was present at the meeting – this is not mentioned in the minutes, but in an advertisement in *The Times* only the day before – and heard the members unanimously resolve:

'That it is the opinion of this Meeting, that Mr. Park has obeyed his Instructions as far as was practicable, and executed the purposes of his Mission with a degree of Industry, perseverance and ability that entitle him to the warmest approbation of this Association.'

This was a pleasing tribute, but rather limited. Banks evidently decided to play this meeting in a low key and to defer a more vigorous oration to the next year, after Park's own book would have been published. The meeting agreed to Park's keeping any profits from it, but as yet he had barely started on the work. Meanwhile Edwards's *Abstract* was in members' hands, and to some extent became public property.

It is surprising that Park never read any paper to the Linnean Society on the botany of West Africa. He had come home with up to perhaps eighty plant specimens, and through making two of them scientifically known he is commemorated in the botanical names. These are the shea tree, *Butyrospermum Paradoxum*, with a sub-species *Parkii*, and the locust bean tree, in the genus *Parkia*. The majority of his specimens of plants in the British Museum of Natural History, South Kensington, probably come from this journey, although they have perhaps been mixed with some from Bencoolen and the three known to have been sent back from the start of his second journey.[4]

It was six months after his return before Park was free to travel to Scotland. He went in early June, and was reunited to his family after a separation of four anxious years for them. At Foulshiels there were now only his mother and John, apart from Adam, who was just completing the surgeons' course at Edinburgh. The youngest sister Isobel, or Bell, was housekeeper on his farm to Archibald, who paid Mungo part of his entitlement under their father's will at this time. Alexander Park's first marriage to Esther Turnbull, a distant cousin, contracted in 1795 when Mungo was sailing up the Gambia, had soon ended with her death, possibly in 1796 when giving birth to their son Mungo. He was now preparing for his second marriage to Allison Veitch of Selkirk, to take place in November 1798. No doubt they all gathered together, with his sister Jean Thomson from nearby Ashkirk, to welcome back Mungo, now famous beyond anything they could have dreamt of.

Whilst at Selkirk he worked hard on his *Travels*, from the notes already used for the *Abstract*, supplemented by his memory. He worked all morning, going out only in the evenings for walks down by the Yarrow, except occasionally when he took a day off for a longer walk in the countryside which he loved. With his inexperience in writing, however, his progress was slow.

Sometimes he found it easier to concentrate by going to write at the house of a Mrs. Currie, who had been a school companion. Her opinion of him as told to her son was '. . . that she had never had experience of a better Christian man – so unselfish – so charitable and benevolent even to his enemies'. Of the latter he had few, but perhaps he expressed forgiveness even of Ali![5]

He spent hours with the Revd. Dr. George Lawson, enjoying a smoke, and telling him about Africa and its peoples. Dr. Lawson was especially interested in discussing the probabilities of the Africans' speedily 'stretching forth their hands unto God'. He was then engaged, on the side of toleration, in a church controversy at home; later he was even to give back to the students he taught for his Church's Ministry a copy of Thomas Paine's *Rights of Man*, once the Government had removed the legal ban on it. His influence with Park can never have been in the direction of an intolerant or aggressive religion.

From Lawson's Manse to the Andersons' house was but a few yards. Probably Mungo went there at first to pay his respects to the doctor and to renew his friendship with Alexander. But before long the main cause of his visits was to see Allison, now grown into an attractive young woman of eighteen years. Soon he proposed and was accepted, and it was agreed they would be married the next year. It must have been in a somewhat confused state of mind that he returned to London in early September, uncertain what he wanted to do next, but having to take a decision on a plan already put to him by Banks before he had gone home.

CHAPTER XVI

'Of a very Close mind'

The Australian proposal

———— ಐಐ ————

Sir Joseph Banks had never lost his interest in the southern island continent he had visited aboard the *Endeavour* with Captain Cook in 1770. Dutch seamen had touched on it long before and had named it New Holland. Captain Cook's voyage was the first along the whole eastern coast, and he also had the first – and nearly fatal – encounter with the Great Barrier Reef. Cook's expedition collected numerous specimens of the continent's strange plants and fauna, and named the first natural harbour they visited Botany Bay. Cook claimed this coast for the British Crown under the name of New South Wales.

Fifteen years later a committee of the House of Commons was pondering what to do with the surplus criminals overflowing the prisons and river hulks of England, now that they could no longer be shipped to the American colonies. One proposal was to dump a number of convicts on an island far up the river Gambia and to leave them to form their own society in 'freedom', or more probably to die of fever and hunger, with a garrison at the river mouth to prevent their escape. Fortunately Banks's rather more humane proposal, to send them instead to settle at Botany Bay, won the day. It was 1788 when a squadron arrived under Captain Phillip, the first Governor; ten years later, after much hardship in the early stages, the little colony was firmly established.

The rest of the continent was no better known than to Captain Cook. Banks was worried that no exportable materials had been found to send to England, and he thought that some navigable rivers might lead inland to the useful materials that must surely exist. In May 1798 he mentioned his thoughts to Park, who responded – as Banks no doubt hoped – by volunteering to go himself, regarding it as the height of his ambition to accomplish the plan with honour. Banks drafted a letter and read it over to Park, who accepted it. Thereupon Banks wrote in its terms to Under-Secretary John King in Whitehall, on 15

May, highly recommending Park for the journey. He also proposed
Lieutenant Matthew Flinders from Banks's own county of Lincolnshire to take charge of the nautical side.

From this first stage the seeds of a misunderstanding sprouted. Park
had not been happy with the remuneration Banks had proposed, but
as Banks had said that the commendation he hoped to secure from the
African Association should put matters on a very different footing,
he did not press any objections. The letter to Under-Secretary King
said:

'He is very moderate in his terms, he will be contented with 10s. a day and
his rations *and happy if his pay is settled at 12s.* The amount of his outfit for
Instruments, arms, presents, etc., will not I think exceed £100.'

The italicized passage, not quoted before, evidently contained the
minimum Park was seriously prepared to consider. With those words
omitted it might look as if Park reneged on an accepted rate, but that
oversimplifies. The African Association's commendation was duly
given at its meeting on 25 May, but it did not have the effect Park
had hoped for.

After returning from Scotland to London, Park went to Whitehall
on 9 September by appointment. Before he arrived John King had
talked with Lieutenant-Governor Philip Gidley King, who was preparing to return to New South Wales. Unfortunately Banks's letter
could not be found and the two Kings discussed *de novo* what to offer
Park. John King thought 6s. to 10s. a day, probably the latter, would
do. When this was in fact offered, with no mention of any outfit money,
Park was taken aback, and said so.

For the next fortnight correspondence passed to and fro. Park raised
another objection, that he could not be ready to go in ten days' time,
which was when Lieutenant-Governor King hoped to sail in the *Porpoise*, complete with an array of plants and a gardener called Sutter,
provided by Banks to tend them. Money remained the main item in
dispute, however, and after a long discussion with Park, Banks wrote
to Whitehall again on 21 September, as a result of which the Government raised its offer to 12s. 6d. a day. Banks assured Park that he personally would see that he was adequately outfitted. It was all in vain,
and the Duke of Portland, the Secretary of State, who had already
prepared a despatch to Governor Hunter of New South Wales an-

nouncing Park's coming, had to add a postscript saying Park had now declined.

The correspondence between Park and Banks became increasingly strained. At one stage Park wrote, 'I feel that those triffling misunderstandings have considerably damped that enthusiasm which prompts to, and is necessary to ensure the success of such an enterprise.' Banks retorted that he had never previously noticed Park's concern over money matters, and continued, 'I am astonished to find your Enthusiasm damp't by the small difference between the Pay you had taught yourself to expect and that really offered to you; because real Enthusiasm, which you certainly possess, is very little swayed by pecuniary motives.' Banks then complained that Park seemed to be putting the blame on him, but Park's final rejection of the revised offer stiffly denied this:

'. . . I declined the Engagement; and I am far mistaken, if any Plea was necessary to justify my Conduct – pecuniary concerns, however contemptible in themselves, serve as a good criterion by which to estimate the importance or inutility of any office or pursuit; and, tho' my fancy had painted this as a Voyage of some Importance, I found that Government considered it in a very different light: – all this I understood perfectly, but I cannot see how any blame could reasonably fall upon you: it must therefore rest with me . . .'

Official inefficiency and seeming indifference exacerbated Park's hurt pride.

Banks's irritation cannot have been helped by an attack of gout he had just then. He apologized to the Government for the trouble caused 'by my having put confidence in this fickle Scotsman', and, in passing on Park's final rejection, he said, '. . . By the tenor of his answer, it appears that he totally disregards my offer, and treats yours very slightly indeed.' All the same, it is noticeable in this correspondence that whilst Park's style grew stiffer and more formal, signing himself, 'Your Humble Servant', Banks signed himself, 'Your friend and well-wisher' or 'Your friend and Servant'. He also tried unsuccessfully to winkle out of Park an admission that he had another motive for declining.

He had good reason for thinking this, for he had received a letter from James Dickson which, in its artless way, throws light on the characters of both Park and Dickson himself:

'Sir,
     As I have had your Friendship for many years, it is my duty ever to retain it. I inform you that I have not in any way been a cause of Mr. Park's

not agreeing with your encouragement; men can soon find an excuse, if they are not willing to do a thing; you may think it Singular that Mr. Park and I, that is friends and have lived upon the best of friendship, the day we left you at Spring Grove we niver entered into conversation upon what you had said to him. Mr. Park is of a very Close mind; and I suppose he thinks I wish him to; so I do, but I shall not tell him so for this reason, when he went to Africa some of his friends was so imprudent as to say I was the cause of him being sacrificed, for they were sure he would niver return; as the saying is, I have got my neck out of that halter I will not put it in again. I shall be very sorry if he does not make use of your kind and good intentions to serve him. I have found out from his Sister, which is my wife, that thier is some private connection, a love affair in Scotland but no money in it, (what a pity it is men should be such fools that might be of use to their country), that is the cause of it, and should such a thing take place, he is burying himself and his talents, a thing which both his Sister and me disapproves much of: I much disapproved of his going to Scotland at the time he did.'

This letter's simple candour and unintentional humour assuaged Banks's annoyance and probably saved his friendship with Park. Even if he could not get Park himself to admit it, Banks continued to believe that Dickson's explanation was the true one. When reporting the following May to the African Association he told them that 'Mr. Park, however, on his return from a visit to his Relations in Scotland, where he seems to have formed a prospect for his future proceedings more satisfactory to himself, desired to relinquish the undertaking...'*

Dickson had indeed hit on one of Park's leading characteristics in describing him as 'of a very Close mind'. He told his family at Selkirk the bare fact of his intention to travel to Australia, and when the misunderstanding arose he wrote to tell them he would not go after all, but when John Whishaw was collecting material for his Biographical Memoir he could only say, 'The particulars of this transaction are not known to Park's family.' This is not the only time in his life when such extreme reticence can be observed: whilst he had a high notion of his value, he neither advertised himself nor easily opened his mind to others.

It has been held that the Government's offer to Park was renewed

---

*In the 1810 *Proceedings* a more explicit statement was added, probably by Banks himself, 'He proposes, when settled in Scotland, exercising his profession of Surgeon, but has declared, that he shall hold himself in readiness at all times, to proceed again to the Joliba, in case Government should think fit to establish a colony on its banks, and his services be required.' (See Hallett, *Records*, pp.166–7).

5. Mungo Park at Kamalia, from an engraving in the *Travels*

6a. Mungo Park at the bridge over the Ba Fing river, from an engraving in the *Travels*

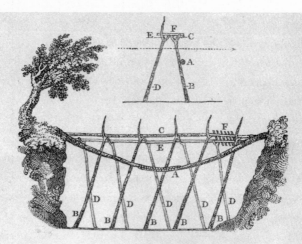

A. Trees first laid across.
B. First range of forks.
C. Trees supported by first range.
D. Second range of forks,
E. Trees supported by ditto.

F. Cross sticks for walking on.
If the river was dried up, the structure would have somewhat of this appearance.

6b. Diagram of bridge construction, from an engraving of Park's own drawing reproduced in *The Journal of a Mission to the Interior of Africa in the Year 1805* by *Mungo Park* in 1799 and again refused. The only evidence for this is a statement in the Biographical Memoir which misdates to that year the negotiations carried on in 1798, and does not point to any second round of proposals. The Government would have not reopened matters without consulting Banks, or probably unless he urged them to do so. In the official files, in the *Historical Records of New South Wales*, and in the surviving letters of Sir Joseph, there is no trace of any intention to renew the plan.

Indeed all the circumstances point the other way. Within a month of Park's refusal Banks had selected a botanist, Robert Brown, to replace him. Due to what would now be called a series of technical hitches, the *Porpoise* remained over a year longer, with Sutter aboard tending his plants and Lieutenant-Governor King waiting ashore. Banks corresponded with King during this time and never alluded to Park until King left in another vessel in November 1799. Nor did he mention him in correspondence with Flinders after he arrived in England in 1800 with news of his discovery of Tasmania's separation from mainland Australia, and made ready for his departure with Brown the next year for their famous voyage round Australia. It is not true that the Government proposal was ever renewed.

Whishaw's information from the Park family probably confused the 1798 negotiations with some ideas that began with Park himself in 1801 but which got nowhere; they will be mentioned later. With Flinders just about to set off with Brown, Banks had no need of Park for Australia then. It is perhaps as well too that he did not go; otherwise he might have had to share with the unfortunate Flinders several years' internment on the way home by the French in Mauritius, and he might never have had his chance to see the Niger again.

CHAPTER XVII

'It has nothing to recommend it, but truth'

——— ∾ ———

It must have been in Park's mind that if he were to set off for Australia in 1798 the publication of his *Travels* would be indefinitely delayed. On returning from Scotland he could send Edwards only the first third of the book in draft. When telling Banks this, Edwards commiserated with him on Park's recent 'fickle and perverse conduct', but soon they were discussing progress on the book as if nothing had happened; the storm quickly passed and left no serious damage behind it. Edwards had to work to animate the early chapters, but from Ludamar onwards Park got into his stride, and Edwards's role became increasingly one of minor editing. Later he told Banks enthusiastically, 'Park goes on triumphantly – He improves in his style so much by practice, that his journal now requires but little correction; and some parts, which he has lately sent to me, are equal to any thing in the English language . . .'[1]

So much for the assertion made by, *inter alia*, Sir William Young, the next Secretary of the African Association, that Edwards was the real author of the *Travels*. When Young referred in a posthumous edition of the *History of the West Indies* to Edwards's 'judicious compilation and elegant recital of the Travels of Mungo Park', Park crossly took the matter up with him. Young then said he had only meant that Edwards had 'assisted in the general arrangement of the materials you supplied'.[2] It can now be seen that Edwards's share was no more than this, although he must be credited at least with the immaculate spelling and punctuation. Park was also stung by the suggestion that he had allowed Edwards to foist his own opinions on to him, especially with regard to the slave trade and to race relations. A comparison of Edwards's *Abstract* and Park's *Travels* weakens this supposition too. The latter included almost all the material from the *Abstract*, but as that was mostly narrative, and the finished work was six times as long, what counts more is the little that was in the *Abstract* but *omitted* from the *Travels*.

Park had had an honourable reception by King Desse of Kaarta, but he refrained from putting into the King's mind the thought that 'Major Houghton was the only European he had ever before seen; and he had conceived the highest idea of the superiority of the whites to the blacks, in all possible respects'. Nor did he incorporate in the *Travels* Edwards's reflection on his receiving King Mansong's gift of 5,000 cowries: 'it was not on this occasion only, Mr. Park derived advantage from the high estimation and honourable light in which the Tobauboes (or whites) are held throughout the Negro territories in this part of Africa'. Park's general conclusion was rather that the Africans 'look upon us, I fear, as little better than a race of formidable but ignorant heathens'.* The third small but notable omission was of Edwards's own views on slavery, which were replaced with something quite different in the *Travels*. That Park deferred to Edwards's views is not proven on this evidence; whether he did so in fact is looked at further in the next chapter. It was probably when they were working closely together that Park declined a job offered by Edwards on an estate in the West Indies.³

At the end of January 1799 he was still writing about his return journey along the Niger's bank, but the book was finished on time to be published in April by George Nicol of London. Rennell's *Geographical Illustrations* were included, with the rights made over to Park, and also verses by the Duchess of Devonshire, based on the song of the women in the little village near Segu, 'Let us pity the poor white man; no mother has he.' The author thought himself highly honoured in being permitted to adorn his book with it, but alas! neither the poem nor the music to which it was set by Mr. G.G. Ferrari really improved upon the original.

The book was an immediate best-seller. About four hundred subscribers, headed by His Majesty's Library, took copies, and the whole first edition of 1,500 copies was sold out before the month of April had gone. By the end of the year three editions had been issued; there was a fourth in 1800; and the sixth was reached in 1810. In spite of the war, a translation was published in France in 1799, and a German

---

*The contemporary Captain Philip Beaver expressed similar views, with justification forcefully shown by many white traders' behaviour, in his *African Memoranda*, published in 1805.

translation and American editions followed in 1800. With no copy-right conventions then, Park would not have gained from these foreign editions, but on the first London edition he cleared over 1,000 guineas, and more money came in, although more slowly, over the years.[4]

The *Travels* received a mention in the *St. James' Chronicle* as early as 18 April. Already they had been cited by the Bishop of Durham at a meeting of the Society for the Promotion of Christian Knowledge, endorsing Park's suggestion that Arabic New Testaments be printed for distribution in Africa.* The article ended by saying that Park's own host at Kamalia had been a slave on the very ship which took him to America. Thereupon 'Humanus' wrote saying that the Bishop or Park himself should have begun, not with printing New Testaments, but with liberating his host. 'Hypercriticus' rejoined that this was un-fair to Park who was impoverished after his journey. Both gentlemen should really have read the book first.

The African Association had continued to pay him while he was writing his book, until the General Meeting of 25 May 1799, when he ended nearly five years on their payroll, including eighteen months in Africa on double pay of 15s. a day. He had received over £90 before leaving England and £615 after his return, and the final total was £866 12s. 6d., plus all his expenses. The overall cost of his journey came to £1,307 15s. 8d., all paid from members' subscriptions. Park's expedition remained the Association's one complete success in West Africa, and also its most costly, throughout its existence down to 1831.[5]

When the Association met in May Banks saw that, with the *Travels* an instant success, this was the moment to move forward. Park, who had left for Scotland, Edwards, who was ill, and Rennell were all warmly congratulated. Looking back, Banks saw bad luck in Ledyard's death, and poor choices in Lucas and Houghton. Then he continued:

'Mr. Park however has done credit to their [the Committee's] election. Strength to make exertions, constitution to endure fatigue and Temper to bear insults with Patience, Courage to undertake hazardous enterprises when practicable, and judgement to set limits to his exertions when his difficulties were likely to become insurmountable, are every where exemplified in his Book.'[6]

---

*The Bishop's suggestion was not taken up, unlike a similar one the next year by Zachary Macaulay, Secretary to the Sierra Leone Company (information by Mr. Arthur E. Barker, Archivist and Librarian, S.P.C.K.).

This was a better and juster tribute to the physical and mental qualities that had earned him his success than the 'Warmest approbation' Park had heard the previous year, and one hopes it was passed on to him.

Turning to look ahead, Banks declared that Park had '. . . opened a Gate into the Interior of Africa, into which it is easy for every Nation to enter and to extend its commerce and Discovery . . . A Detachment of 500 chosen Troops would soon make that Road easy, and would build Embarkations upon the Joliba – if 200 of these were to embark with Field pieces they would be able to overcome the whole Forces which Africa could bring against them.' Probably he had in mind the French, the Moors, and the local states, in that order. Scientific methods could increase the production of gold a hundredfold, and soon the trade would be able to pay for its own protection. If Britain delayed action, then 'some Rival Nation will take possession of the Banks of the Joliba, and assert by arms her right of Prior possession'. Here is already foreshadowed the Scramble for Africa that took place eighty years later, although in 1799 Banks seems to have thought of establishing a kind of Gold Coast fort on the Niger, with a protected line of communications, rather than of conquering wide territories.

After such a stirring address there was little difficulty in securing the unanimous approval of a Resolution empowering the Committee to take up again with the Government '. . . the Plan of appointing a Consul for the District of Senegambia, and sending there a sufficient force to take possession of the Banks of the Joliba, and explore the Interior from thence . . .' With the war against France and the prospect of gold to spur it on, the Association had travelled far away in just nine years from Beaufoy's vision of 'means as peaceable as the purposes are just'.

Although Banks had deduced from Park's account that there were great commercial prospects in the area, the *Travels* were rather vague about these, and we may suppose that Rennell's contrary assessment was known to Banks. Rennell expressed this some years later as follows: the gum trade was based further north and, 'The odious traffick in men must remain, as it is, confined to the sea ports; and then *Gold* alone seems to be the main staple that remains . . . over and above that which already comes into Europe by way of *Morocco, Barbary* and . . . the Coast of Guinea, there can be but little I perceive.'[7]

Sticking closely to what he had observed and avoiding generalization, Park had left the situation open to contrary interpretations.

Lacking adequate historical knowledge, Park could not convey to his readers the full force of the incipient upsurge of Islam from the Gambia right across Africa, which was to be the dominant theme in the history of the area for the next eighty years. He correctly observed the signs of Islam's diffusion through the schools, the distribution of Arabic texts, and the influence of traders; he saw how the Muslims lived apart from others, trying to practise their religion and law within the constraints of pagan states, and being allowed to exercise influence but not power; yet he did not perceive here a great historical movement.

The reviews of Park's book in the periodicals were favourable. Those in the *Gentleman's Magazine* and the *Annual Register* share an identical opening paragraph, and so may have come from the same hand, although the tone of one is very different from the other. The former, printed four months after the *Travels* emerged, was still based on Edwards's *Abstract*. It stressed the importance of Park's contribution to geographical knowledge, although this dealt with only a small part of the vast continent, and summed up in a sentence what Park had shown of African life: 'The Negroes of these districts are not to be considered as an uncivilized race; they have religion, established governments, laws, schools, commerce, manufactures, *wars*!' The later review, written with the full *Travels* available, chose instead to interpret Park's descriptions in the least favourable way, seeing 'no consummate polity and pure religion; but forms of government, weak, imperfect or oppressive; the wildest fanaticism and the most debasing superstition'.[8]

Any unbiased reader of Park's *Travels* must find this writer's first summary much nearer the truth than his second, strangely jaundiced account. There was nothing weak in, say, Mansong's government in Segu, nor oppressive in Bondu. Park had shown the existence of states with well-established governments and laws, with schools, manufactures, commerce, and pilgrimage routes linking them to a wider world stretching out to north Africa, the Middle East, and even beyond. Africa might not have 'pure religion' as Christian Europe understood it, but Park had met devout Muslims and had partly penetrated the religious character of traditional beliefs and customs. On the other hand there was some gross superstition, as the Muslim reformers

would have agreed, and it was to this, along with poverty and ignorance, that the context shows him to have been referring in his rare
laments on the 'barbarous' state of Africa.

He would have agreed that Africans 'are not to be considered as an
uncivilized race'. He rejected any notion of their living, as the pro-
slavery writers maintained, in lawless savagery, rife with witchcraft
(which he never encountered) or cannibalism (cautiously accepted by
him to be practised only in respect of Minianka) or nakedness (seen
nowhere). The most accurate part of the second review was the observation that 'The author found . . . what has been found in all
countries, a mixture of good and evil.' Park had convincingly shown
that African societies lived under moral codes as certainly held as in
any other country. Life for most people might offer limited opportunities, but it was lived out in an intelligible, dignified, and humane
way. Hospitality to strangers was more the rule than the exception,
and for the women in particular he had nothing but praise: 'I do not
recollect a single instance of hard-heartedness towards me in the
women. In all my wanderings and wretchedness, I found them uni-
formly kind and compassionate.'

The only major exception to this generally favourable assessment –
the Moors apart – concerned the recurrent stealing or exactions from
him. Even there, he pointed out that Africans rarely stole from each
other, and that as an unprotected stranger carrying very tempting
objects he was in a special category. An Indian carrying a box of
jewels through England would, Park thought, if he were without
legal protection, most likely suffer the same way (but he did not discuss why legal protection might be lacking).

What Park offered was, in fact, the first realistic, detailed, and objective description for other parts of the world, of everyday life in the
interior of West Africa. Arab travellers such as Ibn Battuta and Leo
Africanus had tended to move largely amongst traders and scholars,
often of their own nationality, and to take the greatest interest in
court affairs, rarely noticing at all closely or favourably the common
people. In its wealth of carefully observed detail, and its lively and
fair description of many individuals and local communities, Park's
book is in another class altogether. Surprisingly, for one so reserved
and shy, he was at his best in bringing people to life. Beyond his
geographical revelations, his greatest single achievement was to get
across convincingly that between Africans and Europeans no difference

existed 'in the genuine sympathies and characteristic feelings of our common nature'.

In his Preface Park had said of his work, 'As a composition, it has nothing to recommend it, but *truth*. It is a plain, unvarnished tale; without pretensions of any kind, except that it claims to enlarge, in some degree, the circle of African geography.' The *Annual Register* gave full credit to Park's veracity: '. . . he seems to have described things as he saw them, and to have consulted his senses rather than his imagination; he is unwilling to glut credulity by the narration of wonders; he draws no exaggerated picture of his sufferings and dangers; nor does he ascribe to his own sagacity any event which resulted from chance or accident . . . if what is described be not real, at least that which is invented is probable . . .' His book, of course, contains errors of detail, having been written largely from memory and no doubt sometimes from inaccurate or misunderstood information, but its essential truthfulness has stood unchallenged. It is probably because it was plain and unvarnished that it was subsequently overshadowed, but if a corrective is needed to later, more lurid, sensational, and damning versions of Darkest Africa, one could do a lot worse, even today, than start with Mungo Park's depiction of people and their lives in West Africa.

His modesty and shyness made the fame that he had earned a doubtful gain. He had made some money, but not enough to keep him indefinitely. He had drawn three main lessons from his first expedition. There was the sense that his turning back at Silla, however unavoidable, was a defeat to be reversed and overcome; his life's work was there, and unfinished. Even stronger than the desire for fame was the urge to solve the nagging question, 'How does this great river end?' Next, his captivity in Ludamar had left a deep mark and a determination never to repeat such an experience, and he thought he saw the answer in travelling in a caravan. Lastly, it was in Africa that he had finally matured, that the barriers of his reserve had been temporarily lowered, and that he had achieved a realistic sense of his position before God and men. He had been stretched to his limit and nearly beyond it several times, but in responding he had found himself. Reading the *Travels* with their poise, fortitude, sanity, humanity, and quiet good humour, one can hardly avoid the conclusion that, come Ali and captivity, come thefts, come fever, hunger, and any other hardship, at heart Park had found his experience in Africa fulfilling and exhilarating.

CHAPTER XVIII

'Neither within my province, nor in my power, to explain'

Park and slavery

——— ∾ ———

'That such a system should so long have been suffered to exist in any part of the British Empire will appear to our posterity almost incredible.' So said William Wilberforce,[1] the Parliamentary leader of the Abolitionist movement, and it is because he was right that it is so difficult to understand individuals' attitudes in the controversies before abolition.

Since his own time Park has been held to have taken a dubious stand. At the end of the chapter on slavery in his book, when his readers must have been agog for a magisterial pronouncement, all they found in fact was:

'How far it [the internal slave system] is maintained and supported by the slave traffic, which, for two hundred years, the nations of Europe have carried on with the natives of the Coast, it is neither within my province, nor in my power, to explain. If my sentiments should be required concerning the effect which a discontinuance of that commerce would produce on the manners of the natives, I should have no hesitation in observing, that, in the present unenlightened state of their minds, my opinion is, the effect would neither be so extensive or beneficial, as many wise and worthy persons fondly expect.'

Elsewhere in the book he let the facts speak openly and sympathetically of the miseries the slaves endured, but nowhere save in that one place, and never again in public, did he make any general observation on slavery or the slave trade.

This led to the curious position described by Whishaw in the Biographical Memoir, '. . . that while the supposed *opinions* of Park have always been appealed to by the advocates of the Slave Trade, his *facts* have as constantly been relied on by their opponents'. In Parliament and elsewhere he was quoted or misquoted by both sides. George Hibbert claimed in the Commons that Park had told him, during a conversation about his *Travels* at a meeting of the Linnean Society, that 'not only every fact, but every sentiment of it was his own'.

Hibbert understood this to mean that Park agreed with his own opposition to the Abolition Bill, but in fact it did nothing to illuminate the
wording of the book.[2]

Whishaw was a Director of the African Institution, an anti-slavery
body, but he was judicial and fair in his assessment of this question.
He was convinced, with great confidence, by what the family told him,
that Park did express a great abhorrence of slavery and the trade whenever these subjects occurred in private conversation, but there is no
doubt that the family was uneasy on the matter. One of them wrote
a memorandum specially for Whishaw about it, which is not now
available. In 1814 Mungo's brother Adam commented to Alexander,
on Whishaw's enquiry whether there were any manuscript fragments
relating to the first journey, 'What else could they wish but a private
opinion on some leading topic, as the Slave Trade, etc.'[3] Yet if
Whishaw had only wanted politely to indicate, 'This is what the
family say, and I have no evidence to refute them,' he need not have
stated his conclusions so positively.

He believed that Park, as a young and inexperienced writer, had
deferred to Edwards, and had allowed himself to be persuaded against
expressing his own convictions. In trying to take up a position of
neutrality he had only seemed to pour cold water on the arguments of
the Abolitionists and to give comfort to their opponents. Some later
writers, including Joseph Thomson and Lewis Grassic Gibbon, have
believed that his reticence shows that, whilst sympathetic to individual
slaves, he was not in the least opposed to the institution of slavery.
How a man could be an enemy of slavery, as Whishaw described him,
but not an Abolitionist, may indeed seem a paradox in need of explanation.

In the previous two centuries when Britain had been prominent in
the slave trade, enormous vested interests had become involved in the
triangular traffic from Britain to Africa, from there to the West Indies
and America, and back again to Britain. How far the support that
developed for the Abolition movement was due to humanitarianism,
and how far to a shift in British economic interests, especially after the
jolting loss of the American colonies, is a matter of continuing historical debate which need not detain us. At the time, there was a very
abrupt change in sentiment away from the general acceptance of the
trade as regrettable, perhaps, but necessary. This acceptance had been
bolstered by theories which kept away disquieting thoughts, and pre-

viously, apart from the Quakers, only isolated individuals like John Wesley and Dr. Johnson had seen through them. Suddenly the scales dropped from the eyes of many like Thomas Clarkson and William Wilberforce, and Abolition became a definite movement, with a view of the trade as a monstrous evil that no economic argument could justify.

The Abolition movement began effectively only in 1787, but within five years its organizing committee had secured the passage of a motion through the House of Commons to outlaw the trade in 1796. However, the Lords blocked it, in the more conservative atmosphere generated by the war with revolutionary France and a successful slave rebellion in the French colony of San Domingo (Haiti). Thereafter the cause lost momentum until Wilberforce revived it again from 1804 onwards. When Park wrote it was largely dormant. There were relatively small groups in Parliament firmly committed to stand for or against Abolition, and in the middle was a large group of 'Moderates', who accepted abolition in principle, only not yet, and who favoured compromises that the Abolitionists rightly feared would be ineffective.

Accepting the Abolitionist programme involved adopting three propositions: that the trade should be abolished at a stroke and not by stages; that abolition must be imposed by the British Parliament, and not left to the autonomous West Indian Assemblies; and that action should be taken by Britain alone without waiting for a united decision of the European states. Some 'Moderates' no doubt hoped to postpone action indefinitely, but others jibbed at one or more parts of the programme, while genuinely desiring to see the trade ended. One could, therefore, be against the trade but not an Abolitionist. Events proved the Abolitionists right on the first two points, but largely justified the Moderates' doubts on the third.

Contrary to the received opinion, Edwards would probably have regarded himself as a Moderate. His history of the West Indies suggests an uneasy conscience on slavery, although he vehemently opposed the Abolitionists as mischievously stirring up trouble. In the third edition, written in 1796 but published in 1801 after his death, he made a forceful appeal to the West Indian planters, '. . . of themselves to restrain, limit and finally abolish the further introduction of enslaved men from Africa'.[4] After the San Domingo slave rebellion, the writing was on the wall. Consistently with this, in 1797 he supported a motion which was passed against Wilberforce's opposition, calling – in vain – on the

West Indian Assemblies to initiate a gradual abolition.[5] He suffered the fate of most men who try to take up a middle position in a tense debate; to the Abolitionists he was simply against them, whilst the diehard George Hibbert could say, '. . . and Mr. Edwards, Sir, when he edited that book [Park's *Travels*] was either an Abolitionist, or at least was wavering in his opinions . . . the West India body, who always respected his abilities, could seldom depend upon the determinations of his judgment.'[6] Edwards defended the interests of the West India body *as he saw them*, rather than the slave trade as such.

Even then, it seems unlikely that Park deferred to Edwards's urgings. Nothing in his history indicates a pliability in accepting the views of others against his own considered judgment. Nor does Edwards seem to have counted on his agreement. In the *Abstract* he said, 'Mr. Park himself will, in due time, suggest what has occurred to him on this subject, with candour and impartiality.' In April 1798 he said in the House of Commons, 'Mr. Park was not an advocate for the Slave Trade, but wished to collect facts on the subject,' but in the same speech he misconstrued Park's evidence, which nobody else had yet seen, and this may have helped to create the impression that Park was in his pocket.[7]

Banks believed that slavery was a matter to be judged by what worked best in practice, and not a moral issue, and he was apparently against Abolition.* Park had been indebted to two slavers, Laidley and Karfa Taura, but there were influences the other way too. Major Rennell, as we have seen, abhorred the trade, and several committee members of the African Association were Abolitionists. The Selkirk Burgh Council was one of hundreds to petition for abolition in 1792, and the Revd. Dr. Lawson was among the many individuals who abstained from sugar in protest against the trade.

Clearly Park rejected the mythology by which Edwards and others consoled themselves that the trade had its brighter side. In his *History* Edwards had said that in being transported the slaves were 'removed to a situation infinitely more desirable'. At home in Africa they had '. . . no security for property, nor protection for their persons; they

---

*Banks's view here is quoted from a letter in Rhodes House, Oxford, Br. Emp. MS. r. 2 (see Dawson, *Banks Letters*, p.899). In 1817 he expressed very different views: 'To see a set of human beings emerging from slavery and making most rapid strides towards the perfection of civilisation, must I think be the most delightful food for contemplation.' (Quoted from *William Wilberforce* by Oliver Warner, 1962, p.139.)

exist at the will and caprice of a master, who is not amenable to any law for his ill-treatment of them, and who may slaughter them at his pleasure'.[8] Park's *Travels* might be taken as almost a systematic refutation of such views, and also of others then common, that there was no civilization or education in Africa, and that Africans would not work unless forced.

Among some notes Park jotted down on morality, probably in 1799, he commented on 'Servile Duties' as follows:

'He who feeds another has a right to the labour of him he maintains and to the fruits of it, and he who labours for another has a right to expect that he should support him, but as the labours of a man are of more value than food and cloathing he has an undoubted right to rate and dispose of his service for certain wages above mere maintenance.'[9]

The word 'servile' here has a wide meaning, but this passage seems an unlikely basis for justifying slavery.

It may be objected that Park did buy three slaves as crew for his boat on the second journey into Africa. He presumably intended to emancipate them at the end of the journey, which would not have put him far out of line with the Abolitionists' own imposition of a transitional stage of 'apprenticeship', a long way short of complete freedom, upon the recaptured slaves at Sierra Leone.[10]

My conclusion agrees with Whishaw's, that although not an Abolitionist Park was in principle against the trade, and I would place him as a Moderate of some sort, to the 'left' of Edwards. Yet I can find precious few clues as to precisely what he *did* think, or *why* he concealed his opinions so steadfastly. Whishaw could only say, '. . . he expressed his regret that an improper stress had been laid upon certain passages in his *Travels*, and that a meaning had been attributed to them which it was not intended that they should bear'; Park took no steps to clear up the misunderstanding.

He certainly believed slavery to be embedded in Africa independently of the external trade,[11] and a clue may perhaps be found in the phrase 'the present unenlightened state of their minds'. Quite possibly he agreed with his less inhibited contemporary, Captain Philip Beaver, who had led an experimental agricultural colony on Bulama Island (now in Guinea-Bissau) from which slavery was excluded. Beaver did not believe that either legislation or a direct maritime assault could beat the slave trade. Instead he held that legitimate trade and agricultural development could open up new vistas for Africans and provide alternative means for them to buy what they wanted from overseas.

Another clue is provided by Whishaw: '... he considered the Abolition of the Slave Trade as a measure of *state policy*; for which reason he thought it would be improper in any work he might give the public, to interpose his private opinion relative to a question of such importance, which was then under the consideration of the Legislature.' A last clue can be found in Park's Preface, in which he showed that he regarded himself as just a humble *employee* of the aristocratic African Association – which never admitted him to membership – and maybe he felt it that it was not his place to risk splitting it down the middle. His duty was done by stating the facts; it was up to others to draw conclusions. It would, however, have been out of character for Park simply to bow to the will or entreaties of Edwards or Banks, and his decision to say no more must have been his own. Half of him sought fame; the other half was intensely private, with a deep aversion to public controversy. His cool rationalism had enabled him to depict Africa objectively, but it also muted his genuine sympathy for the oppressed.

CHAPTER XIX

'My lovely Allie'

At Selkirk, 1799–1801

———— ဏ ————

Park left London for Selkirk early in May 1799, not waiting for the African Association meeting on the 25th, and leaving Banks to arrange for the second edition of the *Travels*.[1] There was a strong reason to go home: to prepare for his wedding. This followed upon the marriage in April of his eldest brother Archibald, now aged nearly thirty-two, to Margaret Lang of Selkirk. At the same time Archibald had taken on a larger farm in the district.

The banns were called on 20 July, and the entry in the register was, as regards his occupation, as much prophecy as record:

'Mungo Park (the African traveler) in the parish of Selkirk and Miss Allison Anderson in said parish gave the names to be proclaimed in the Church of Selkirk in order to marriage.'

The wedding took place on 2 August 1799. Nothing is known of how Mungo's acquaintance with Allison, begun at least fourteen years earlier, developed into matrimony, but that they were in love is amply shown by the later letters that have survived. He was now nearly twenty-eight, tall, handsome, moderately well-off, and regaining his strength after his illnesses in Africa, although he suffered for years from indigestion, linked to his nightmares of Ali's camp. Allison, nineteen years old, was also tall and handsome and, it is said, 'amiable in disposition, with no special mental endowments, and if anything somewhat frivolous and pleasure-loving'.[2] To Mungo, she was 'My lovely Allie'.

He could afford to maintain a wife for the present. Their marriage contract provided her with a life interest in half his property should he die, unless they then had more than one child, when she would receive one-third, or one-sixth if she remarried.[3] Allison joined him at Foulshiels, along with his mother, his brother John, and Isobel, who returned home from being Archibald's housekeeper once he had married. With the rest of the family now away, the newly-wed couple probably had a room of their own.

Mungo no doubt resumed his walks along the Yarrow and in the hills that he loved, going further afield as his vitality returned. He felt a need to think out afresh his beliefs and principles. Some notes on this have survived, made on leaves from a small notebook dated April 1799, but probably used later.[4]

In the month of his marriage he took on full church membership and made his first communion; this was usually done earlier, on reaching adult life. He kept in close touch with the Revd. Dr. Lawson. His sincere Christian faith ran, however, along undogmatic channels, bypassing the Calvinist doctrines of Salvation, Election, and Predestination.

To the traditional Calvinist God is known by faith, and to look for proofs of his existence is, if not impious, at least beside the point. Yet one of Park's notes made at that time sets out a 'Demonstration of the Being and attributes of God', from the impossibility of an infinite series of causes. It reads as though it were his own work, and it did not come from Dugald Stewart's books. Probably he was seeking to reconcile the arguments of reason with his existing faith.

His review of moral principles, now incomplete, begins with Fortitude, Humility, and Resignation. The first he defined as 'That calm and steady habit of mind which either moderates our fears, and enables us bravely to encounter the prospect of ill or renders the mind serene and invincible under its immediate pressure'. This aptly describes, but probably not consciously, how he himself had faced tribulations and would do so again. Then follows a list, with short descriptions, of men's duties under various conventional headings: Filial, Fraternal, Matrimonial, Parental, Servile (as quoted earlier), then Social Duties of a Private, Commercial, or Political kind.

Lastly comes his view of man's Duty to God:

'Wherever right conceptions of the Deity and his providence prevail, when he is considered as the inexhaustible source of light, and love, and joy, as acting in the joint character of a *Father* and *Governor* imparting an endless variety of capacities to his creatures and supplying them with every thing necessary to their full completion and happiness; what *veneration* and *Gratitude* must such conceptions thoroughly believed excite in the mind . . .'

A comparison of the Divine nature and our own engenders humility and repentance; God is forbearing. Reason gives us some grounds to expect this, and Natural Religion will teach the humble theist to await revelation and to carry out his duties:

'This is the completion of Morality – to the hopes of pardon must be added – *Worship*, *praise*, and *thanksgiving*, both internal, external and Public.'

Thus Park reconciled his rational beliefs with revealed truths, but the whole process of thought, and even the language, were far removed from the style and concerns of his Covenanter forbears. It was also an entirely optimistic faith, the binding force and the reflection of his personality. The problems of evil were hardly visible in the quiet of the Scottish countryside and in the happiness of his marriage.

Nor was he troubled as yet by mundane considerations of how he was to earn a living. Presumably the possibility of his joining Dr. Thomas Anderson in Selkirk was discussed, but now that Alexander Anderson had joined his father there was no room for another surgeon.

He must have known that Banks was pressing the Government to mount an expedition to the Niger. That was where his heart was set, as it had never been set on the Australian expedition. His recent marriage created a problem, but optimistically he could have thought again, 'It is a short expedition.' When it was done, then he could settle down to raise a family.

After some months of waiting he went to London at the beginning of 1800. From there he wrote to Allison on 10 January:

'My Dearest Allie –
    I have done little or nothing since I wrote to you. My first object was to consult Sir Joseph on the subject ... I informed him of my present situation and solicited his advice and assistance concerning my future prospects. He assured me that he was always ready to serve me and would do his utmost to procure me a situation – I hinted to him the China appointment but he said he was affraid it would not answer my expectations – I then enquired if he thought there was any Chance of obtaining a situation at home, he said he had none in view at present but he would think of it and advised me to bestir myself among my friends as soon as they came to town at the meeting of parliament ... on the 21st Jan^y.

'I Dinned with Mr. Nicol yesterday ... he says that the profits upon the three Editions will be about two thousand pounds. I have been constantly running about since I came here but I am far from happy as my mind is always anxious about my Allie. I hope my love that you will write me as soon

as you can and I shall lose no opportunity of informing you of the welfare of him who is ever yours,
    Mungo Park.'[5]

The China appointment that Banks dissuaded him from was probably some post under the East India Company. There is no clue what kind of post he might have hoped for at home – a botanist at Kew Gardens perhaps? His friends in Parliament, whoever they were, turned up nothing for him – Bryan Edwards had been seriously ill for months and in the coming July he had, as he put it, 'a much longer journey to undertake than poor Park's'.[6] Banks probably told him the Government had not even responded to the African Association's memorandum on the Niger, being preoccupied with the war in Europe, where Napoleon was triumphant, the union with Ireland, and discontents at home. There was nothing for it but to go back to Selkirk and continue waiting hopefully.

On 28 May 1800 a son was born to Mungo and Allison Park, named Mungo after his grandfather, like Alexander's eldest son then aged nearly four and Archibald's eldest, born the next year. In July news came that Gorée had been captured from the French in April, and Park promptly wrote to Banks urging that this should be the signal for a fresh expedition. 'If such are the views of Government, I hope that my exertions in some station or other, may be of use to my country. I have not as yet found any situation in which I could practice to advantage as a surgeon; and unless some of my friends interest themselves in my behalf, I must wait patiently, until the cloud which hangs over my future prospects, is dispelled.'

Still there was silence from the Government. He had never been a man to sit idly, but all of the year 1800 he waited. Perhaps he filled in some time, with however little enthusiasm, brushing up his medical knowledge. In the New Year of 1801 he became restless again. A letter to Nicol written 'at the commencement of the 19th Century' asked for an account relating to the third and fourth editions, and said that if he did not hear he would have to come to London, 'though such a trip would be much against me in my fresh situation'.[7] Against him or not, he was soon in London. On 5 February he passed an examination and became one of the early Members of the Royal College of Surgeons of London, recently reconstituted from the Company of Surgeons, a qualification necessary if he were to practise.[8]

Nevertheless he still had other plans, as a letter written to Allison from London on 12 March shows:

'My lovely Allie –
Nothing gives me more pleasure than to write to you, and the reason why I delayed it a day last time was to get some money to send to you. You say you are wishing to spend a note upon yourself. My sweet Allie, you may be sure I approve of it. What is mine is yours, and I receive much pleasure from your goodness in consulting me about such a trifle. I wish I had thousands to give you, but I know that my Allie will be contented with what we have, and we shall live in hopes of better days. I long very much to be with you, my love, and I was in great hopes of having things settled before now, but Sir Joseph is ill, and I can do nothing till he recovers.

'I am happy to know you will go to New South Wales with me, my sweet wife. You are every thing I can desire; and wherever we go, you may be sure of one thing, that I shall always love you. Whenever I have fixed on this or any other situation I shall write to you . . .

'My lovely Allie, you are constantly in my thoughts . . . My darling, when we meet I shall be the happiest man on earth. Write soon, for I count the days till I hear from you, my lovely Allie . . .'[9]

The object of going to New South Wales was clarified in a letter he wrote to Banks in October 1801 after moving to Peebles:[10]

'I left London, as you may easily suppose, a little down-hearted: the romantic village which my fancy had erected on the shores of New Holland, as a habitation for myself and family, had completely disappeared.'

This was clearly no revival of Banks's proposal for Park to explore Australia, nor were negotiations with Government involved. It was a suggestion from Park himself that he should settle there. Doubtless Banks told him plainly that there were no 'romantic villages' there, but still only convict settlements.

Park's letter to Banks continued:

'I journeyed towards my native country with the painful but not degrading reflexion, that I must henceforth earn my bread by the sweat of my brow. On my arrival in Scotland, it was my wish to occupy a farm; but the high price of cattle and the enormous rents which landowners everywhere expected made it rather a dangerous speculation: in short, I was again compleatly at a stand . . .'

Park did negotiate for a farm with the Earl of Dalkeith, the heir to the Duke of Buccleuch, who was well-disposed to him, but this came to nothing. A severe winter in 1799 had killed many farm animals, and of course this drove prices up, but Park did have appreciable capital, and probably his heart was not in this plan.

'At this juncture,' Park continued, 'a surgeon of considerable eminence died at Peebles; and, as I was tired of a life of indolence, I resolved to succeed him.' As an early biographer tactfully put it, he was also 'urged by the importunity of his friends', no doubt led by Dr. Anderson, anxious about the inactivity of his son-in-law!

In late September 1801 Park travelled with Dr. Anderson to Peebles to interview Dr. James Reid, the surviving surgeon of the town. The elderly doctor wanted Park to accept, as his recently deceased half-brother Robert Marshall had done, one-third of the profits but to do half of the riding out of town. This proposal Park refused and the negotiations broke down. He decided instead to set up in Peebles on his own, and in early October he moved over from Selkirk, with his wife, young Mungo, and his daughter Elizabeth, born on 9 September.[11]

In the same month he heard from Banks, that in consequence of the Peace – about to be concluded, but lasting only until 1803 – the Association would certainly revive their project of sending a mission to Africa, to penetrate to and navigate the Niger; if the Government agreed, then Park would certainly be recommended for it. This may have cheered Park, but he had waited too long in vain to wish to defer his present plan unless something definite emerged.

CHAPTER XX

The Reluctant Surgeon

At Peebles, 1801–1803

———— ∞ ————

The reluctance with which Park resumed his profession as a surgeon was frankly stated at the end of his letter to Banks in October 1801. He wrote:

'I was induced to take this step, because it would afford me present employment; and in the event of obtaining something better, I could resign my situation to my younger brother [Adam] or my brother-in-law [John Anderson] ... In the meantime I hope my friends will not relax in their endeavours to serve me. A country surgeon is at best a laborious employment; and I will gladly hang up the lancet and plaister ladle whenever I can obtain a more eligible situation.'

Nevertheless he worked to establish both his home and his practice, the latter based in a room in the High Street rented for his surgery. At first he lodged with Mr. Oman, the retired schoolmaster of Peebles; then he took a small house, still marked as having been his, in the Northgate nearby. Peebles had almost exactly the same population as Selkirk, and was likewise a quiet market town with many scattered farms and cottages for miles around. The lawyer Lord Cockburn once quipped, 'As quiet as the grave – or Peebles!'

To build up his clientèle of patients in the face of Reid's established practice was probably easier, given the latter's age and reluctance to go out riding, out of town than in it. That meant tiring and unremunerative work, no pleasanter for being started as winter was coming on. A vivid account of such a practice was given by Park's friend of later years, Sir Walter Scott, in 'The Surgeon's Daughter':

'Like the ghostly lover of Leonora, he mounts at midnight, and traverses in darkness paths which, to those less accustomed to them, seem formidable in daylight, through straits where the slightest aberration would plunge him into a morass, or throw him over a precipice, on to cabins which his horse might ride over without knowing they lay in his way, unless he happened to fall through the roofs. When he arrives at such a stately termination of his journey, where his services are required, either to bring a wretch into the world, or prevent one from leaving it, the scene of misery is often such, that, far from touching the hard saved shillings which are gratefully offered to him, he bestows his medicines as well as his attendance – for charity. I have heard the celebrated traveller Mungo Park, who had experienced both courses of life, rather give the preference to travelling as a discoverer in Africa, than to wandering, by night and day, the wilds of his native land in the capacity of a country medical practitioner. He mentioned having, once upon a time, rode forty miles, sat up all night, and successfully assisted a woman under influence of the primitive curse, for which his sole remuneration was a roasted potatoe and a draught of butter milk. But his was not the heart which grudged the labour that relieved human misery. In short, there is no creature in Scotland that works harder and is more poorly requited than the country doctor, unless, perhaps it may be his horse.'

After one such visit the shepherd followed him along the path and, when asked why, explained, 'Deed, sir, my wife said she was sure you must be an angel, and I think sae tae [so too]; so I am just keepin' ahint [behind] to be sure I'll see you flee up!'[1]

Scott once described Park's attitude slightly differently, 'that he would rather brave Africa and all its horrors, than wear out his life in long and toilsome rides over the hills of Scotland, for which the remuneration was hardly enough to keep body and soul together'. Eighty years after Park's death, on the strength of this remark alone, the writer John Ruskin denounced Park's almost total absence of the instinct of personal duty; of belief in God who chose for him his cottage birthplace, and set him his life-task beside it; of interest in his profession; and of compassion for the poor. In a word, he detected Avarice. Ruskin was right about Park's lack of interest in his profession, but wrong on all the other counts. Apart from his quaint idea of how a man's place in life is determined, Ruskin created his own problem by ruling out in advance any possibility that Park could reasonably put his singular talent for exploration ahead of his replaceable skill as a country surgeon, and also by supposing that money, rather than fame, was his principal personal motive. It is not even certain that Scott correctly quoted Park's words. In what seems to be a third version of the same comment, Park said that a few inglorious winters of country practice at Peebles were a risk as great, and would tend as effectually to shorten life, as another journey in Africa. This misdirected attack is only worth mentioning because of Ruskin's own stature as a writer.[2]

Not all of his life at Peebles was so wretched or irksome. He enjoyed many visits to the home nearby of Dr. Adam Ferguson, who had retired from being Professor of Moral Philosophy at Edinburgh University before Park went there as a student. There he also met Ferguson's successor, Dugald Stewart, whose first book he had taken to Bencoolen. Two friends in town, Mr. Oman and Mr. James Chambers, whose sons founded the famous Edinburgh publishing firm, possessed telescopes with which he learnt more about astronomy. He translated some botany lectures from French, and he is said to have hoped to have Banks's recommendation to succeed Professor Rutherford in the Chair of Botany at Edinburgh. Rutherford in fact continued in the Chair until 1819.

Park also acquired both friends and patients amongst the local gentry, including Sir John Hay, Sir James Montgomery, and Colonel John Murray, who welcomed him to dine in spite of his low place in the social hierarchy. It was under Montgomery that Park enrolled in the Yeomanry, the 'Home Guard' formed some years before because of fears of a French invasion. Park's rumbustious brother Archibald was a volunteer at Selkirk, and Walter Scott was a keen officer at Edinburgh. In the renewed war period after 1803 Napoleon did plan to invade, but Park's sailing for Africa came just before the one occasion when the Yeomanry were called out, for a false alarm as it proved.

The Yeomanry's activities had a social side. For one such event in camp Park wrote and sang, to enthusiastic applause, the 'Song for the Tweeddale Cavalry', sung to a tune finely called, 'Willie was a wanton wag.' Possibly other verses of his had more literary merit than this war song. It is the only surviving example of his verse – unless his 'Sleep on sweet baby', said to be in a Collection of Scotch Songs by Ross, can be found.[3] The third and final verse ran:

> 'But freedom fair will ne'er forsake
>   The sons of Caledonia:
> What Roman courage couldna shake
>   May laugh at blust'ring Frenchmen a'.
> United let us draw our swords:
>   United let us stand or fa':
> Let Gallia land her savage hordes,
>   United we shall bang them a'.'

Hardly great poetry, but it does show a more relaxed Park than commonly appears!

The comments of those who knew him at this period converge with what has been reported of him earlier, and do not seem to be unduly influenced by piety to the dead. All agree that to strangers his manner was reserved, serious, and shy, conveying coldness. One of his unre-munerative patients put it well, 'He was a dacent man, Dr. Park, but he hadna muckle to say for himsel'.'[4]

With friends his conversation was described as 'that of a well-informed man on all subjects, though not very communicative; and particularly shy when his *Travels* were introduced – very fond of a good joke.' He had no small talk – perhaps another bond of sympathy with Banks. Even with friends, the presence of one stranger would inhibit him. He objected to people trying to draw him out by indirect questions, which he felt led to misunderstandings.

But with relatives or his closest friends he could relax and talk about his adventures, especially on a convivial occasion. He enjoyed his pipe and a drink of strong ale, and he sometimes went to the pub with companions. His *Travels* show that his taste in humour was not prudish. He did not object to direct curiosity, for example from Dr. Ferguson who, on his first visit, showed him a large map of Africa and made him go over his journey stage by stage.

It seems that the unreservedness he achieved with only a few select friends at Peebles he managed with all manner of men in Africa. Perhaps this was a factor in his longing to return. Some of those who knew him best at Selkirk and Peebles described him 'as having always the appearance of brooding over some secret confined to his own breast'. Next to his letters to his wife, these recollections of him give us the best clues to his interior personality.

During these two years at Peebles there was little encouragement to think he would ever return to Africa. He may have been quite out of touch with what little in this regard Banks had been able to do. Park's letter to Banks of October 1801, written just after moving to Peebles, bears a note in Banks's hand, 'I recommend him a copy of Sir Wm. Younge's account of Hornemann,' but nothing further.[5]

Hornemann, a young German, had been engaged by the Association and sent off in June 1797, before Park's return, to Cairo, where Napoleon's invading force soon arrived. Napoleon befriended him but, setting off westwards with a caravan of traders and pilgrims returning from Mecca, Hornemann soon found that the invasion was sending messages of pain and alarm along the nerves of Muslim communications into the heart of north and west Africa. His guise of a Muslim traveller was challenged but he bluffed his way through, whilst his German servant, who really was a Muslim, was in panic. After a fascinating journey inland across the north African desert to Murzuk in the Fezzan, he managed to send an informative report back to England from Tripoli.

He had heard at Murzuk about the Tibu and the Tuareg of the desert lands to the south, and about the countries east of Borno towards the Nile. This description tallied with the report of W.G. Browne, a traveller not engaged by the Association, who had been as far from Cairo as Darfur, in the west of the present Sudanese Republic, from 1793 to 1796. Hornemann also found out that 'Haussa' was the collective name of the group of states which included Kano and Katsina, and not a separate state. He even secured a sketch map showing more or less correctly their relative positions. Yet Rennell persisted in misconstruing 'Haussa' as an Empire. (Unity of the Hausa states was about to be achieved for the first time, through a Fulani-led Holy War of reform.) Within ten years much had been filled in on the 'wide extended blank'. From Timbuktu to the Hausa states and Borno, and from there southwards to near the coast, was the principal area in which the main features had still to be made clear.

One great puzzle continued: what happened to the Niger after Timbuktu? All of Hornemann's informants agreed that it flowed east through Hausa, where it was known as the 'Gaora' – the first mention of its Hausa name, Kwara – on through Borno, where it was called the 'Zad' – a confusion with Lake Chad – and then eastwards until it joined the Nile, as Herodotus had said. Rennell still rejected this view, being able to call Browne to his aid, and adhered firmly to his belief that it ended in a great lake in Wangara, just west of Borno. Park agreed with the rejection of the Nile theory, but was unconvinced by Rennell's own view. No doubt he longed for the chance to return to Silla, and to penetrate beyond it.

After Hornemann left Tripoli, only two short letters sent from Murzuk in 1800 were ever received. In 1805 he was reported to have been in Katsina two years before; only long afterwards was it heard that he had continued south and had perished of dysentery at 'Bakkanee' in Nupe, possibly Bokani, near the major road junction about thirty miles north of Jebba on the Niger, below the furthest point Park ever reached.[6] He was within 300 miles of the coast and of un-ravelling the mysteries of both Hausaland and the Niger. Once more, as with Ledyard and Houghton, had Hornemann lived, Park's career would have been radically changed.

Meanwhile Park's commitments to home and family grew. His second son was born at Peebles in March 1803, and was called Thomas after his maternal grandfather, Dr. Thomas Anderson, to whom Park repaid his debt by taking his son Thomas as his apprentice. On 15 September Dr. Reid died, and Park prepared to take over the whole medical practice of Peebles. He wrote to James Dickson to send all of his dividend on his London stocks so that he could keep a second horse.[7]

A fortnight later came a letter that knocked aside all such plans. It was from Sir Joseph Banks at his Lincolnshire estate:

'To Mr. Park – I am requested by Lord Hobart to desire your attendance immediately at his Lordship's office in Downing Street, where you will be pleased to enquire for Mr. Vansittart, and send in your name and mine to him.

'I have every reason to believe that the expedition which is on foot, of which I am not allowed to acquaint you with the particulars, will suit your wishes, and that proper terms of engagement will be offered to you.'[8]

This must have been a testing moment for Allison, as Africa had always clearly been her one rival for her husband's affections. Perhaps she had hoped that marriage, three children, and a growing practice would hold him to her, but any such hopes were soon dashed. Within days the lancet and the plaister ladle were hung up, and Park was down to London as fast as any coach could carry him.

CHAPTER XXI

'Another trip into the Centre of Africa'

First plans for a second journey

———— ༚ ————

Only a little of what lay behind the Government's sudden call can ever have been known to Park himself. The African Association began its efforts to arouse Government interest only a few days after its 1799 meeting, with the submission of its resolution and an explanatory memorandum in beautiful copperplate handwriting to the Board of Trade. At the same time Banks, being an appointed member of that Board, wrote to its President, Lord Liverpool, giving his personal view that the greatest benefits would ensue if Britain were to annex the whole coastline from Sierra Leone northwards to 350 miles north of Gorée, or at least to procure the cession of the river Senegal, a much smaller target: gold first 'to almost any given extent', the conversion and better government of the Negroes, and the greatest practicable diminution of slavery. This comprehensive annexationist and 'civilizing' policy looked far ahead of Banks's own time; and its definitive form was not to crystallize for another eighty years.[1]

The Government was then too preoccupied in Europe and at home to take action. In 1800 the Association could only be told that the resolution had been submitted; in 1801 the plan was still held in reserve, to take effect at a more advantageous time of peace. One small step was taken in April 1800 with the capture of Gorée, and the island was occupied by a British force under Colonel John Fraser. It was this news which caused a flutter of Park's hopes that he might be sent for. St. Louis in the mouth of the Senegal was unsuccessfully attacked the following Christmas Day, but nothing happened after that. Fraser sat out the short-lived Peace of Amiens from 1802 to 1803 on Gorée, as orders sent, after a previous set had been issued and then countermanded, telling him to hand back the island as provided in the peace treaty, took five months on the way and reached him too late.

Before that, in 1801, war-weariness had brought down Pitt's government, and it had been replaced by Henry Addington's, in which

Lord Hobart occupied the newly created post of Secretary of State for War, to which the Colonies were transferred from the Home Office with just one clerk! John Sullivan, M.P., was his Under Secretary. When peace came, the African Association did not attempt to revive its plan. Its final West African effort was to send Henry Nicholls in 1804, to penetrate inland from Calabar in south-eastern Nigeria. Nicholls died there. His attempt was unconnected with Park's affairs.

Banks acted on his own in August 1802 when he wrote to Sullivan, drawing attention to a book by S.M.X.Golberry just published in France. Golberry advocated a policy of annexation even wider than Banks's own, taking in modern Liberia. Sullivan appreciated the danger Banks had pointed out that the French might pre-empt the West African trade, and he wrote a memorandum on 12 August about it. He advocated the reoccupation of James Island fort in the Gambia, establishing trade 'factories' and free-trade treaties up the river and across to the Faleme, and also inland from Sierra Leone and Bulama. Consulting such experts as were available, he found that Captain Beaver was still in favour of penetration from Bulama Island up the Rio Grande, while Zachary Macaulay preferred the Senegal and the Gambia – but had the Government thought of using the Gold Coast Forts as a starting-point? – and Rennell was doubtful whether anything more than exploratory consular contacts for trade purposes as far as Bamako would be worth while; interference with the Moors' trade would call for strong forces.[2]

Even before Rennell wrote, the Government had decided to do no more for the present than send a small exploratory mission, as Sullivan explained in a Most Secret letter to Banks on 13 October:

'. . . our little Flotilla for African Discoveries should proceed as soon as possible and I have reason to think every thing at the Admiralty will be ready in ten days. The immediate objects are to ascertain how far the Gambia and the Rio Grande may be navigated, at the most favourable time, by small craft; and at what distance, from the points where their waters may fail us, we may be able to avail ourselves of any other rivers to shorten our Course to the Niger – I have gathered much from Moore's book, from Park and from the publications of your Association, but this only tends to make me the more anxious to have the lights of your mind upon the subject . . . The opportunity well improved [? handwriting illegible] may enable us to lay our ground broadly for another expedition. The present will consist of two small Frigates, some Gun Brigs and small craft, to be augmented by as great a number of large canoes and African navigators as Captn. Beaver who is to command may think proper to employ.'³

Captain Beaver seemed quite unaware of this when he wrote the preface to his *African Memoranda*, and described how he then enjoyed his first long home leave for many years; and it seems that this expedition never in fact went. It would have been typical of these years if the Admiralty had said that its resources were so strained that no ships could be spared for a sideshow.

The next sign of activity was in July 1803, when a Colonel Charles Stevenson was authorized to raise a corps to go to West Africa.⁴ In November Fraser, at Gorée, was ordered to prepare for an attack on St. Louis or on a solitary French trading-post in the Gambia. Between these two events, out of the blue came the seemingly unconnected summons to Park, on 10 October, to report to Lord Hobart. Banks's hint of secret operations is only intelligible on the assumption that the Government wanted to economize on shipping by sending Park out at the same time as Stevenson's corps, or alternatively that it did not want to alert the French prematurely to renewed British interest in the Senegambia area.

The object of Park's own mission can, in the absence of any mention in the official records, be deduced from his correspondence; it was exploration pure and simple. On his way back to Scotland after seeing Lord Hobart, he wrote about 20 October to Banks:

'. . . When I waited on Lord Hobart, I found that his Lordship wished me to take another trip into the Centre of Africa, with a view to discover the termination of the Niger, that a guard of 25 soldiers would be allowed me, and that I should have 10(s) per Day for subsistence, and £200 per annum during my stay in Africa. It would be cruel in me to engage in an expedition of such magnitude without first acquainting Mrs Park ... I shall wait for your letter before I return my decisive answer to Lord Hobart.'⁵

It is noteworthy that he was now prepared to accept a lower daily rate than the final offer for the Australian expedition; the £200 per annum was presumably for the upkeep of his family, which had not existed in 1798. Can these terms be called Avarice?

For the first time a proposal was made, by whom is not indicated, for Park to travel with a protective escort of troops. Traders and their servants commonly banded together in Africa for security, negotiating their way by the payment of fairly well-defined tolls. Whether Park's party would be accepted as such a caravan would depend on various circumstances, especially on their readiness to act similarly, and above all, on their following frequented trade routes.

It is probably correct, as has been generally held, that his mind was made up before ever he saw Allison at Peebles. It is also said that she did not try to deter him, although there are ambiguities in the record here. Banks's reply to his letter, encouraging him to go, would have removed any lingering doubts, and he informed Lord Hobart of his acceptance. However, he spent two months at home, and during this time Alexander Anderson asked to be included in the expedition. About the New Year of 1804 he made his farewells and journeyed south.

On 4 January he arrived back in London, and the next day he wrote to Alexander:

'Dear Brother – I arrived here last night, and this morning had an interview with Sir Joseph and Mr. Sullivan, and find that it is the wish of Government to open a communication from the Gambia to the Niger for the purpose of trade, and they do not wish me on any account to proceed further than I shall find it safe and proper. 200 pick't men embark this day at Falmouth for the expedition.

'I mentioned you as my companion, and that you expressed a wish to accompany me. They readily offered you 10s a day, and the Government allowance, with a promise of their interest in your favour.

'With respect to myself, I have their most solemn promise that in case of my success I shall be put in a comfortable situation at my return, and should I die, I have asked and obtained that £100 shall be settled on my dear Allie and family during life.

'If you have made up your mind you should lose no time in coming to London ... I think we shall not sail for a week or ten days. If you go by Peebles bring me particular word how my dear Allie is ...'[6]

Apart from the financial insurance provided for his family, what stands out most is that the plan for the expedition had been changed. Instead of going with 25 men to explore the termination of the Niger, he was to take 200 men to open a communication *to* the Niger from the Gambia for the purposes of trade, but he probably still secretly hoped that a chance to travel down the length of the river would somehow emerge. Some new outline plans, it seems, had already been accepted in principle by Lord Hobart, although only detailed on paper over the next three months. These plans came from Colonel Stevenson.

Stevenson's proposal was for a major military expedition from the Gambia to the Niger, proceeding downstream to seize Timbuktu in order to control the whole trade of the region in gold. The product would be enormous, he thought, if worked by Europeans. He confidently, though with extremely little evidence, believed that 'That part of the District to be occupied is, unquestionably, the richest in the world'. In letters to Sullivan between January and April 1804, he detailed his plans for the use of 1,200 West Indian troops with some white artificers and an unwholesome mixture of army deserters and other military or civil prisoners sentenced to transportation, to be followed by more the next year. He was most insistent on using only the dry seasons to advance, for health reasons. He was ready, if ordered to advance during the rains, to leave a statement of this opinion with a friend in order to vindicate him if disaster occurred. By March he was already looking forward to the next dry season, and he was anyway far from being ready. Months later he was still complaining about slow recruitment due to unfair competition from the Navy's press-gangs.

By April 1804 the Government, never strong, neared paralysis, a process hastened by the King's having had in February a recurrence of an earlier mental illness, conjuring up visions or fears of a Regency, and likely political changes. The King recovered in April, but the Government did not, and it resigned in May. Thus the planning had been done by a Government powerless to execute the plans, if indeed it ever got as far as approving them. In March Sullivan set down a much reduced version of Stevenson's grand design. This incorporated Sullivan's own earlier exploratory ideas using Bulama, Sierra Leone, and the Gambia, but it also proposed an advance in the next dry season to the Niger and down to Timbuktu. Park was to lead the way with 150 men. He was always to negotiate his way peacefully, and there was no discussion of what would happen if he were refused permission to go ahead. Stevenson was to follow with a larger force but, unless he encountered any French posts, he was to be strictly enjoined never to use force except defensively. It is doubtful whether Park even heard of these plans, so that we have no idea what his views on them would have been. In the event, the significance of the plans was to keep alive the idea of some form of West African expedition and of the importance of using the dry season.

Meanwhile, Park had been waiting around since the New Year,

hoping to leave, at the latest, by February 1804. There is a look of
hurried improvisation about all the arrangements. Park and Anderson
were to be ready to go at a few days' notice, with no time to prepare
any specialized equipment, and no written instructions seem to have
been issued to Park. Stevenson found himself being switched around,
first to go to Ceylon to deal with a temporary crisis there, then to go
back to Gorée when it was learnt that the French had taken it in
January. Only days later, he was told to stay at home, when news
arrived that the British Navy had recaptured Gorée in March. On
Gorée itself, Fraser had kept getting instructions to prepare for an
assault on Senegal; these were regularly followed by cancellations, and
arrangements were made several times between December and February to send him reinforcements from England (as shown once in
Park's letter to Anderson) but these reinforcements never went. 4
February 1804 seems to have been the date of the final cancellation of
instructions for that dry season; they had been issued only the day before! These instructions would not in fact have found Fraser on Gorée
any longer, for he was captured with the island in January. He was
freed on parole and sent back to England, and was replaced at Gorée
by a Major Richard Lloyd. After the postponement of action to the
following dry season, Park stayed on in London for a month, probably
in the vain hope that his future would be made clear. Then he went
home, little the wiser.

Colonel Stevenson met Park once at a party, and can be imagined
expounding his views to him in a lengthy monologue. He later referred
to Park favourably as having been a prospective colleague, but his one
comment made at that time was: 'This Expedition must be made with
a view to a permanent and important Establishment, and not as an
attendant on a rambling Individual, who wishes to have the honor
of ascertaining the course of the Niger or the Source of the Nile'!
Had they ever had to try working together, it is hardly imaginable
that, with their divergent interests and personalities, they could possibly have formed a harmonious partnership.

7. Mungo Park, from an engraving after the portrait by Henry
Edridge reproduced as the frontispiece to the *Travels*

8a. Major James Rennell,
from a drawing by
George Dance, 1794

8b. The 1st Marquess
Camden, from a drawing by
Francis Chantrey, 1830

CHAPTER XXII

'Freits follow those who look to them'

Scotland, 1804

———— ∞ ————

Park returned to Peebles at the beginning of March 1804, leaving Anderson in the south, where he became a Military Surgeon at Gosport near Portsmouth. Park took with him Sidi Ombark Bouby, a Moroccan by birth, who had come to London as interpreter to the Egyptian Ambassador. Park had engaged him in early January to teach him Arabic. Ombark Bouby now made (but we do not know whether he ever *wrote*, as Lewis Grassic Gibbon hoped he had) his Travels into the Interior of Scotland. He caused nearly as great a sensation at Peebles and Selkirk as ever Park did in Africa.

As a devout Muslim he regularly said his prayers and observed the rules of his religion, but people in rural Scotland knew little about these, and were never sure what belonged to his religion and what should be ascribed to 'prejudice'. Abstaining from all alcoholic drinks, he was once angry with Park – who should have known better – for serving a pudding containing brandy. What seemed most odd to the local people was that he would eat meat only from animals slaughtered by himself in the Muslim fashion, slitting the throat and letting the blood drain. He was often to be seen in the early morning at the slaughterhouse. If he were going out to dine he either ate a vegetarian meal, or sent meat in advance to his host to be cooked for him. On the other hand, his faith in dreams struck a chord in the populace, especially after he had told Park he had dreamt his mother was dead, and shortly afterwards had received news that this was actually true.

Ombark Bouby was with the Parks at Peebles up to May 1804, teaching Mungo Arabic. Park also studied astronomy to help him in fixing positions in Africa. At Whitsuntide he finally closed his surgery at Peebles, and moved with his family and Ombark Bouby to the farmhouse at Foulshiels, where the lessons continued. A visiting would-be portraitist there was nearly stabbed by Ombark Bouby, wroth at the disregard of the Muslim prohibition of depicting any living creature.

Despite such upsets, he was favourably remembered in Peebles and Selkirk as an intelligent and worthy man, who conversed freely with all who displayed friendliness to him. He too greatly enjoyed his sojourn with the family, and especially playing with the children, which he re-called in a touching letter of thanks he sent to Mrs. Park after return-ing to London, 'I will never forget how happy I was at Fowlshiels . . . I never in my life will forget you.'

Park would have liked Ombark Bouby to accompany him to Africa, but Ombark Bouby would not agree, and constantly affirmed that if Park went he would never return. After Park's departure, a story went round in London that Banks had offered, or knew that Ombark Bouby had been offered, £500 to go with Park, but that he had re-fused. Ombark Bouby was deeply hurt and asked Banks to deny this rumour, as he did.[1]

About the time that the Parks moved to Foulshiels, Walter Scott, then just beginning to earn repute as a poet, rented a house called Ashestiel, over the hills in the neighbouring Tweed valley. This was so that he could attend more fully to his duties as Sheriff of Selkirk-shire, a judicial office. He wanted to meet Mungo Park, and Archi-bald, for long afterwards a friend of the Shirra', introduced them. Scott must have also been acquainted with Alexander Park through his official duties. Scott and Mungo Park had only four months of contact, but their shared interest in the border legends and ballads quickly opened the way to a wider friendship. Mungo soon found in Scott one of those friends to whom he could open his mind, and with whom he could enjoy an evening of relaxed conversation and amuse-ment, so much so that Scott became one of Whishaw's principal in-formants for his portrait of Park in the Biographical Memoir.

One day early in their acquaintance Scott, having been redirected from Foulshiels, sought Park out on the banks of the Yarrow. He found him tossing in pebbles and counting the time for the bubbles to rise, as he explained he had done in Africa to help judge the depth of rivers. Though no more was said, Scott at once divined that a return to Africa was in his mind. This is a remarkable instance of Park's secretiveness, even if he did have the additional motive of official secrecy. He can have had little to hide, after once making his fare-wells, then returning and closing his practice, with Ombark Bouby accompanying him to teach him Arabic.

Another new contact was made in this period but only by correspondence, as a planned meeting did not take place. George Maxwell, who had been a trader operating down the western coasts of Africa, wrote to Park in July propounding a new theory about the Niger. In essence it was very simple: the upper Niger was known, a great river needing an outlet, and Maxwell had also seen the mouth of the Congo, large enough to be that outlet, and with no known origin. Modestly and tentatively, he wondered whether they could be the two ends of one river. The argument was supported by considering the time at which each river was in flood, which, in the case of the Congo, did not tally with the timing of the local rains. This theory evidently struck Park as the answer to a conundrum that had puzzled him; he accepted that the ground levels were all wrong for it to be possible that the Niger joined the upper Nile, but he could not accept Rennell's theory that it petered out in a lake in the heart of Africa. Such a great river demanded an outlet to the sea. He adopted Maxwell's theory, which led him to expect to have to make a journey of at least 3,000 miles by river from Sansanding.*

William Pitt had returned to office as Prime Minister on 14 May, with his friend Earl Camden as Secretary of State for War and the Colonies, and Edward Cooke as his Under Secretary. Colonel Stevenson soon began to work on them to persuade the new Government to adopt his strategy. Between July and December 1804 he sent Camden ten memoranda, had interviews with him, and even managed to see Pitt. He also wrote to Addington at his usual length, but Addington was then out of power and could do nothing.

As he was to continue doing for years, Stevenson sought to flatter the Government with grandiose hopes of success: 'This expedition, like that of Columbus, appears calculated to rescue from Chaos another World and may prove as important to England as South America has been to Spain.' On a less exalted level, he went on to point out that the Government could avoid the unpopularity of sending troops from Britain to reinforce Gibraltar, where a plague was raging, and could instead recruit and send Africans. Being ignorant of English,

---

*Appendix IV to the Biographical Memoir quoted Maxwell's letters (originals in Add. MSS. 37232K, ff. 52–3 and 56–9) and analysed the current theories about the Niger, including the correct one that it enters the Gulf of Guinea, first put forward in 1808 by the German geographer M. Reichard. This was rated a rather poor fourth to Rennell's, the Nile, and the Congo theories, mainly because of the Kong Mountains – 'Of the existence of these mountains, there appears to be no doubt'! It was only in the 1880s that their non-existence was finally accepted.

'They would only conclude it was an unhealthy season.' Fortunately Africa never had to suffer the ministrations of the colourful and obnoxious Stevenson. He later deluded himself that only Pitt's death stopped the adoption of his plans.

Camden was busy by August with his own plan. He wanted to send Colonel Fraser and 600 men to attack Senegal, but the Navy was too stretched, blockading France and watching Spain, as it edged closer to war, to spare ships. His objects, very different from Stevenson's and Sullivan's, were to prevent the French destroying British trade, and to hold Gorée and Senegal as bargaining counters to extract French support at the end of the war for a general European treaty outlawing the slave trade. He hoped thus to outflank the objection that if Britain alone prohibited the trade, her rivals would carry it on even more vigorously.

In September Camden hit on the brilliant idea, which evidently appealed to the Admiralty, of putting Fraser's Corps into a large convoy well known to be destined for the West Indies, and then secretly detaching it at sea to go to attack Senegal.[2] Here he saw the opportunity to get Park on his way in October, with the whole dry season ahead of him. Sometime in September he summoned Park to London, but not disclosing any details.

Park's whole life had been attuning him to hear this call: his ambition for achievement beyond what Selkirk could offer; his education, scientific interests, and association with Banks; his earlier travels and the unslaked urge to penetrate the Niger's obstinate secrets – all of these, forming a unity rare in any man's life, prepared him to take an opportunity that might never recur.

There was one flaw in this unity. In the years of waiting he had built up contradictory commitments to his family. If he could quickly succeed and return, he could reconcile the two, but if not . . . He did not find it easy to part from his wife and family. Allison was six months pregnant with their fourth child. There are conflicting stories of his departure. One was told much later by his sister, Mrs. Jean Thomson. According to her, Mungo and Allison had been staying at her husband's farmhouse, then at Myreton, Clackmannanshire, north of Edinburgh. She and Allison tried once more to persuade him not to go because of the dangers of the journey, but he became impatient. He mounted his horse and galloped off, calling out, 'Tell these tales to old wives!' Although Mrs. Thomson stated firmly that this occurred at his final parting, she may have confused the occasion with his leaving the previous year.[3]

A quite different but equally circumstantial account of his departure was given by Sir Walter Scott. When the time was near, Park paid a farewell visit and slept at Ashestiel. Next morning, he and Scott rode slowly up the Williamhope ridge between the Tweed and Yarrow valleys. On the way, Scott tried to dissuade him from going with a military escort, arguing that while it would be inadequate for conquest it would be large enough to excite suspicion. In Scott's recollection, 'He refuted my objections by referring to the subdivision of Africa into petty districts the chiefs of whom were not likely to form any combination for cutting him off and whose boundaries were soon traversed. He referred also to their habit of seeing coffles or caravans of all nations pass through their boundaries on paying a small duty so that the march of such a party as his own had nothing in it to alarm them with fears of peril or invasion.'[4]

Park next told Scott that he could not face a formal leave-taking. Allison was agreed to his going but he feared that at the last moment one or other of them would break down. He was determined to tell his family that he had some business in Edinburgh for a day or two, and to send them his blessing from there, without returning home. Many years after the event, the Parks' housemaid reported that he did in the end nerve himself to face a leave-taking and, in an emotional scene, offered not to go if Allison asked him to stay, but she replied, 'No, go and do your duty.'[5]

Callousness to his family was a second charge made by John Ruskin, who thought such a journey pointless anyway. What Scott's version shows is, rather, that he was under a great tension. Had he been able to go some years before, with no family commitments, how much easier it would have been. His actions were also probably influenced by his being uncertain what awaited him in London; it might not be a final parting at all. He later wrote to Alexander Williamson, Town Clerk of Peebles, 'When I saw you at Edinburgh I had every reason to believe that all thoughts of the expedition were for the present laid aside. On my arrival in London I was informed that the Ministry were still desirous to send out the expedition . . .'[6]

When Scott and Park had reached the top of the ridge, and were looking down through autumn mists hanging over the Yarrow, these friends of so short a time prepared to separate. In crossing a small ditch

Park's horse stumbled and nearly fell. 'I am afraid, Mungo,' said an anxious Scott, 'that is a bad omen.' With a smile Mungo quoted in reply from an old border proverb: 'Freits [omens] follow those who look to them.' Then he struck his spurs into his horse, and Scott never saw him again.

CHAPTER XXIII

'His Majesty has selected you'

Final preparations

—— ᕫᕬᕪ ——

Park reported to Lord Camden in London on 26 September 1804, and the impressions of both of them are available. Park wrote at once to Alexander Anderson:

'Dear Brother – I am just returned from Ld. Camdens. I had a long conversation with his Lordship, he said that if I would undertake to go on an Embassy or rather a Journey of discovery to the *Niger* (we should be absent from England about 18 months) a sufficient force would be allowed to me and if you went with me he said Government would have no difficulty in allowing you one thousand Pounds and four thousand to me to be settled on my wife and family in case of my Discease. You will perhaps be amazed at the great disproportion of our Sallaries but I assure you we shall not differ on that point. Pray write by the Next post what you think of it, it is certainly much more advantageous than the former. The only uneasiness I feel is on account of my Dear Allie and when I think of her I feel that I am indeed a Coward, to part with her seems the very bitterness of Death . . .

'P.S. My hand trembles so that I think I shall not write to Allie till I hear your opinion.'[1]

The nature of the journey and the provision made for his family, of which Alexander had none, were both to Park's satisfaction. This is also seen in his letter to Williamson: 'The alterations appeared to me very judicious . . .,' with particular reference to a much reduced number of troops. But it was indeed proving hard to part from his family.

Lord Camden's opinions were expressed the same day in a letter to the Prime Minister:

'Dear Pitt – Mr. Parke has just been with me. He is inclined to attempt the expedition proposed for the sum I mentioned – viz. £4,000 for himself and £1,000 for his Friend – An expedition upon the scale stated in Mr. Sullivan's memoire is *now* quite out of the Question and it is therefore to be determined in what manner a Journey of discovery and of Enquiry for commercial purposes can best be attempted. Mr. Parke seems to think that he shall be able to travel with less suspicion and therefore with more Effect, if he was only accompanied by 2 or 3 Persons on whom he could depend. He has however promised to consider and to give me his Sentiments in writing. I think it will be advantageous you should see him – I have apprized him you wish it and he is ready to come down to Walmer on any Day – You will find him a very conversible and well-behaved man . . .

'I much doubt whether we shall be able to establish any advantageous Intercourse – but the discovery and Enquiry are well worth the Sum of Money to be expended in these Enquiries.

Most sincerely yours, Camden.'[2]

Scott's arguments must have turned over in Park's mind on the journey south, and had had more effect than he had allowed to appear or than Scott ever suspected. His faith in the caravan principle was weakened.

Lord Camden is the only known person to have found Park 'very conversible', perhaps because he met him where his closest interest was aroused. It is unrecorded whether or not Park travelled down to Walmer Castle to see the ailing Pitt. After these preliminaries, Camden practically handed over to Banks the direction of the new, limited mission, writing to him on 28 September, '. . . I should anxiously hope that you would either give him your Instructions or desire the most scientific Man of the African Committee to communicate with him confidentially . . . it is material Mr. Park should sail by the Middle of October.'[3] Too little was known to warrant framing confident plans like Stevenson's; the British Government was prepared to send Park out on a journey of exploration, without even any firm hopes of promoting trade.

Meanwhile Park acted on Camden's request to set down his ideas in writing; there was a more businesslike approach than was ever visible in Hobart's time. His memorandum, perhaps partly written before he came to London, was submitted to Camden on 4 October. The objects of his journey, he wrote, would be 'the extension of British Commerce, and the enlargement of our Geographical Knowledge'. He would investigate the most practical and safest route to the Niger, the trade prospects, 'the general fertility of the country, whether any part of it might be useful to Britain for colonization, and whether any objects of Natural History, with which the natives are at present unacquainted, might be useful to Britain as a commercial nation'. He would ascertain latitudes and longitudes, the course and

if possible the termination of the river, and the kingdoms on or near
its banks with an account of the inhabitants.

He would require 30 European soldiers, 6 carpenters, and 15 or 20
Gorée Negroes, most of them artificers. His faith in the caravan principle had firmly recovered from its temporary wavering. 50 asses and
6 horses or mules should be bought on the way in the Cape Verde
Islands. Then he specified in detail the trade goods for making purchases and presents, the clothing, arms, and packing materials needed,
and the food: two tons of rice. He included the equipment for con-
structing two 40-foot boats on the Niger.

As for the manner of carrying out the expedition, 'Mr. Park is
sensible that difficulties will unavoidably occur; but he will be careful
to use conciliatory measures on every occasion. He will state to the
native princes the good understanding that has always subsisted between them and the English, and will invariably declare that his present journey is undertaken solely for the extension of commerce and
promotion of their mutual interests.'

He would start as before, going through Wuli and Bondu to Kajaaga
but then, instead of going on through Khasso and Kaarta, he would
turn southwards to Bambara. There he would try to win Mansong's
favour and his protection as far as Jenne. Beyond that he had no personal knowledge, but he would survey Lake Debo and continue by
Kabara, the port of Timbuktu, on through Hausa, Nupe, and Katsina
to the kingdom of Wangara, 1400 miles from his place of embarkation,
and supposed by Rennell to be much farther inland than where Lake
Chad actually is.

'If the river should unfortunately end here,' he said with masterly
understatement, 'Mr. Park would feel his situation extremely critical.'
To return up the Niger would be impossible, and he almost ruled out
the routes to the north or east; only the route southwards to the coast
held out any hope of success. He then explained why he believed that
the Niger and the Congo would prove to be one and the same river.
He wound up by declaring:

'Considered in a commercial point of view, it is second only to the discovery
of the Cape of Good Hope; and in a geographical point of view, it is certainly the greatest discovery that remains to be made in this world.'

Lord Camden was well satisfied and he soon sent for Park and told
him so. Neither party seems to have reflected that to do all that Park

aimed to do would need a leisurely rate of advance and a long time spent on enquiries. Before any definite commitment was made, Camden sent Park off to Brighton to consult Major Rennell. As we have seen, Rennell was sceptical about the commercial possibilities. He also held firmly to his idea of how the Niger ended, and was unmoved by Park's arguments about the Congo. He had grave forebodings about the trip as a whole, and in his solicitude for Park he pressed his doubts so forcefully on him as to convince him that he ought to relinquish the undertaking.[4] As in the case of Scott's advice the effect was purely temporary, and as soon as Park left Rennell to return to London his faith that the journey could and should be undertaken reasserted itself. He reported Rennell's doubts to Camden, but also restated his willingness to go ahead. In this, and also over the Congo theory, he was supported by Banks, who said quite frankly he regarded the expedition as one of the most hazardous ever undertaken, but it was only by taking such risks that great geographical discoveries were to be expected.[5]

Everything was taking shape for Park to leave in October with the West Indian convoy, giving him the whole dry season to reach the Niger and start down it. By 13 October Camden had secured the King's approval of the Senegal expedition, but by then a hitch had occurred. Colonel Fraser wrote to Camden on the 10th that he had learnt from two American traders who had come on a vessel from Senegal that the French had a larger force there, and were better prepared against an attack, than had been believed. Previously so confident of success, Fraser now argued that a larger attacking force would be necessary. With relations with Spain now at danger-point, this small extra force could not be spared for a minor operation. On 20 October Camden therefore had to write to the King again, to recommend postponement.[6]

This is the prime reason why Park's expedition was delayed, with such serious eventual results. The arrangements were back to the starting-point; linking his explorations for transport purposes with military plans had now delayed his departure by a year, and then the plans themselves had all fallen through. Nevertheless it was soon decided that his expedition should go on. Camden wrote to Banks confirming this on 1 November, and saying he was sending Park to see him, to 'receive any Hints which your Experience and Knowledge can suggest'.[7]

Park told Alexander Anderson in a letter dated 10 November that

as Banks was pleased with things relative to the expedition, 'You may therefore be almost sure that it will go on. [Under Secretary] Cooke is also very bright on it.' He explained how busy he was, 'John [Anderson] and I have had sad running about among the City Merchants, if all trades fail I believe I may set up as a Broker. I am quite up to 10 Per Cent Disct. for prompt 2½ Commissions etc. etc. etc.'!
His postscript must have been especially welcome to the devout Alexander: 'We can have Arabic New Testaments and Psalm Books for Nothing,' and they did take some.[8]

For his journey Park bought over £1,600 worth of goods from one supplier alone (which the Colonial Office neglected to pay for until interest was charged) and other goods from another supplier. With his characteristic optimism Park told the shipping agent 'that as the vessel sailed with convoy, he did not think it would be necessary to insure the Goods'.[9] All this took time, and so would finding new transport, and collecting stores for the Gorée garrison. Anxiously Park did all he could to speed matters up. The delay was probably due to the fact that both a major war and numerous colonies were being run from an office with only an Under Secretary and about six clerks.

Some of Park's friends continued their efforts to dissuade him from going, but a new volunteer came forward, George Scott, another Souter or Selkirk man, also son of a tenant farmer. He too had attended the Grammar School, but he was eight years younger than Park, being then aged twenty-five. He had been apprenticed to an engraver in London. By chance he became known to Walter Scott – no relative of his – whose recommendation led the Duchess of Buccleuch to obtain for him a post under the Ordnance Department in the Tower of London. Stirred by a longing for adventure, he preferred instead to go as draftsman to Park's expedition.

In December Ombark Bouby's instruction in Arabic came to an end, and early in 1805 he was apparently able to fulfil his dearest wish by returning home to Morocco. Also in December, Park received word from home of the birth on the 16th of Archibald, his third son and fourth child, whom he never saw, but through whom his line and name have continued.

Two of the best travelling months had passed by, and 18 December had arrived, before Camden was able to move things on. Then he was worried whether it were not after all too late, and he anxiously consulted Banks. Sir Joseph checked from the *Travels* and deduced, how is not clear, that the Niger was navigable for boats from about 8 July. If Park could leave England by 8 January that would give him six months, divided thus: two months from England to disembarking up the Gambia, two months from there to the Niger, and two more for building his boats. It was a tight schedule to follow.

Nearly two more weeks went by before Camden obtained the King's approval. Finally on 31 December the Colonial Office sprang into action. On that day Camden wrote a stately letter to the Lords Commissioners of the Admiralty, conveying the King's command that he desire their Lordships to appoint a proper convoy for the *Crescent* transport, then ready to sail from the Thames to make a rendezvous at Portsmouth, in order to take Park to Africa.[10]

On 2 January 1805 Camden issued Park's formal instructions:

'Sir,

It being judged expedient that a small expedition should be sent into the interior of Africa, with a view to discover and ascertain whether any, and what commercial intercourse can be opened therein for the mutual benefit of the natives and of His Majesty's subjects, I am commanded by the King to acquaint you, that on account of the knowledge you have acquired of the nations of Africa, and from the indefatigable exertions and perseverance you displayed in your travels among them, His Majesty has selected you for conducting this undertaking . . .'

Following earlier advice by Banks, Park and Anderson were granted brevet military commissions, and Scott was selected as draftsman. Park might engage up to forty-five of the garrison at Gorée with such inducements as appeared best and also, 'by purchase or otherwise', as many black artificers from there as he needed. He could travel from the Gambia to the Senegal and the Niger by such route as he should find most eligible.

'The great object of your journey will be to pursue the course of this river to the utmost possible distance to which it can be traced; to establish communication and intercourse with the different nations on the banks; to obtain all the local knowledge in your power respecting them; and to ascertain the various points stated in the Memoir which you delivered to me on the 4th of October last.'

He could then return by whatever route seemed best. Finally, he could draw up to £5,000 for expenses. Another letter two days later authorized him to hold out a Royal and Free pardon to any troops at

Gorée who would accompany him. Both Camden and Cooke instructed Lloyd at Gorée to give him every necessary assistance.[11]

Another important letter was sent to him by Cooke on 19 January, formally setting out his financial terms. After his departure £1,000 was to be paid to James Dickson, whom he had made his attorney, for the use of Mrs. Park. There remained, 'To be paid to Mr. Park on his producing a chart of the River Niger, £3,000.' If he died in the course of the journey this was to be paid to his wife or executor. Anderson was to receive £1,000 on the successful termination of the expedition; or it would be paid to his father if he died. Should they not be heard of within two and a half years of sailing, they were to be considered dead. In retrospect this seems most unfortunate wording; Park's family would be provided for if he either succeeded or died on the journey. The third possibility, that he might do his utmost but have to return alive but defeated, was not covered at all. In fact he was probably already determined to exclude that possibility, but the terms of this letter would have served to harden that determination.

The last known letter he sent to Allison before leaving England was dated 8 January 1805 – the day for sailing in Banks's timetable. It shows the agony in his mind over leaving her, and dispels any charge of callousness:

'My Beloved Wife,

I have waited with great anxiety for these two days for another letter from you, ah my sweet Allie I never knew till now how much I loved you. I admire every part of your conduct and I have no doubt but it will soon be in my power to shew you how sensible I am of your worth. I should like much to hear again from you before we leave England, it will make the whole Voyage pass chearfully away. I believe that every thing will be shipped this day and tomorrow or the day following the vessel will be ordered round to Portsmouth at which place we must join her – She will not arrive at Portsmouth before Sunday or Monday next so that I shall have time enough to receive a letter from you. Give my Compts. to your Father tell him I shall write him before we sail. We are all extremely well and have got through the bustle of business and shipping which was to us very troublesome ... I have got every thing I wished, yesterday I was made a Captain and Sandy a lieutenant, we are not obliged to wear any uniforms but have these Commissions to keep the soldiers in proper order ... I met my uncle the other day in the Street, he seemed to be on his high horse so we did not converse long ...

'Give my kind compts. to my Dear mother, John and Bell.

'I remain, my beloved Wife,
your Mungo Park.'[12]

It was still a fortnight before he could leave London, after drawing
£500 worth of silver dollars. One of his last preparations must have
been to buy a copy of Mendoza's *Astronomical Tables*, for they were
published in 1805. On 22 January Park, Anderson, and Scott coached
down to Portsmouth, where he collected another £500. The next day
they were joined by four carpenters for building the boats on the
Niger, released to him on his presenting a pardon to the captain of the
Captivity Hulk. He had then to chase around getting them bedding
and suitable clothes.[13] On the 25th he wrote to his father-in-law, enclosing Cooke's letter about their pay. They were to sail the next day
if the wind held up, and he was already looking forward with anxiety
to his return, but his trust in God maintained his spirits. Dr. Anderson
would, he hoped, advise his dear Allie for the best and see she was
comfortable, and he would write to her whenever he could.[14]

The wind did hold up, but the final arrangements took yet a few
days more. His last known letter from England, to Alexander Williamson at Peebles, was written on 29 January. It was blowing so hard
that it was difficult to write on the rolling ship, but they expected to
be away in a few hours. He, who had thought insurance unnecessary,
was now hoping to see a fight between the escorting *Eugenie* and
French privateers! None of these last letters betrays any of the concern he must have felt at their leaving over three months later than
originally planned, and more than three weeks behind the timing Banks
had indicated to Camden. Even now, when all seemed set, one final
small delay had to be endured, for in moving over to be near the
Eugenie, the *Crescent* fouled her rigging on another ship's, and had to
waste a precious day in repairs before she could sail.[15]

CHAPTER XXIV

'The undertaking worthy of the Best of Governments'

The second journey begins

———— ∞ ————

The *Crescent* and the *Eugenie* sailed in the early morning darkness at about 7 o'clock on 31 January 1805. To be starting at last must have been a relief to Park although mingled, even in him, with anxiety. His margin of safety and his scope for adjustments to meet problems threatened to vanish altogether unless all went well.

From the start things did not work out well. It took five weeks, instead of the usual three, to reach the Cape Verde Islands, then under Portuguese rule. Winds were contrary and gales blew in the Bay of Biscay, but basically both ships were slow. When the *Eugenie* tried to close with a troublesome privateer, one of several seen, it made off at double her speed and nearly caught the *Crescent* just before dark. The overwhelming British naval victory over France and Spain in the Battle of Trafalgar had still to be won, in October when Park was at Sansanding, and clearly the cream of the fleet could not be spared for his expedition.

They passed near to the island of Madeira without calling, because 'Mr. Park was so desirous of getting forward before the commencement of the rainy season,' as George Scott wrote to his father. He also related how, in the Cape Verde Islands, they first sighted St. Nicholas and then Fogo, 'the most sublime object I have ever seen ... with a volcanic mountain of an immense height', before correctly finding St. Jago, where they landed at Porto Praya. It was 8 March when they reached there, exactly the date on which, in Banks's timetable, they should have been disembarking far up the river Gambia.

At a dinner on 10 March the Governor promised his help and named a price of $8 for each donkey. Three days later 28 asses were produced, but Park objected to five as being too small, whereupon the price was raised to $10 each, which he decided to pay. The next day the Governor refused any further help and imposed a tax of $1 on any sales. A man named Nicolai helped increase the purchases to 45 asses, but he finally absconded with one of them. Before leaving Park wryly noted having heard that two men had been imprisoned for selling below Nicolai's price, and that the asses were bought in the interior for $4 each! He embarrassed the Governor by insisting on having some corn brought before him for a proper valuation price; even more so by immediately handing over the $20 saved to a priest to distribute to the poor. There was perhaps a touch of Protestant feeling about Catholics here.

Their departure was three or four days later than he had hoped it would be when he wrote to Lord Camden and James Dickson, taking place on 20 March.[1] Strong winds held them back and led to two asses dying the first night and to others being injured before they landed. In two days they made just three miles forward, and it was not until 28 March that they completed the 450 miles to Gorée. Park went straight to the Commandant, Major Richard Lloyd, to deliver the Colonial Office letters, and returned to him the next day.

This was one stage of the journey free from unnecessary delay, and Major Lloyd deserved the royal approbation he received. In the course of a day he and Park had settled the terms, left to their discretion, to encourage troops to volunteer and a Garrison Order had been issued, a Lieutenant John Martyn had immediately offered his services, and Lloyd had also arranged the issue of clothing 'adapted to the service', including an extra pair of shoes per man and two flannel vests, which were then regarded as healthy wear in the tropics! He agreed to the *Crescent* being only partly unloaded of provisions for the garrison before sailing up the Gambia, and thus enabled the departure to take place a week after arrival. During this time Anderson went to the village of Dakar on the mainland, giving away an Arabic New Testament whilst there.

What kind of escort did Park manage to collect at Gorée? Martyn, probably aged about twenty, was an enthusiastic man who knew his troops, and had joined the garrison two years earlier as an Ensign. In January he had successfully led a small boat party which had captured a Spanish vessel in the Gambia estuary. He had the good sense to make a will before leaving Gorée.[2]

Park could make his choice, with the help of the officers, from the garrison's other ranks, amounting to 20 N.C.O.s and 194 rank and file, nearly all of whom soon volunteered. Physical fitness and some manual skills were qualities looked for. Subsequent events showed how unfit they must really have been; there had been sickness amongst them, and the garrison had been short of supplies since the previous March, as the naval officers in charge of Gorée's recapture had sold the provisions on the island as prize![3]

A former Royal African Corps commander, probably Fraser, when later a Major-General, told a friend that he had become a Lieutenant-Colonel by offering general service, 'And they took me at my word, and gave me the Royal Africans! A precious time I had with them for the next two or three years on the coast of Africa! They were the sweepings of every parade in England, for when a man was sentenced to be flogged, he was offered the alternative of volunteering for the Royal Africans, and he generally came to me. They were not a bad set of fellows when there was anything to be done, but with nothing to do they were devils incarnate.' Can one acquit Lloyd of irony in referring in his Garrison Order to the 'Steadiness and Alacrity for service which distinguishes the Royal African Corps'?

Most likely the prospect of 'anything to be done' prompted them to volunteer, and Park may therefore have seen them in their best light. The terms offered, double-pay (i.e. 2s. per day) and above all a free discharge if their conduct was well reported upon, probably also over-persuaded them to apply for a service of which they could have had little conception. In fact they seem to have behaved well, and not once was there a need for any disciplinary action. Their background is given to show how little prepared they could have been, physically or morally, for their arduous journey.

Two sailors volunteered from H.M.S. *Squirrel*, then at Gorée. Their terms included, as well as double-pay, future freedom from the press-gang, which had probably been the cause of their being there in the first place. Besides Park himself, there were the keen but untried Anderson and Scott, the enthusiastic Lieutenant Martyn, 2 sailors, 4 carpenters, a sergeant, a corporal, and 33 privates, a total of 45 Europeans in all. Significantly not one of the few African artificers on Gorée could be induced to volunteer to leave the relative security of the island for the interior.

Before leaving Park wrote to Allison, showing his usual calm optimism, 'I need not tell you how often I think about you; your own feelings will enable you to judge of that. The hopes of spending the remainder of my life with my wife and children will make every thing seem easy; and you may be sure I will not rashly risk my life, when I know that your happiness, and the welfare of my young ones depend so much upon it. I hope my Mother does not torment herself with unnecessary fears about me. I sometimes fancy how you and she will be meeting misfortune half way, and placing me in many distressing situations. I have as yet experienced nothing but success, and I hope that six months more will end the whole as I wish.' His desire to spare his family anxiety at home sometimes led to his writing in terms far removed from his true situation.

They now parted from Staff Surgeon Heddle, who had been a fellow-passenger on the voyage, and with whom they stayed at Gorée. He served at Gorée from 1800 until at least 1812, being especially commended for his actions at the time of the French capture of the island in 1803; he was later to be a sympathetic enquirer for news of the party. Park also left with Lloyd $2,000, an unneeded half of the sum he had drawn in England.

On 6 April the party sailed from Gorée with loud cheers to be going on active service, whose importance Lloyd had impressed upon them. Soon after entering the Gambia the next day both ships grounded on a sandbank near Fort James, but they worked free after a few hours. At Jillifree just beyond, they met an American and a Prussian ship. The former provided a grisly reminder of what the slave trade involved, as the slaves on board had revolted, and the captain had only suppressed them by scuttling his ship and shooting fourteen slaves.

Touching briefly at the small port, Anderson gave away another New Testament. Here the *Eugenie* left them after firing a 17-gun salute, Captain Webb taking a short report to Cooke at the Colonial Office. The captain's steward later wrote, under the name of Reuben Traveller, *The Last Voyage of Mongo Park* (sic), a dull poem with small gleams of interest in it. A footnote says that Park had dined several times with Captain Webb, and that, 'Concerning his conversation, I am best able to speak: it was at all times free from licentiousness, which is too often the principal feature of ship talk; it was principally on moral and religious topics [which Reuben would have greatly approved], or such as turned more immediately to his transactions in the world as a public traveller. But when I reflect upon how much he knew from the searchings of his mind, and the variety of views that must have passed before his eyes, I considered him a man of little conversation . . .' Here he sided with Park's impecunious patient in Scotland rather than with Lord Camden! He also had one shrewd remark on the readiness of the soldiers to volunteer, 'They willing came – for many there had died.'[4]

Having continued upstream in the *Crescent*, they disembarked on 15 April at Kaiai, where Park had parted from Dr. Laidley on his earlier journey to sail back to England in 1797. Some goods were bought from the traders there, Thomas Dean and another slaving doctor, Forbes; the purchases included asses to replace those lost or crippled on the voyage. The party was soon busy sorting out the stores into bundles for transport on the asses.

Park had been told at Gorée that his old friend Karfa Taura was near by, but this proved incorrect. Still no African was found willing to accompany him until finally he met a man called Isaaco, a trader who was willing to join his own group to Park's to go as far as the Niger, '. . . and when I drink of the water I am to pay him two slaves money' (about £40). Isaaco travelled with some of his family and a retinue of unstated but clearly appreciable number. Park did not describe his background in the Journal, but what can be learnt about him is given in Appendix II.

Before leaving Kaiai, Park wrote up an account of his purchases from Portsmouth onwards. He had spent £358 15s. od., which, with what he had bought in England, meant that he had over £2,000 worth of animals and stores, excluding army issues to the troops: a vastly greater amount than his humble belongings on his first journey.[5] He also completed a record of his journey up to 26 April for Lord Camden. In it he said that one of the soldiers, sick before leaving Gorée, had recently died, reducing the number of Europeans to 44.

The same day he wrote to Banks, Dickson, and Allison. Park had asked Camden to let Banks see the main report, so Park confined himself in this letter to some botanical observations, accompanied with specimens, sending his compliments to Major Rennell, praising the accuracy of his timepiece, which should enable him to survey Africa by feet and inches, and asking Banks to keep any unfavourable reports out of the newspapers or from otherwise reaching his wife and mother.[6] To Allison he gave assurances that everything looked favourable; the soldiers were in the highest spirits and would be an adequate safeguard, and he hoped to be home by December, possibly before she had heard from him again. To Dickson he said he was busy, and expressed even more confidence in the soldiers, 'the most *dashing* men I ever saw', and if all went well, 'this day six weeks I expect to drink all your healths in the water of the Niger.'

In fact his position was a very serious one. He was now seven weeks behind Banks's timetable, and he ought to have been nearly at the Niger. He could afford no more than six weeks to reach there before the rains came, as he knew. Even then, with the most strenuous part of the journey over, there was no guarantee that the party would remain healthy in the rains. For 500 miles in a direct line, and longer by winding paths, six weeks was an optimistic but not impossible target; Park had spent over nine weeks on his way back before. They were now to travel at the hottest time of the year and, although the soldiers wore their red uniforms only on special occasions, they all had heavy clothes and those flannel vests, so that it was bound to be a gruelling march.

To turn back before the *Crescent* left him would have meant months of delay, a total loss of the spirit of his men, and an uncertain response by the British Government, possibly cancellation of the expedition. To go on was a gamble, and Park seems to have been blind to what could happen if it failed. His instructions gave no final date for him to leave the Gambia, an omission no doubt welcome to him, and, with his characteristic optimism, he decided to go ahead and risk not merely his own but also over forty other men's lives. In retrospect it seems a clearly wrong decision but given that he had perhaps an even chance of success, to a man of his temperament and determination no other was possible. Nothing he wrote either then or later suggests that any other course seriously suggested itself to him. Nor, apparently, did he consider travelling fast and light with a smaller party; he was determined to have his own 'caravan'.

At the last moment, on 26 April, he made a will. In it he asked his brothers and father-in-law, as guardians, to give his children as good and liberal an education as possible, 'particularly to have them instructed in the knowledge of the Christian Religion, which has been the solace of their Father in this Vale of Tears'. He left an annuity of £20 to his mother. Otherwise the will did little more than recite his assets and reaffirm the terms of his marriage settlement, which he must previously have thought sufficient, but the act of making it suggests that he then saw his death as a closer possibility than ever before. It was not witnessed, even by his brother-in-law, and it was sealed in an envelope addressed to Dr. Thomas Anderson, to be opened only in the event of his death. In a covering letter he stressed that 'I did not do this from any thing like second-sight, but merely to guard against a possible occurrence'.

This letter gives us one of our few glimpses of Alexander Anderson's personality. Park wrote, 'I receive great benefit from Alexander, who is as systematic, cautious and careful as ever. I sometimes think he has forgot his old maxim, "Take it easy." '[7] There is no indication that Alexander's opinion about proceeding with the journey was ever sought or offered; on the available evidence, he was just a steadfast and hard-working lieutenant helping with the day-to-day organization, until ill health made him incapable of doing anything. Park alone made the decisions. This is borne out by the letters Anderson and Scott wrote from Kaiai to their respective fathers. Anderson's letter has much to say about his rheumatism, then cured, about their sending back trunks of surplus clothes, and about the field for Christian mission endeavour in the Gambia, but it never discusses the prospects for their own mission. Nor does Scott's letter, although it is more descriptive of the journey up river, and the shooting expeditions they had been able to make.[8]

One item of clothing which Park decided was superfluous was a red officer's jacket of the Royal African Corps, probably presented to him at Gorée, and he gave it to Captain George Gibson of the *Crescent* transport. In 1823 Captain Gibson passed it on, for reasons unknown, to a branch of John Martyn's family, with whom it remains to this day.[9] Then, all being set, with a final hasty note to Banks[10] written on the morning of 27 April 1805, Park, seated on an ass's saddle, and saluted by the *Crescent* and some other vessels at Kaiai, led most of his party by land close to the Gambia, whilst Anderson went some way further up-stream in a shallow-draft boat with the baggage. The tone for the mission was set in the rather sententious conclusion of Park's report to Lord Camden, 'If I succeed I shall reckon myself the happiest man on Earth, and if I should fail I will enjoy even in my last moments the pleasing reflection that I have done my utmost to execute the undertaking worthy of the Best of Governments.'

CHAPTER XXV

'Thunder, Death and Lightning – the Devil to pay'

From the Gambia to the Niger

———— ⟨⟩ ————

Their route lay, at the beginning, close to the one followed by Park when returning previously from Bamako, which was the most direct way to the Niger. In his memorandum to Lord Camden he had proposed striking further north towards Segu, but on that route Khasso had recently fallen victim to internal strife followed by an invasion from Kaarta, which drove the people of Khasso across the Senegal.

On the first day three asses stuck fast in a muddy rice-field and, while they were being extricated, some of the party under Martyn took a wrong road and only rejoined the others after a long, broiling day. The temperatures had risen to 100 °F (38 °C) or more by day in the shade and 135 °F in the sun, with hot breathless nights. The next day, however, brought them with less trouble to Mr. Ainsley's house at Pisania. Seniora Camilla, the first English-speaker Park had met on his previous return, was astonished to see him again. Anderson arrived up-stream two days later.

A week was spent at Pisania sorting stores and buying more asses, and when they did get away on 4 May recalcitrant asses still caused hold-ups. The soldiers were as unused to managing asses as most of the asses were to carrying loads, but lack of organization was not the cause of the trouble, as has been suggested.[1] Scott and one of Isaaco's people led the march, Martyn was in the centre, and Park and Anderson brought up the rear. The soldiers were divided into six messes, each man allotted his ass and load, marked with numbers in red paint. What the party lacked was adequate time to sort out the problems of an untried form of expedition before setting off in earnest.

At Samee, Park made presents: two jugs of rum to a very drunk headman who wanted ten, and some amber to the 'Mumbo Jumbo boys'. At Tabajang, where Isaaco's mother lived, they spent three nights. Not for the last time more asses had to be bought there, either to reduce overloading or to replace losses. It took a week to travel from Pisania to Medina, capital of Wuli, compared to three days on Park's first journey; his larger party, whatever its protective value, was a liability that lost him what mattered most now: time. On the way Park had met one of those who had accompanied him back to the Gambia before, and the son of the Mansa of Wuli whom he had known, who warned him the traders there were 'jealous' of the expedition. The new Mansa coldly demanded a much larger present than Park at first offered him, and even water had to be bought at Medina.

Each morning they started at sunrise, rallied, no doubt, by the regimental trumpet Park had bought at Gorée. They rested during the heat of the day, and then continued in the evening. This routine limited the distances covered, and there were other delays too. They wasted a day in avoiding paying some village women for water. Finally a soldier had himself lowered down a well to recover a canteen dropped 'by accident', and then filled all the soldiers' kettles! On 14 May they omitted the evening march, so as to avoid woods where brigands were feared to be. They stayed at Kussai, where the chief was enraged to see a soldier collecting the pods of the *nitta* or locust bean tree (*Parkia*), kept under taboo as a safeguard against famine. Park calmed him down by telling him they had not known of any such ban.

From Kussai, Park wrote to Dean at Kaiai saying he found Isaaco, like all Serahuli, very fond of money, but he would try not to quarrel with him.[2] Isaaco in fact warned Park that word was going about that they had plenty of goods for plundering, and he slaughtered a black ram on the road with a long prayer for their success. However, although Park gave orders for the soldiers to march with their muskets ready and loaded, no bandits showed themselves. The next evening they had the first fatality since leaving the Gambia. After reaching camp, Private John Walters fell down in an epileptic fit, probably compounded with some other disease that caused his death an hour later.

The following night Park observed with his telescope a transit of one of Jupiter's moons, and to his surprise found that his watch, which had kept excellent time on the voyage, was $3\frac{1}{2}$ minutes fast. Partly because of this, his estimates of longitude on the journey were quite inaccurate. An unnoticed handicap was that he had made an entry in his *Journal* at Pisania for 31 April instead of 1 May, which caused all his earlier estimates of latitude to be much too far north. If the error was sustained, all dates from then onwards should be one day later than he recorded them, but I have retained here the dating he used. (He may have made a compensating error afterwards, for the sightings of Jupiter's moons were correctly dated in the *Journal*, and his latitudes of places on the Niger were nearly accurate.)[3]

Still they proceeded by rather short stages. At Tambico on 20 May the head of a neighbouring village, nominally subject to Wuli but used to exacting his own considerable customs from passing caravans, took hostage Isaaco who had been sent to see him, flogged him, and put his boy in irons. Isaaco's wife and child sat crying under a tree with his dejected followers. Rather at a loss what to do, Park consulted Anderson and Martyn, and then decided against making a night attack to release Isaaco lest innocent people were killed. They proposed, however, to attack next morning if Isaaco were not released. Early next day Isaaco was sent back with his boy, although without his gun and sword. The incident ended, after more haggling, with Park paying a third of the duty originally demanded.

On 26 May another incident nearly ended the journey. While they were unloading some asses by a creek a swarm of bees was disturbed and forced men and animals to scatter. In the panic a cooking fire threatened to burn all the baggage, without which they could not go on, but it was saved and they reassembled as evening drew on. None of the men had suffered serious injury, but six asses were killed by bee stings or lost.

At Badoo on 28 May they met a slave caravan going to the Gambia, and Park wrote letters to his wife and to Banks. In both of these he said that he expected to reach the Niger on 27 June, even though they were only one-third of the way there after one month. It is amazing to read in his letter to Allison, 'I am happy to inform you that we are half through our journey without the smallest accident or unpleasant circumstance. We all of us keep our health, and are on the most friendly terms with the natives . . .' Presumably it was from this slave caravan that Banks heard, through Dr. Heddle, that Park had been seen 'sixty miles from the Niger', but Banks should have been able to deduce the inaccuracy of this.[4] They were still only four miles from the Gambia, which they saw for the last time the next day.

Soon after this, some of the men had left Julifunda with every appearance of mutual goodwill when the local chief, living up to an avaricious reputation, suddenly demanded considerable extra goods. If they were not given, he said, he would ensure that the party would be plundered in the woods. Recalling the advance guard, Park made one gift after another but finally dug in his heels and refused to give more. On they went and the chief, pleased with what he had extracted, let them be.

Their first and last celebration was held on 4 June. Halting outside a village they feasted on beef and saluted the King's birthday, toasting the health of His Majesty with water in their canteens. Even a few days later, celebrations would not have been in order.

Then the dreaded rains came upon them. On 8 June old James, a carpenter, died of dysentery. The next night five soldiers who stayed out in the rain, probably because of the heat in their tent, fell ill. On the 10th Park arrived at Shrondo long after most of the men; he had stayed behind with one of the sick on his own horse, and was driving fatigued asses ahead of him. Before they could pitch their tents a tornado caught them which, the *Journal* says, '. . . had an instant effect on the health of the soldiers, and proved to us, to be the *beginning of sorrow*. I had proudly flattered myself that we should reach the Niger with a very moderate loss . . . But now the rain had set in, and I trembled to think that we were only half way through our journey. The rain had not commenced three minutes before many of the soldiers were affected with vomiting; others fell asleep, and seemed as if half intoxicated . . . June 11th – Twelve of the soldiers sick . . .' It was probably pure coincidence that an acute infection from a recent meal caused the soldiers to vomit just as the rain started, and this, with fatigue, would explain the abnormal drowsiness. But from then onwards, the party was chronically sick. Martyn had a fever on 12 June but soon recovered. Park himself had fever two days later.

This was the moment, if any, when the expedition should have halted or turned back. But the crucial errors had already been made, by the Government in despatching them so late, and by Park in deciding to leave the Gambia when the onset of the rains was already near. Any decision he took thereafter would only affect the degree of the disaster, not avert it.

For those then sick, to stay put would have given the greatest chance of recovery, but with recurring sickness the party could have dwindled away with nothing achieved. Food problems might in any case have ruled out this alternative. Kaiai was nearly as far back as the Niger was ahead, and if they had returned they might have had to wait for a ship to take them to Gorée, with sickness taking its toll meanwhile.

Apart, then, from his own desire to press on, Park could well have argued that to go ahead was the best of the bad alternatives. He was asking a lot of his men but he drove himself hardest of all. The average daily march fell from perhaps ten to five or six miles a day, although some stages had to be much longer. The results suggest sheer ruthlessness but, given the initial errors, could he have done any better?

Whilst the men rested for a day, Park visited some gold mines near Shrondo and reported in detail on the processes used, but later there was little opportunity for such excursions. By now he had veered northwards from his former route, across the Faleme river, to avoid the Jallonka wilderness; sick men were soon afterwards struggling up a steep rocky hill, with untended asses in confusion and local villagers coming amongst them pilfering. Twice in the next exhausting day Park had to hold sick soldiers on horses and drive them on until he could manage no more. The redeeming feature of the day for him was meeting Fankooma, the 'good old schoolmaster' from nearby Malacotta, who had accompanied him back from Kamalia in 1797. They walked together for the day and Park gave him a present including an Arabic New Testament, the third he had given out to date, one previously having been given to a brother of Karfa Taura whom he had encountered.

From this stage the expedition began to disintegrate. The rains produced slippery paths and swollen streams. Sometimes storms caught them in the open as night fell, with violent thunder, lightning, and fierce winds. Soon, as is normal in West Africa, rain came in the daytime as well.

The rains brought more mosquitoes and dirty pools, and the health of the Europeans was undermined with fevers and dysentery. A note in Banks's memorandum made months before, when he was advising the Colonial Office, was all too prescient, although unanswered: 'What are the Provisions for carrying sick men if any are dangerously ill? The whole expedition may be marred in waiting for one man too ill to be moved with safety, unless the mode of moving sick persons is effectual.' In the circumstances the expedition could not wait, and the mode of moving sick men, weakened by the loss of fluids and body chemicals through dysentery, had to be by holding them on horses or asses. When they could no longer travel that way, or there was nobody able to help them, they could only be left behind, where possible at a village with some payment to the chief for looking after them.

Almost daily men fell out, and each must have wondered when his turn would come to have to give up in sickness and exhaustion. From 8 June to 19 August when they reached the Niger 31 men, or two-thirds of the party, were lost, one drowned in the fast-moving Senegal, a few perhaps falling victims to wild animals or brigands, but the great majority killed by disease (see Appendix II). Twenty-two of them were left behind, or simply failed to turn up at the end of the day's march, and were never seen again. On one dreadful day, 27 July, five men were left behind. That same day Park saw far-off mountains beyond which, he knew, lay the Niger. 'I thought of nothing all the way,' he said, 'but how to climb over their blue summits.' In struggling over them on the last day's march another three men, including the sergeant, dropped out and were lost. Park spent much energy doing what he could for his men, but his comments in his *Journal* on the losses were usually terse. He seems, however, particularly to have regretted having to leave behind William Allen, who had often cheered their evenings with Scottish songs, and Private Roger M'Millan, who had given long service to his country: 'He had been thirty-one years a soldier, twelve times a corporal, nine times a sergeant, but an unfortunate attachment to the *bottle* had always returned him into the ranks.'

Sometimes a rainstorm prevented Park's party from cooking a meal, and at one stage they were also short of rice, the harvest being still some time ahead and food scarce. There were often too few fit men to manage the beasts properly. As a result the compact and orderly marching which seems to have been achieved before the rains came broke down. Park was constantly having to go back or to send somebody, either during the day or after the main group had wearily made camp, to look for missing men, animals, or loads.

When the caravan's strength had crumbled, it became a tempting target. Before entering Bambara the travellers passed through areas with little central state authority; the Fouladou area had been battered alternately between Segu and Kaarta. Demands for customs increased and their weakness made them more ready to concede these demands, but at Kimbia on 23 June they resorted to a show of force when attempts were made to seize their baggage.

At Maniakorro a parade of the fit soldiers, wearing their red coats and firing a salute, seemed to please the chief, but in the end Park cursed that place more than anywhere else. The chief had numerous sons who led the people in the most brazen thieving, both there and for a week afterwards along the road. Whenever a man turned his back someone would dash in and grab something, and if a soldier was weak they did not wait for him to turn away, but even stripped off his clothes. Asses, muskets, pistols, greatcoats, knapsacks, were all carried off. On one occasion Park himself had his musket wrenched out of his hand. Another time, he shot a thief in the leg, but refused urgings from his local escort to kill him. The asses that were not stolen died, until none was left by 30 July of the 44 from St. Jago, purchasing which had occupied nearly two weeks of valuable time.

In 1879 the French officer Gallieni was told near Maniakorro by an old man how once, long ago, before he was born, a white man had appeared across the river and called out without making himself understood. Then he had leapt across the river on rocks and had later been joined by a number of other white men. The old man spoke of how hospitably the party had been received and how generous they had been. As this story led up to the proposition that the new and wealthier visitors should be even more generous, and as Gallieni found the same cavalier attitude to travellers' property, this last part of the story must be taken with a grain of salt![5]

To add to their trials, they also had uncomfortably close encounters with lions. One night several lions stampeded the asses and came charging after them through the camp, near enough for a soldier to try cutting at one with his sword. Later, when Park was guiding the sick Anderson, he heard strange noises and found three lions approaching them. Fortunately these ran off when he advanced towards them and fired, but it was with fear that they continued that afternoon. 'Wolves' (probably hunting dogs) too caused trouble, trying to attack the asses at night. A very sick man resting under a tree near the camp one day woke to find them sniffing at his feet. They set up a horrid howl as he raised his head and, feeble though he was, his terror brought him to his feet and rushing for safety to the tents.

If the party maintained some coherence, this was due first of all to the pluck and dogged perseverance of the men, who went on as long as they had strength, and who seem always to have been orderly in their behaviour. There was only one serious incident on 1 August when Isaaco, flustered by thieves pressing around, struck two soldiers, and one of them nearly bayonetted him but fortunately was prevented by Anderson. That tempers were not more often frayed implies effective leadership.

Secondly, it was due to Isaaco. He acted as guide, negotiated with chiefs, sent his own men to buy provisions, and once made them build a bridge over a swollen stream, which Park found time to describe in detail. On additional payment, he also sent his men to look for missing men and animals belonging to Park's party, and made them get the animals across rivers and carry packages up the bank, or load them on to the asses when Park's men were too weak even to do that. The party could hardly have got through at all without him. There was a near disaster on 4 July, when Isaaco was attacked by a crocodile while driving some asses through a river. With wonderful presence of mind he twice freed himself by thrusting his fingers into its eyes. The party was held up for nearly a week while his leg wounds healed.

Finally, the survival of the remnant was due to Park's own exertions. He was everywhere: driving off thieves or wild animals, repacking loads to prevent damage by the rain, rallying or going back for the sick, sometimes holding them on a horse or an ass or carrying their loads, and making what arrangements he could for their care when they had to be left behind.

Anderson, Scott, and Martyn played a part in the work of the expedition when they were fit, but they all had periods of sickness, sometimes acute although at first brief. Scott had not fared too badly until 15 August, only a few days' journey from the Niger, when he was suddenly stricken, had to be left at Koomikoomi, and died there, as they learnt later, that same day. At the same period Anderson's life hung in the balance, and he had to be carried in a cloak slung like a hammock.

Park did try medical treatments on the men, contrary to Lewis Grassic Gibbon's belief that he kept his medicines for himself. Twice, on 18 June and 6 July, he recorded that he daily boiled for them a kettle full of a strong concoction of chinchona, containing quinine. This was already a recognized treatment for fever, but its effectiveness varied according to the chinchona's quality, and was negligible if the fever being treated was not malaria. At Bangassi, where they rested for four days, he bought milk every day to try to restore the men's strength. He later treated Anderson's dysentery with calomel, a mercury preparation; this incident is not recorded in the *Journal*, so that the *Journal*'s silence concerning medicine for the soldiers proves nothing.

A letter was published anonymously in several newspapers in 1806,

probably by Banks. It included part of a letter Park wrote from Sansanding to 'a friend at Gorée'; we may suppose this was Dr. Heddle:

[All went well until] 'we entered Minsoodo: here, alas! the rainy season commenced, and the soldiers were affected with fevers. The fever had at first the
appearance of typhus, but in a few days the yellow tinge of the skin convinced
us that we had a more dangerous disease to contend with. [Here he relates
his method of treatment which, he says, he has every reason to believe would
have been very successful, had they had proper convenience, and not been
exposed to the heat of the sun.]'[6]

The words in brackets were unfortunately not fully explained in
the newspapers. 'Typhus' according to the usage of the times may
have meant any prostrating and debilitating fever. The yellow tinge
of the skin was much more likely to have been due to jaundice, or to
severe anaemia following malaria, than to yellow fever. Either of these
would explain the general fatigue and debility of the affected men. At
all events it is clear that at a time when the causes and cures, and even
the nature, of most tropical diseases were unknown, Park did for his
men whatever current medical science and his circumstances made
possible, albeit with little success.

During the latter part of the journey, in spite of his other exertions,
Park did not give up his geographic interests. He described in detail,
in late June, some beautiful country they were passing through. It
had a diversity of rock pinnacles, in one place like a Gothic abbey
with niches, windows, and staircases in natural rock, and later with
little villages picturesquely situated below rocky precipices up to six
hundred feet in height. At another place he watched closely a process
for smelting gold. He continued to observe Jupiter's satellites and to
determine the latitude from the sun. That he wrote up his daily notes
is remarkable when there was so much else to do. His additions to
geographical knowledge on this journey were, however, very small.

On 15 August, the day Scott was left behind, Park was happy to
meet Karfa Taura, his saviour and homeward guide in 1797. Hearing
that a white man called Park and speaking Mandingo was passing
through the country, Karfa Taura had come via Bamako with slaves
ready to help Park, but the *Journal* does not say whether they stayed
together for more than just one evening at the end of a long day's
march.

At Kaiai, Park had estimated that they would reach the Niger in six weeks; at Badoo, in two months. In fact it was after more than three and a half months when, in the afternoon of 19 August, Park went a little ahead of the remnant of the party up a ridge, and '*once more saw the Niger* rolling its immense stream along the plain!' Reflecting on his losses, and the lack of carpenters to build the boats, he conceded that 'The prospect appeared somewhat gloomy.' Besides himself, only Martyn, a very sick Anderson, six soldiers, and one carpenter, ten men in all out of the forty-four who had left the Gambia, had reached the Niger alive. (In fact twelve men reached there; two stragglers may have come in after Park wrote this note.)

He was, however, pleased to reflect that 'I had always been able to preserve the most friendly terms with the natives', presumably meaning that there had been no open fighting. He believed he had demonstrated, '1st, that with common prudence any quantity of merchandize may be transported from the Gambia to the Niger, without danger of being robbed by the natives: 2dly, that if this journey be performed in the dry season, one may calculate on losing not more than three or at most four men out of fifty.' These conclusions could be inferred from the experience of the first part of the journey, and were probably correct; what had actually been *demonstrated*, however, was that with the existing ignorance of the causes and treatment of tropical diseases, sending a European expedition in the rainy season was an almost unmitigated disaster. The aptest description of this terrible journey was produced by Lieutenant Martyn, 'Thunder, Death and Lightning – the Devil to pay'.

CHAPTER XXVI

'Lonely and friendless amidst the wilds of Africa'

From Bamako to Sansanding

———— ∞ ————

After their arrival at the Niger or Joliba at Bamako the survivors rested for two days, but not entirely undisturbed; one night 'wolves' tore the bowels from a live bullock tethered only ten yards from their tent door. Park occupied himself salvaging rain-damaged items from the stores.

A request for canoes to take them down-stream produced only one small one. Park, who had dysentery, decided to go with Anderson, whilst Martyn and the other men travelled overland. The river was swollen with rain and a mile wide, moving at five miles an hour; it was two miles wide at a series of rapids, where 'the velocity was such as to make me sigh'. After a night of pouring rain in the open canoe they came to Maraboo where they disembarked; the others joined them later that day. Anderson was able to walk from the river to the village, but he continued in a state of debility from the combined effects of malaria and repeated dysentery.

As agreed, Isaaco was paid goods to the value of two slaves and some articles on top. Park wanted him to arrange matters quickly with King Mansong before the Moors and Muslims at Segu stirred up feeling against them, and for this he promised him all the horses and remaining asses. Isaaco set off on 28 August with part of Mansong's present. Park then decided to take a very strong dose of calomel to deal with his dysentery. He was unable to speak or sleep for six days but the cure worked – or at least he survived it; such mercury treatments were later generally abandoned as ineffective and dangerous, although lingering as a purgative in the *British Pharmacopoeia* until 1958.

For some days nothing but worrying rumours came up-stream, and while they were waiting Private Thomas Dyer died. On 8 September Mansong's 'singing man' Bookari came with six canoes and a welcoming message. They left on the 12th, Bookari requisitioning an extra

9. Mungo Park, from a watercolour by Thomas Rowlandson, c. 1805, shortly before his second African journey

10. Island of Gorée, from an engraving in Joseph Corry, *Observations upon the Windward Coast of Africa* (1807)

canoe next day with blows and extortion. They travelled to Samee, not far short of Segu, in four days, where they disembarked whilst Bookari went ahead. In the middle of the night of 19 September Isaaco arrived by canoe, bringing back the presents so that Park might give them himself to an emissary. Mansong had said he would let the party pass, but whenever Isaaco had spoken about them he had drawn squares and triangles with his finger in the sand. This seemed to support the belief that Mansong was superstitious about meeting white men; the next European visitor to Bambara, Staff Surgeon Dochard in 1819, was refused entry to Segu allegedly on the same grounds. He heard that Mansong's death had been attributed to Park's coming, although it is actually dated to 1808.[1]

Three days later Mansong's Chief Minister Modibinne came with four companions. Modibinne was, said Park, 'a Mahomedan, but not intolerant in his principles'. The next morning Park explained to them in their own language why he had come. He recalled Mansong's kindness in giving him cowries on his previous visit. He said he was seeking the outlet of the Niger, so that the European goods Mansong's people now purchased at high prices from the Moors could be brought more cheaply by water. He ended by asking them, no doubt vainly, not to let this news reach the Moors. Modibinne replied that their journey was a good one and Mansong would protect them, but he, Modibinne, must first go and report to the King. Before they went they approved the presents Park showed them, but they insisted on examining his baggage and satisfying themselves that he did not have similar presents to give further on. In return he was promised two large canoes.

That the Chief Minister should come to see Park was a notable change from 1796. His return must have conveyed to them his seriousness of purpose; and this time he was not an unknown and penniless wanderer, without status, goods, or comprehensible motive, but an accredited representative of his Government, with interesting goods and some protection. Segu was then at the height of its power, undisturbed by a chastened Kaarta preoccupied with Khasso; it had been to some degree enlarged by campaigns to the south against Mossi and other states, and had newly reasserted, for a few more years, its intermittent and limited suzerainty over Masina and Timbuktu. Any European military threat would have seemed remote, and could not have been anticipated from Park's broken handful. The Bambara

leaders could be confident of themselves, and they apparently decided
that it was worth seeing whether Park and his compatriots could really
bring greater commercial benefits than the Moors did. If not, then
the Moors and their local partners would soon get over their present
fear and anger. Segu's links with the Moors were based on practical
convenience, not conviction.

The day after Modibinne left, two more soldiers, Seed and Barber,
died. In 1888 when the French had occupied the area, Lieutenant
Hourst and another naval officer were shown the grave, then thought
to contain only one body. They also saw a Chinese vase which Park
had given the inhabitants of Samee, or Samba-Marcalla as it had become, adorning the minaret of the mosque, and the officers managed
to exchange it for another vase, taking it to Paris. A few years later
Félix Dubois, travelling from Bamako to Timbuktu, heard many
times on the river favourable recollections of Park's generosity. He
was remembered as 'Bonciba-tigui', the man with the large beard,
which he had left to grow again. As far as this late evidence goes, he
showed the same humane characteristics as in his first journey.[2]

On 25 September Modibinne returned, bringing two bullocks and
a sheep and an entirely favourable answer from the King. They could
travel in whatever direction they wished with his protection, and they
could choose any place on the river to build a boat. Park decided on
Sansanding, as it was quieter than Segu and as Mansong did not want
to see him. Setting off the next day, an intolerably hot one, in open
canoes, they needed only one night to reach Sansanding, where they
passed nearly the next two months. A few days after they arrived, on
2 October, two more soldiers, Marshall and Garland, died. One they
buried but the body of the other was taken away in the night by
'wolves', in this case probably hyenas, as hunting dogs do not eat
carrion.

Sansanding was said by Counti Mamadi, again Park's kind host, to
have 11,000 inhabitants. Park had more chance to look at it than he
had had before. In the large market square, where crowds thronged
daily, a wide variety of goods was sold from specialist stalls: beads,
indigo, cloth, antimony, copper and silver rings, salt, excellent beer,
and other things, whilst from some houses fronting the square Moroccan silks and other exotic goods were sold. Every Tuesday a neighbouring open space was also packed with people from all the countryside around for a weekly market.

By 8 October, not yet having received the promised canoes from Mansong, and observing a four-inch drop in the river level that morning, Park decided to open his own shop and sell off surplus goods in order to be able to buy two canoes. The shop's success did not endear him to the merchants who, he heard from Modibinne when he came, spread stories that his object was to kill Mansong by charms so that the white men could come and seize the country. But Mansong rejected their proposals for taking his baggage and getting rid of him. Park said that 'two thirds of the people of Segu, and almost all Sansanding' were against him, but this could not have included the common people who thronged his shop, so that he sometimes needed three tellers. In one day he took over 25,000 cowries, which sounds a great deal, but it was equivalent to just over £5! Whishaw computed that on most of the goods sold Park made only about 100 per cent profit over the price in England, which would not be enough to cover the costs of transport, escort, duties, gifts to chiefs, etc. He wondered whether, in his anxiety to raise money, Park had sold goods more cheaply than necessary, which would not assist further trade.

At last on 15 October Modibinne brought a canoe, but half of it was rotten. There was some going to and from Segu before Isaaco eventually returned on the 20th with another, also half-rotten. Park worked with Private Abraham Bolton until 15 November, joining the two good halves together, taking out rotten pieces, repairing all the holes, and sewing places. This last suggests that they adopted the local method of boat-building and repairing, as described by the later travellers, Caillié and Hourst. Sawn planks were pierced and tied together with ropes, the apertures were caulked, and a second tying with ropes drew them really tight. A decking was then laid on the top. In this way canoes up to 100 feet in length and carrying 100 tons were made. They could be paddled, poled, or towed, but they were rather fragile and any cross-wind made them hard to manage.

On 1 October, whilst waiting for the canoes, Park had written to George Scott's father:

'Dear Sir – I am extremely sorry to be the messenger of bad news, but the friendship I had for your son and the respect I have for your family compels me to acquaint you with an event which sooner or later must reach your ears. Your son George, who conducted himself with the greatest propriety during a long and tiresome journey, and who would one day have been an honour to all connected with him, is, alas, no more! He died of the fever (which has proved fatal to so many Europeans in hot climates), at the village of Koomi-koomi in Bambarra, on the 15th day of August, 1805. His death was much lamented by all the party, and by none more so than by Mr. Anderson and myself, who lost in your son the only acquaintance in whom we could put confidence during our present journey.

'I sympathise with Mrs. Scott and you for the loss you have sustained, and sincerely hope that you may derive that comfort from above which the changeful scenes of this world can neither give nor take away.'[3]

By the time this letter could be sent Park had added a sorrowful postscript. Alexander Anderson had seemed to be slowly recovering, but on the night of 24 October he was attacked by acute dysentery. An opiate relieved his pain but calomel could not arrest the dysentery, and his constitution was now too weak to resist it. Park sat up with him each night, and Alexander spoke of his approaching death with Christian resignation, and of his friends at home with warmth. Finally, early on 28 October, with his last words, 'Thou knowest my state, O Lord,' he died peacefully.

In his *Journal*, intended for Lord Camden's eyes, Park did not feel able to say more than, 'I shall only observe that no event which took place during the journey, ever threw the smallest gloom over my mind, till I laid Mr. Anderson in the grave. I then felt myself, as if left a second time lonely and friendless amidst the wilds of Africa.' By 'gloom' here we should probably understand despair rather than sorrow, in the context. Later he wrote to Alexander's father a letter of nearly 700 words, unfairly described by Lewis Grassic Gibbon as a 'short cold note', the central part of which outlined Alexander's illness and death, but which began and ended as follows:

'My dear Father – I know not in what manner to tell you the most sorrowful tidings that ever reached your ears, and I sincerely pray that the supporting spirit from on high may sustain and comfort you under this severe dispensation of Divine Providence. You will readily anticipate what I am going to say – your son, my dear, dear friend, has shut his eyes on the scenes of time, and opened them on the glories of eternity . . .

'My dear father, endeavour to comfort my beloved wife; tell her not to be uneasy on my account. I am in excellent health, and the healthy season is now set in. If every thing succeeds, I expect to be in England in the month of May . . .'[4]

As the time for departure came near, other final letters were written. One from Martyn to Ensign Megaw at Gorée has survived:

'Dear Megaw – Thunder, Death and Lightning – the Devil to pay; lost by disease Mr. Scott, two sailors, four carpenters and thirty one of the Royal African Corps, which reduces our numbers to seven, out of which Doctor Anderson and two of the soldiers are quite useless, the former from one disease or other has been for four months disabled; we every day suppose he'll kick it – Capt. Park has not been unwell since we left Gorée; I was one of the first taken sick with fever and ague – had a hard pull of it for a few days, but my constitution soon got the better – had not an hour's illness since – I send you for the information of the inquisitive, the names of the four men with us, viz. Abraham Bolton, John Connor, Thos. Higgins and Joseph Mills (the last two sick but recovering fast – Higgins from a fever and Mills from an old wound in the ancle) – Capt. Park has made every enquiry concerning the River Niger, and from what we learn there remains no doubt that it is the Congo – We hope to get there in about three months or less – We had no fun on the road – met no opposition the whole way – We were well received by Mansong, King of Sego; to whom Capt. Park made very handsome presents, and at our arrival at the River, he sent Canoes upwards of 200 miles to carry us and baggage, and also made us a present of one which we are now fitting out, as we intend going down the river in it – Capt. Park is this day fixing the Masts – Schooner rigg'd – 40 feet long – 6 feet wide and 5 feet high in the side, all in the clear – Excellent living since we came here (Aug 22) the Beef and Mutton as good as ever was eat – Whitbreads Beer is nothing to what we get here . . .

'p.s. Dr. Anderson and Mills dead since writing the within – my head a little sore this morning – was up late last night drinking Ale with a Moor who has been at Gibraltar and speaks English – got a little tipsy – finished the scene by giving the Moor a damn'd good thrashing.   J. M. Nov. 4.'5

This letter was from one young subaltern to another. Hands have been needlessly raised in pious horror over the reference to Whitbread's beer, but the general tone is distasteful and suggests a pretty limited usefulness to the expedition. The *Journal* never mentions Martyn after August, and from it and from one of Park's final letters it seems, in spite of Martyn's 'we', that he took no part in the work on the boat. He was not an acquaintance in whom Park could confide. Discrepancies between Park's dates and Martyn's do not suggest close contact between them. Not too much, however, should be made of Martyn's absence from the *Journal*; the last part is the scrappiest, with few entries for October and November, no reference to Anderson except briefly about his death, Private Mills's death omitted – the only such instance – two entries misplaced which refer back to Maraboo

and Samee, and the whole tailing off without conclusion. Perhaps Park
was more exhausted than he allowed to appear. He evidently succeeded
in concealing all his periods of illness from Martyn. Surprisingly, his
own letter to the 'friend at Gorée' had also said that he had not had a
day's sickness since leaving Gorée.

Park wrote to Banks on 16 November, Lord Camden on the 17th,
and Thomas Dean at Kaiai and his wife on the 19th. In none of
these final letters did he state his continued belief that the Niger and
the Congo would prove to be the same river, although he had so
written to Dr. Heddle, as the doctor told Dickson. He said to Camden
that he had heard nothing he could depend on, only that he believed
'that it can end nowhere but in the sea'. He wrote to Banks that his
new guide was a native of Khasso but had travelled to Cape Coast
Castle in the south, to Borno in the east, and to Katsina, which was
where he would leave Park. This guide said the river continued southwards after Katsina. He had never heard where it ended, but it did
not end at Katsina or in Borno. They would encounter the Moors
only at Timbuktu, but they would find Tuaricks (Tuareg), resembling
the Moors in colour, on the banks of the river elsewhere; they were
also called Surka or Mahinga in certain districts. Park still could not
get clear where 'Houssa' lay.

His letter to Camden struck a similar note to the one sent from
Kaiai, but with less optimism and more defiance:

'Your Lordship will recollect that I always spoke of the rainy season with
horror . . . [he then gave a summary of their losses] . . . From this account I
am afraid that your Lordship will be apt to consider matters as in a very hopeless state; but I assure you that I am far from desponding . . . though all the
Europeans who are with me should die, and though I were myself half dead,
I would still persevere; and if I could not succeed in the object of my journey,
I would at last die on the Niger . . .'

The letter to Dean commended Isaaco, who 'has behaved very
well . . . I never found him guilty of telling lies. Any attention you
can show him I will esteem it a favour.'[6]

He naturally tried to console his wife, in his letter to her, on the
death of her brother and to reassure her he was well himself and still
sufficiently protected. It was evidently written at the last moment:

'We have already embarked all our things, and shall sail the moment I have
finished this letter. I do not intend to stop or land anywhere, till we reach
the coast; which I suppose will be sometime in the end of January . . .

'I think it not unlikely but I shall be in England before you receive this – You may be sure that I feel happy at turning my face towards home. We this morning have done with all intercourse with the natives; and the sails are now hoisting for our departure for the coast.'

Possibly there was another letter which has not survived. The Revd. Dr. Lawson, who had a phenomenal memory, wrote in 1819 about the last letter received in Selkirk from Park, which included thoughts not reflected in the known letters, 'And I never forget one of the observations made in it, which I believe has been since that time verified. He said that he hoped the death of his friend, and his dying behaviour, would be a happy means of preparing him for his own death when that event should come.'

The correct dating of Park's letter to his wife might have been either 19 or 20 November 1805, depending on whether the later dates in his *Journal* are correct or not. That was presumably when he set sail from Sansanding, accompanied by Martyn and the three soldiers, Amadi Fatouma the guide, and two slaves. One soldier had gone mad, probably the sick Higgins. Seven of the twelve Europeans who had reached the Niger three months earlier had died, and they now numbered five.

The boat in which they sailed was christened by Park 'His Majesty's Schooner Joliba'. His description adds to Martyn's that it was flat-bottomed and drew only one foot when laden; this was a useful property in shallow water but did not improve manoeuvrability. What seem to have caught people's eyes most on the way were the white sails and a 'house' built at the stern. An awning of bullock hides had been erected to protect the travellers from the spears and arrows of the Surka.[7]

When Amadi Fatouma had said he would take them in two months to Katsina he must have used the name loosely to refer to the Hausa states, for Katsina stands about 250 miles north-east of the closest point on the river, near Yauri. Park's letter to Allison shows that he was reckoning on emerging at the coast in only a little more than two months and, if we understand him correctly, he expected to reach the mouth of the Congo, at least twice as far away. He was in haste to complete his business and return to his family.

To fulfil all his instructions would have needed more time than was ever envisaged. Much of his original memorandum had probably reflected what he supposed the Government wanted of him; in the

event, he exerted himself but little on investigating commercial questions. By this stage he had largely, although not entirely, abandoned
that part which was 'to establish communications and intercourse with
the different nations on the banks; to obtain all the local information
in your power respecting them . . .' He had narrowed down his objectives essentially to the one which had all along mattered most to
him, as expressed in that last letter to Lord Camden, 'the fixed resolution to discover the termination of the Niger or perish in the attempt'.

It was not feasible with his depleted band to strike northwards
across the desert, through the country of the Moors whom he dreaded,
or southwards to Cape Coast, through completely unknown territory.
To retrace his steps once more to the Gambia would have seemed a
more ignominious retreat than before, when he had been alone. Trust-
ing in his party of five having the same deterrent effect as the original
forty-five, Park decided to suppress what Banks had termed his 'judgement to set limits to his exertions when his difficulties were likely to
become insurmountable'. In so doing he made himself act in ways
which friends would have described as out of character.

It seems not to have occurred to him to ask for a letter from Mansong to the authorities in Masina and Timbuktu. The experience of
later travellers shows that the pen of a known sovereign, African or
otherwise, was often mightier than the sword in ensuring protection.
Nor does Mansong seem to have had much confidence in his ability
to protect the party as far as Timbuktu, in spite of his nominal sover-
eignty over the area. He sent Park a message bidding him begone before the Moors at Timbuktu heard of his coming. This may, of course,
have been an oblique way of seeing Park off before the merchants at
Segu caused trouble for Mansong himself.

CHAPTER XXVII

The quest for Mungo Park

———— ‍ ————

The first report to Lord Camden and the letters sent from Kaiai were carried on the *Crescent* and reached London on 1 August 1805.[1] Banks received the letter from Badoo on 8 October. Thereafter there was a long interval before the letters Isaaco carried from Sansanding in November reached England. Dr. Heddle had received his letter at Gorée by 23 July 1806 when he wrote to Dickson, but the *Journal* and other letters were then still in the Gambia aboard an English slave ship, the captain of which refused to give them up for speedier transmission. As late as 12 October Banks had not heard of their arrival.[2] Whenever they did come, they brought the last news received from Park's own hand. However, others passed on some information. On 7 December 1805, Dean wrote to Banks from Kaiai that a man had told him he had seen Park at Segu. Between April and May 1806 Banks noted down other brief reports giving a not too inaccurate picture of the situation, including the losses, up to Sansanding, but confirmation was still awaited.[3]

In April, Allison Park wrote to Dickson expressing natural anxiety,[4] which must have deepened as the months passed with no definite news. Two stories of 'apparitions' of Park need no supernatural explanation. In late 1805, not long after receiving a letter from him, his sister Mrs. Jean Thomson heard the sound of horses one night and believed she saw Mungo enter her room and walk up to her bed. She tried to embrace him but was distressed as her arms folded on her breast, enclosing nothing, and her husband had to comfort her. Another story (which, admittedly, could relate to the time of his first journey) was told to the biographer Stephen Gwynn, that at Foulshiels one night Park's mother heard the latch of the door raised. Unthinkingly she called out, 'Is that you, Mungo?' and, hearing an answering 'Yes', she turned over and went to sleep.[5] The Revd. Dr. Lawson's biographer said of that time, 'On each visit to Foulshiels the subject was again and again discussed, till the hearts of all became sick with deferred hope, and the days of mourning for the dead began, but were not here ended.'

How the reports came which touched off formal enquiries is not clear. On 10 July 1806 *The Times* reported that a letter had been received from the Gambia, saying that Park and nearly all his party had been murdered in the interior, a few survivors having reached Ouidah on the Dahomeyan coast; these supposed survivors were never heard of again. Even earlier, on 1 July, the *Charleston Courier* in America had published a circumstantial report from the Rio Pongus, south of the Gambia, saying that the King of Segu had shown the travellers round his capital but had then murdered them; this was quoted in *The Times* of London on 1 September.[6]

News had evidently reached the Park family a little before the first notice in *The Times*. The source was probably a paper now in the British Library, with no date or signature visible, but most likely written by Heddle to Dickson, saying: 'I enclose two letters which I kept longer than he desired in the hope that he might return by this Route. I am in the highest degree distressed to have to state that unfavourable Reports have reached us respecting him and his companions. These however are mere reports and I would willingly hope are without foundation. Should I learn anything certain I will not fail to communicate to you.'[7]

It seems almost certain that, like other stories published over the next few years, these reports were only accidentally correct in stating that Park was dead. Even a general account of his end could hardly have got back so early across 2,500 land miles to Gorée, with no frequented through route, and then by sea to England. The story of his murder at Segu was untrue, but the reports probably reflect the fact that he had soon afterwards run into trouble.

On 10 July 1806 John Anderson wrote to Colonel Fraser that the reports 'have plunged his wife, family and relations into the deepest distress', and Fraser passed his letter on to the Colonial Office on the 12th. The same day, Camden's successor Windham wrote to Major Lloyd at Gorée directing him to make enquiries. On 10 October Lloyd replied that he had not yet been able to find any suitable person to send inland, but that reports from Ainsley at Pisania tended to confirm the reports of the party having been murdered *after leaving Sansanding*.[8]

Matters got no further until January 1810. By then Major Charles Maxwell had succeeded Lloyd at Gorée in 1808 and had on his own initiative captured and moved to the sole existing French Senegal post, thereby becoming Lieutenant-Colonel and Lieutenant-Governor. Maxwell managed to obtain Isaaco's services to go and seek news of Park, basing his action on Windham's instructions to Lloyd. Isaaco returned in September 1811 with – a considerable achievement – a description of Park's voyage down the Niger by Amadi Fatouma, whom Isaaco found near Sansanding. The Arabic was translated into English by someone in Senegal, whose annotations suggest fair knowledge and competence. The translation was forwarded to Maxwell, who had again moved up to become Governor of Sierra Leone at Freetown, retaining Senegal and Gorée under his control, and from him it reached London on 31 January 1812.[9]

Even if doubts were expressed about details, the main facts of Park's death at Bussa were generally accepted, except by his family. One lone writer in 1815 did contend that Amadi's Journal was a fabrication by Isaaco to justify his being paid. All his reasons, such as doubts whether Park would have used force, and lack of confirmation at that time of his death at Bussa, were subsequently proved incorrect, thus tending to vindicate the Journal's authenticity.[10] Amadi's account has been regarded ever since as the version to follow, and although it has gaps in it there is no serious reason to doubt it except at one important point.

It is, however, by no means the only source of information on what happened after the expedition left Sansanding. Park's journey clearly created a major sensation, far more than a 'nine days' wonder'. The enquiring traveller anywhere within a very wide radius of Bussa might hear echoes of it for many years afterwards. From Morocco some reports had reached Banks before Isaaco's Journal was received. Ashanti, in what is now Ghana, then on an active trade route passing near Bussa, was another source of information, and stories from there published by Thomas Bowdich and Joseph Dupuis around 1820 deserve rescuing from oblivion. Echoes came from as far away as Ethiopia; reports from there were carried through the pilgrimage to Mecca, on to distant Bombay and Calcutta,[11] and so back to Britain.

There is little direct information on Park's passage by Timbuktu in the writings of the next Europeans to visit there. Whether the American sailor, Robert Adams, was actually taken there about 1812 when in captivity is doubtful, but he said he had heard no reports of white men having been there earlier. Major A. Gordon Laing certainly visited Timbuktu in 1826. Half-way across the desert from Tripoli, he revised his first belief that the experiences of Park's journey would not hinder him from voyaging down the river himself. Approaching Timbuktu he was nearly killed by Tuareg, but he came under the protection of the Kunta clan of Arabs, widely influential as peaceful arbitrators, then living over 100 miles north of Timbuktu. With their support he safely reached and stayed in the cosmopolitan city, but outside pressures obliged him to leave. Going into the desert to the north-west, he was soon afterwards murdered by Arabs, and his journal was lost. He had sent only one short letter from Timbuktu, so that we do not know what he may have learnt there, but he had already found things to say about Park.

The first European to return with a detailed account of the long-sought city was the Frenchman René Caillié. His ingenious and successful cover story was that he was an Egyptian captured as a small boy by Napoleon's forces, and only recently freed, who was now making his way home. This account of himself explained away his imperfect Arabic, his lax observance of the precepts of Islam, and, if need be, his ignorance about Egypt, but it prevented his making any open enquiries about a Christian who had passed there earlier than Laing, about whom he heard much said. However, Caillié's description of his trip down the Niger from Jenne to Timbuktu in 1828 illuminates events in Park's journey over twenty years earlier. For Park's own visit to Timbuktu we have to look to other sources.

Information about the end of the journey had naturally to be sought nearer to Bussa. In 1822–4 Captain Hugh Clapperton, R.N., went on an expedition from Tripoli to Borno and Hausaland, accompanied by Dr. Oudney, who died on it, and by Major Dixon Denham. Clapperton visited Sokoto alone, and found that Park's journey was known about there. Two years later Clapperton travelled inland from Badagry near Lagos, staying for three days at Bussa, where he found some information but also eloquent embarrassment. Again visiting Sokoto, he obtained an extract from the Caliph's records, which must be considered to supersede what he had heard there before. He died at Sokoto, but Richard Lander, initially only his servant but latterly his close friend, returned safely to England with his papers. Lander went back again with his brother John in 1830; having made a longer visit to Bussa and then to Yauri, they voyaged down the Niger from Bussa to one of its outlets at Brass (Nembe), completing Mungo Park's exploration of the river. Their journey is commemorated on the Park–Lander Memorial at Jebba in Nigeria.

Clapperton and the Landers had hoped to recover Park's manuscript journal, but the Landers' final conclusion was given in somewhat stilted language in their book and more plainly in a letter to the Colonial Office: 'Mr. Park's Journal &c. are no longer in existence; they are irretrievably lost.'[12] Nevertheless they produced indubitable proof that Park had reached Bussa. There were the inhabitants' recollections, and the Landers also saw guns, ammunition, and other articles recovered from the boat. The only item they succeeded in getting back to Britain was a copy of *The Hymns of Isaac Watts and the Psalms of David* which had belonged to Alexander Anderson. It was restored to his family at the instance of James Hogg, the Selkirkshire poet known as the Ettrick Shepherd.[13] They also saw, but did not take, Park's copy of Mendoza's *Tables*, inside which there were a few minor notes in Park's handwriting and a dinner invitation addressed to him in London. The book was bought twenty-eight years later by Lieutenant (later Sir) John Glover, R.N., at Lome, a Nupe town southeast of Bussa, and it is now in the library of the Royal Geographical Society in London. Both books are intact and undamaged.

The stories Clapperton and the Landers heard varied much in their details, but Richard Lander put together what he considered the most probable sequence of events, and does not seem to have changed his mind after the later journey. It is frustrating to find that none of them ever commented directly on Amadi's story at its most vulnerable point, even after the Landers had spent some weeks at Yauri and must surely have made enquiries there. Had they done so, matters would be much clearer!

A tragic and unsuccessful search was made by Park's second son Thomas, who set out from Accra for Bussa in 1827 but soon died. Thomas was less than two years old when his father left home for the last time, and this effort of his bears testimony to Allison's abiding love for her husband, which she must have passed on to the children, and to her having fully accepted his decision to travel again in Africa. Her persistent hope that he was still alive was not completely unreasonable. He had emerged from his first journey when the lack of news might have indicated that he was dead, and there were occasional rumours, shown for example in Bowdich's book, of a white man or men being

alive somewhere in the interior. As late as 1830 the Landers could
say at Bussa that 'the white man had a wife and family in England
who would not believe he was yet dead.'[14]

In 1851 Dr. Heinrich Barth followed the desert route from Tripoli
to Borno, and later went westwards to Sokoto. In 1853 he approached
Timbuktu from the south of the river, passing in trepidation through
Tuareg country and calling himself a Syrian. On arrival he cast himself on the protection of the Shaikh El-Bakay, then head of the Kunta
clan; this enabled him, though with difficulty, to stay safely in Timbuktu and to get on good terms with the Tuareg (many of whom believed him to be Laing's son). From them he heard, even at this late
date, several eye-witness accounts of Park's journey. The Shaikh
accompanied him as far as Gao and then sent him on safely to Sokoto
with an influential escort, and he returned to England in 1856 with a
mass of valuable information, historical and geographical. His five
years of travel, and Denham's and Clapperton's two years, contrast
with the haste shown by Park.

Still later, in 1895, Félix Dubois heard the recollections already
referred to, but he could only trace fragments of Park's river journey
from Sansanding to Timbuktu. Subsequent French expeditions on the
lower Niger heard tales too. In the early years of the British occupation of Northern Nigeria in this century faint echoes were still
detectable.

Some of the stories must be discounted as wild rumours or even
gross inventions, and there were suspiciously numerous claims to have
been eye-witnesses. The rumours were followed by more credible accounts but later reports are less reliable. If the more obviously incorrect stories are set aside and the rest superimposed on each other to
form a kind of identikit picture, it will be found that there is sufficient
convergence to be able to draw some probable conclusions. The result
cannot be clear and definite; it is more like an early cinematograph
film in a mutilated state, jerky, with gaps, in places fuzzy, and sometimes open to alternative interpretations.

The following chapters try to show this picture. All those accounts
of the final stages which might have some claim to come from original
sources have been set out together, with the exception of passages
quoted in the text, in Appendix III, for what is believed to be the first
time.[15]

CHAPTER XXVIII

'A boat came having Christians on board'

From Sansanding to Timbuktu

———— ◊ ————

Amadi Fatouma's Journal began:

'We departed from Sansanding in a canoe the 27th day of the moon, and went in two days to Sellee, where Mr. Park ended his first voyage. Mr. Park bought a slave to help him in the navigation of the canoe . . . without landing we bought the slave. We went in two days to Ginne. We gave the Chief one piece of baft and went on . . .'

Here Sellee obviously means Silla, and Ginne means Jenne, but there is a problem in following Amadi's account. He narrated it in one language to Isaaco who wrote it down in Arabic, and somebody unknown translated that into English. It is not surprising that place-names are sometimes hard to identify, but one detail supports Amadi's general veracity. The new moon, which marked the beginning of Ramadan, would have been seen about 22 November 1805, and what Amadi said therefore tallies with the party's having left Sansanding on 19 or 20 November, as indicated by Park's last letters. Amadi gave no indication of timing or distance after Jenne.

On his first journey Park did not visit Jenne for fear of the Moors. This time he had said in his *Journal*, 'We shall not see Jinnie in going to Tombuctoo,' for he had learnt that it was not on the Niger itself but on a large tributary called the Bani or Ba Nimma, joining the Niger from the south side beyond Jenne. He must have found out, however, that there was a curious winding channel called the Koua-kourou linking the Niger to the Bani at Jenne, through land inundated after the rains. As they neared the Bani they would have come upon the prosperous, walled city standing to their right on an island. Its fame as a great mart, rivalling Timbuktu in importance, justified a detour, even at some risk. To Jenne caravans brought produce from the lands to the south and west, whilst Timbuktu received goods over the northern desert route. The river was the vital connecting link, also carrying the food without which Timbuktu could not survive.

Park had been told that although Jenne was nominally under, and paid tribute to, Segu, it was a Moorish city. This probably meant that it still had a governor who belonged to the 'Arma' or 'Ruma', the descendants of the Moroccan conquerors of the Songhai Empire, by now completely intermarried with local populations, and only mis-leadingly described as Moorish. Jenne was almost a city-state on its own. Its population was cosmopolitan, largely Muslim, but whilst the real Moors were influential they were not the rulers. After what he had heard, however, it is understandable that he might have been nervous in his approach.

Had he come after the Fulani Jihad, starting in 1818, which im-posed an austere Muslim rule on Masina, the country around and north of Jenne, he would certainly have been in danger. It was these Fulani who later pressed for Laing and Barth to be expelled from Timbuktu. We cannot judge just how dangerous a visit to Jenne would have been at the time of Park's journey. A letter from Mansong might have helped, and he could then have asked for one from Jenne to Timbuktu. What his actual reception was is far from clear. The records of Caliph Bello of Sokoto in Hausaland bear out Amadi's des-cription of a peaceful visit, saying, '. . . they arrived at Jeris, where they resided as long as God was pleased,' and 'Jeris' can only mean Jenne.[1] The writer should have known, for he was a native of Masina. Barth too believed Park had been well received in Masina.[2]

But these accounts are contradicted by a story Abdel Gassam told Denham in 1823 in Borno: 'Many years ago, before I was born, white men, Christians, came from Sego to D'jennie, in a large boat, as big as two of our boats. The natives went to them in their canoes; they would not have done them any harm, but the Christians were afraid, and fired at them with guns, and killed several in the canoes that went near their boat . . .'[3] He too should have known, being the son of a Fulani chief at Jenne. For reasons shown later the other accounts are more probably correct, but if Abdel Gassam was right perhaps this incident was what lay behind a report in 1809 that the King of Jenne had sent after Park's party and had had them murdered.[4]

After Jenne they would soon have reached the junction with the Joliba, or Niger, where Mopti stands. It was a strange area they passed through, a succession of inland deltas. The Niger sends off side chan-nels which rejoin it miles further on at the shallow Lake Debo. The country is very flat apart from the occasional barren, stony hillock.

With the yearly flooding and recession of the waters there are few trees and little permanent habitation, but the Fulani graze their cattle there and live in seasonal camps. The abundant wildfowl could provide meat for the pot. The current is sluggish and the winds could have been adverse for sailing; they may have had to pole the canoe slowly along in shallow water, with periods of waiting necessitated by strong winds, as Caillié found in his journey twenty years later.

Issuing out of Lake Debo the river divides once more, and also floods on both sides into shallow lakes, which empty out again as the water level falls. From about here, right round its great northern arc, the river takes the Songhai name Isa, which, like Joliba, means 'The (great) river'. Park and his companions seem to have followed the main western branch, the Isa Ber or White River, calling at Sébi. Caliph Bello's secretary recorded that after visiting Jenne, 'They thence went on to Masena, following the river till they came to one of our towns called Seebi, between Jeri and Timbuctoo, that they might cross the way of the river. They sojourned there with the prince, who was one of the sons of the Sultan of Timbuctoo, and whose name was Babal-kydiali. He entertained them, and gave them leave to proceed to Timbuctoo . . .' This is circumstantial and credible, but again we are faced with an apparent contradiction. Amadi Fatouma said: 'In passing Sibby [which the translator mistook for Lake Debo, or Dibbie as Park had called it], three canoes came after us, armed with pikes, lances, bows and arrows, etc., but no firearms. Being sure of their hostile intentions, we ordered them to go back; but to no effect; and were obliged to repulse them by force.'

These were almost certainly the Surka, part of the Tuareg, against whose spears and arrows they had erected the protective awning of bullock hides. René Caillié called them Soorgoos. When the trading boat in which Caillié took passage neared Timbuktu, it came up with others collecting together before braving the Surka, who hung around them for days making whatever exactions they could. As a supposed Egyptian, Caillié was obliged to hide all day below decks, as the Surka believed all fair-skinned people were wealthy. Incorrectly but with feeling he said, 'I conjecture that Mungo Park was murdered by these barbarians.'

As Caillié described them, they had no firearms and they retreated in fear if anyone fired in the air, but they had an undoubted upper hand. There seems to have been a tacit pact not to use physical force.

Had the traders used force on them, they could have cut Timbuktu's essential lifeline, as Caillié heard explained in the city. Had they used force on the traders, even a temporary cessation of river traffic would have removed their source of profit. Whether, faced with a boatload of obvious strangers, they would have been so restrained is of course doubtful. Possibly Park could have got by peacefully had he been willing to submit to some troublesome extortion. Unable to gauge their intentions, and faced with the need for instant decision, he decided to take no chances with these men, who physically resembled the Moors of Ludamar.

After the two branches of the Isa reunite the river turns east. At this point they were close to Timbuktu, having already come 400 miles via Jenne. Only at exceptionally high water can Timbuktu, standing in the desert some ten miles from the main river, be approached by boats. At that time of year, however, they could easily enter the side channel leading off at Koriouma to Kabara, the port of Timbuktu. As at Jenne, Park's geographical curiosity overcame his desire for haste and his fear of the Moors. Timbuktu was, after all, one of the great prizes sought by European exploration, the fabled city of the trans-Saharan trade.

He would have expected to find wealth there, no doubt, but not houses roofed with gold, as Richard Jobson had said. That myth probably sprang from tales of the enormous transfers of gold as booty to Morocco immediately after the conquest of Songhai, but these transfers soon dwindled to a steady trade in the annual output of goldfields developed to the south-east of Bambuk. Secondly, he would have expected an extreme intolerance of Christians, who 'were looked upon there as the devil's children, and enemies to the Prophet'. This was not a matter of European myth but what he was repeatedly told by Africans.

The one extended account Park gave of what he had heard of Timbuktu comes in the *Travels* at the point when he was preparing to turn back at Silla:

'To the north-east of Masina, is situated the kingdom of Tombuctoo, the great object of European research: the capital of this kingdom being one of the principle marts for that extensive commerce which the Moors carry on with the Negroes. The hopes of acquiring wealth in this pursuit, and zeal for propagating their religion, have filled this extensive city with Moors and Mahomedan converts; the king himself, and all the chief officers of state are

Moors; and they are said to be more severe and intolerant in their principles than any other of the Moorish tribes in this part of Africa. I was informed by a venerable old Negro, that when he first visited Tombuctoo, he took up his lodging at a sort of public inn, the landlord of which, when he conducted him into his hut, spread a mat on the floor, and laid a rope upon it; saying, "if you are a Mussulman you are my friend, sit down; but if you are a Kafir, you are my slave; and with this rope I will lead you to market." The present King of Tombuctoo is named *Abu Abrahima*; he is reported to possess immense riches. His wives and concubines are said to be clothed in silk, and the chief officers of state live in considerable splendour. The whole expence of his government is defrayed, as I was told, by a tax upon merchandize, which is collected at the gates of the city.'

What he would actually have found is in some ways easy to state. He would have found Kabara a small town, set amongst marshes, busy with the transit trade between Timbuktu and the south. Had he entered it, his first impression of the famous city itself, then walled, would probably have been disappointment. It is true that Gordon Laing, cannily withholding all details until he should return to Europe, said of it, '. . . in every respect except in size (which does not exceed four miles in circumference) it has completely met my expectations.'5 But Caillié, only eighteen months later, '. . . looked around and found that the sight before me, did not answer my expectations. I had formed a totally different idea of the grandeur and wealth of Timbuctoo. The city presented, at first view, nothing but a mass of ill-looking houses, built of earth . . . There was not as at Jenne, a concourse of strangers from all parts of the Soudan . . . in comparison with Jenne, the market is a desert.' Desert with only stunted shrubs certainly surrounded Timbuktu, and nothing whatever was grown there except a little poor tobacco. The city existed because it had water and because of its strategic position for the Saharan trade. In the end, however, though Caillié could not 'account for the impression, there was something imposing in the aspect of a great city, raised in the midst of sands, and the difficulties surmounted by its founders cannot fail to excite admiration.' It was worth a long and hazardous journey, and most later visitors have echoed both Caillié's initial disappointment and his final admiration.

What is more difficult is to unravel the complex political situation there. The government of the Ruma and the puppet Songhai 'Emperors' they had maintained had crumbled in the preceding century before increasing Tuareg pressures. They had steadily lost their hold on Jenne, Gao, and other places along the river, except, according to Barth, between Timbuktu and Sébi. The Tuareg were supreme up to the city gates, and they exacted tribute from within them but, as on the river, they were careful not to disrupt trade entirely. Distant Segu too is said to have sent an expedition to collect tribute as recently as 1803 (although Barth was sceptical about this). But through all the turmoil a city government of some sort remained in being, controlling Timbuktu itself, Kabara, and – rather precariously – the few miles of road between them. The Kunta Arabs in their northerly oasis also wanted to maintain peace, order, and trade. Unless the Ruma were meant, Park was misled when told that the Moors ruled the city; as Caillié found in 1828, the Moors were influential but were not permitted to take part in the council.

Caillié was terrified that his disguise would be penetrated, but he learnt that the openly Christian Major Laing, though pressed to become a Muslim and called names, was never ill-treated in the city. He moved freely around, visiting mosques, taking notes, drawing plans, and even being allowed to search the city records. The most influential Moors, used to dealings with Christians in north Africa, were contemptuous of them but not inimical. Both the city government and the Kunta Arabs protected Laing as far as they could from pressure by the Masina Fulani, who had just made themselves Timbuktu's overlords, and even these pressures were only exerted to expel him, not to kill him unless he would not go. The same was true later with Barth, although his pages show the kaleidoscopic effects of internal factions interacting with outside forces. It was the Tuareg and the Arabs of the desert who physically assaulted Laing, and who might have attacked Barth but for his protection from the city. Park's reception might, therefore, have been very different from what he had expected.

There was one other important fact that Caillié learnt at Timbuktu, '. . . that there was no traffic or communication by water between Timbuctoo and the country of Haoussa; because . . . the navigation of the river ceases at Cabra.' Where there was no regular traffic, Park could not count on the rules for caravans being effective, and he could have benefited if help was offered at Timbuktu. But with the city authorities so weak, buffeted between the Tuareg – as often as not disunited – the Kunta Arabs, the Bambara, and different factions in the city itself, what the balance of forces and their resultant action at any moment would have been defies analysis. If help had been given, it would probably have had far greater influence than the limited power of the city authorities would suggest.

As Park approached Kabara, having probably travelled peacefully apart from the one clash near Sébi, we can visualize him torn between hope and anxiety. Just possibly he did have some friendly contact there. Caliph Bello's records say that '. . . they arrived in safety, five as they were, at the city of Timbuctoo, where they resided as long as God was pleased.' Abdel Gassam told Denham that they had held a parley with a chief sent by the sultan, and were given provisions. They left abruptly, however, and took no notice of canoes sent after them by the sultan to warn them of rocks in the river. The boats followed them until they came to grief. Denham went on to say that Abdel Gassam had often seen with his father a man who had gone that far, and who had brought the news of the disaster to Timbuktu –

'Their appearance excited a great sensation amongst the people; . . . to this day they talk about them. They had guns fixed to the sides of the boat, a thing never seen before at Timboctoo, and they alarmed the people greatly.'

Abdel Gassam would have us believe that the canoes from Timbuktu followed Park's party for about a thousand miles. Denham found Abdel Gassam an exceptionally bright youngster, a 'prodigy', and most of what he told Denham was sound enough. He was, however, too young to have first-hand knowledge of what had happened to Park, and it is likely that he had listened with half an ear, getting the descriptions of events roughly right but the locations wrong. Or it may be that Denham confused what he was told.

The subsequent course of events makes it far more likely that Park never made effective contact at Timbuktu at all. We must also discount the curious story of Al-Hajj Mahomet Alibali of the 'Timbuctons' killing Park and his party.[6] What seems the most authentic version was received by a Moroccan trader in Mogador, sent by his agent at Kabara in March 1806, and passed on by James Jackson to Banks:

'You will be much surprised to know from me that, a few days since, a boat came to this place having Christians on board: they hoisted a white flag, and remained at anchor in the Niger from the rising till the setting sun: no one went to them; nor did they come (or communicate) with any one: they did not appear (to be) hostile, but on the contrary (they seemed) peaceably inclined, and inoffensive. I think they wished to trade with us, but the meaning of the flag was not understood here, and they returned towards Jennie in the evening since when we have heard nor seen nothing of them nor of their boat.'[7]

Park should have been able to reach Timbuktu by mid-December, unless there were some unrecorded delay on the way. With lunar months overlapping calendar months, this letter could have been sent in February rather than March, and 'a few days since' may be an understatement.

This account does not stand alone. In 1810 Jackson's successor at Mogador, Alexander Court, wrote to Banks:

'In the spring of 1810 a number of persons were here from Tombuctoo, who almost all confirmed the Intelligence you had from Mr. Jackson of a Boat with Christians, having appeared and lay off the port of Cabra – of their having hoisted a white Flag – and of their having passed Tombuctoo without having entered it, or having any communication with it ... at the time of their being off Cabra there were remaining six white persons and two Blacks.'[8]

In 1818 Lieutenant-Colonel Fitzclarence heard a similar story while on a Mediterranean voyage:

'During our conversations, Hadjee Talub mentioned, that eleven years ago, in 1807, when at Timbuctoo, he heard of two white men, who came from the sea, having been near the city. This was the year before he arrived at Timbuctoo, and he understood that the white men sold beads, as they had no money to purchase grain. He adds, that they went down the Nile [the Niger] to the eastward, and the general report stated that they had died of the climate.'[9]

Taken together, these stories conjure up a curious spectacle of the travellers and the people at Kabara watching each other with mixed hope and suspicion, but not hostility; each waiting for the other to make the first move. Eventually, disappointed and probably afraid to remain where they were after dark, Park directed his crew back to the main river the way they had come from Koriouma, rather than risk the narrower eastward channel also leading back to the Niger. Because Amadi Fatouma omits this episode, Park's attempt to open contact with Timbuktu has been neglected, but it is one of the best-documented parts of the journey.

We cannot say firmly that, had he been only a little bolder, he would have received help to ensure his further passage with safety, but as he and his men slipped away from Kabara, all unknown to them their best hopes slipped away too. This marked the point of no return in the journey. Up to Timbuktu he might have been able, if he had had any thought of so doing, to turn around and make his way back slowly to Segu either up-river or overland. Once past Timbuktu, he could only press onwards, down the long river wheresoever it should lead him.

CHAPTER XXIX

'The fixed resolution to discover the termination of the Niger'

From Timbuktu to Yauri

───── ⟐ ─────

Park had not negotiated his passage in advance either at Timbuktu or with the Tuareg. His little band was not an effective deterrent, as forty men might have been; it could not enforce a pause during which parleying could take place. Probably Park did not know that the river east of Timbuktu was not frequented like the stretch between there and Jenne, where there was an interest in letting boats pass even while subjecting them to extortion. He had therefore to trust to luck, in attempting to pass, and to resort to force rather than negotiation if opposed.

Amadi Fatouma omits any account of the unsatisfying entry to Kabara, and the following must apply to their departure:

'. . . we passed Rakbara [Kabara]; three came up to stop our passage, which we repelled by force. On passing Tombuctoo [however that is to be understood] we were again attacked by three canoes; which we beat off, always killing many of the natives. On passing Gouroumo [Koriouma] seven canoes came after us; which we likewise beat off . . .'

These fights would not have been connected with the fight near Sébi, as the Tuareg east and west of Timbuktu had no unity. Amadi gives no indication of the causes. All Barth had to say at this point was that '. . . he had been first attacked by the Tawarek below Kabara, where he had lost some time in endeavouring to open a communication with the natives . . .' One of the earliest reports to reach Banks, demonstrably inaccurate as it was in most respects, probably provides the best clue, '. . . it is customary for all boats passing, to pay a Tribute to the Tuercs, but the Europeans not suffering them to approach were assaulted in this hostile Manner.'[1]

From what Laing and Barth said later it seems that the Tuareg must have believed that Park had been given, but had rejected, an opportunity to deal with them peacefully. What happened never comes into sharp enough focus for us to see whether pacific intentions were signalled unmistakably by either side to the other. Amadi is unlikely to have known enough Tamashek (the language of the Tuareg) to have been of much use at this point. It is probable that each party approached the other as potentially a band of marauders, warily and suspiciously, weapons in hand, until some small misunderstanding or hasty move precipitated a clash. If we transfer the sixteen-year-old Abdel Gassam's story of Jenne to Timbuktu, it fits here. After he had shaken off pursuit Park pressed on, in his optimism perhaps expecting that these attacks were isolated events, the kind of hostility he had anticipated at Timbuktu, and that African hospitality would subsequently reassert itself.

From Kabara the river runs almost due east for about 200 miles, between swamps, alternating with dunes, on its north bank and mainly sand along Aribinda, the south side. Over half-way along this stretch it cuts through rocky barriers which constrict it, first at Bamba to a width of 600 to 700 yards, and later to a mere 150 yards at Tosaye, where the current is very swift. Then it widens again and turns sharply to the south-east. For nearly 200 miles beyond there the Tuareg continued to be dominant. They were knit together in a loose confederation of tribes amongst which, however, feuds were common. Authority was widely dispersed and, lacking a protector and advocate such as Barth later had in Shaikh El-Bakay, Park would have had difficulty even in locating such an authority, let alone negotiating with it.

On this occasion Tuareg unity was shown against the intruder. Barth quoted a Chief Awab as saying that whilst Park had lain hopefully before Kabara, '. . . the Tin-ger-egedesh forwarded the news of his arrival, without delay, to the Igwadaren, who, having collected their canoes, attacked him, first near Bamba, and then again at the narrow passage of Tosaye, though all in vain . . .' He heard too of another attack at the island of Zamgoy, half-way between Bamba and Tosaye, from one of the Tuareg who, encamped with his people on the sandy downs of Aribinda, had been a spectator as the Christians had 'come down the river in a large boat with a white tent [sail]' and had then passed on unharmed.

The manner in which Chief Awab narrated these events 'altogether proved what an immense excitement the mysterious appearance of this European traveller, in his solitary boat, had caused among all the surrounding tribes'. Another group of Tuareg not far away also showed Barth that the 'adventurous Christian who, fifty years ago, had navigated this river ... even after this lapse of time, remains a mysterious and insoluble enigma to them, as to the place from whence he so suddenly appeared, and whither he was going'. The initial astonishment generated suspicion and alarm, and then it only needed a single spark to set the guns blazing for hundreds of miles. The Tuareg were intent on stopping the strangers by force, whilst Park's policy, 'which he no doubt adopted much against his own inclinations ... was to fire at any one who approached him in a threatening atti-tude'. Thus mutual suspicion fed hostility in an unbreakable cycle and, once fighting had begun, there was no chance of either negotiating or beating a retreat.

Amadi may have been referring to Bamba in this passage:

'We lost one white man by sickness; we were reduced to eight hands; having each of us fifteen muskets, always in order and ready for action. Passed by a village (of which I have forgotten the name), the residence of King Gotoijege; after passing which we encountered sixty canoes coming after us, which we repulsed, and killed a great number of men. Seeing so many killed, and our superiority over them, I took hold of Martyn's hand, saying, "Martyn, let us cease firing; for we have killed too many already"; on which Martyn wanted to kill me, had not Mr. Park interfered ...'

So many muskets were needed, of course, because muzzle-loaders could not be quickly reloaded in the heat of action. Whether the Tuareg had guns is never clear; Barth found the double-barrelled gun almost universal amongst them, but that was fifty years later. Martyn's acting in this crazed way, loosing off shot after shot, would go far to explain why, as Barth heard, the Tuareg classed Europeans with wild beasts; he found they hesitated at first to approach him.

They did call at Bamba, as Barth heard in a striking eyewitness account:

'This chief, Woghda, had been present, when quite a boy, at the attack which the Igwadaren at Egedesh made upon Mungo Park, whom all the old men along the river knew very well, from his large strange-looking boat, with its white sail, his long coat, his straw hat, and large gloves. He had stopped at Bamba in order to buy fowls, of which he appears to have endeavoured to obtain a supply at every large place along the river. Woghda further asserted that it was on this occasion that the Tawarek killed two of the Christians in the boat, but this seems to be a mistake, as it appears evident that two of the four valiant men, who, solitary and abandoned, in their boat, like a little fortress, navigated this river for so many hundred miles in the midst of these hostile tribes, were killed much lower down.'

Again, after staying at the place itself, Barth said:

'I was roused at a very early hour by the crowing of the cocks in Bamba, which could not but recall to my mind the fate of the enterprising but unfortunate Mungo Park, who is said by the natives to have stayed here a couple of hours in order to provide himself with fowls, and thus to have given leisure to the Tawarek, lower down the river, to collect together and impede his passage; a story which is also related with regard to Gogo and some other places along the river; though it is more probable that his chief reason for making a halt near the principal places along the river, was to open communication with the natives, and more particularly in order to make astronomical observations.'

It seems, then, that Park had not altogether done with 'communication with the natives', but it is probable that he stopped at non-Tuareg settlements, like the subdued Ruma of Bamba, and the contacts were of a limited kind, not involving serious negotiations.

Rushing through the narrows of Tosaye in the high waters of December or January, as Barth deduced, from there round the bend of the river, and for the next sixty miles they had only one more clash with Tuareg. They faced other problems, however, described by Amadi:

'After passing Gotoijege a long way, we met a very strong army on one side of the river; composed of the Poul nation [Fulani]; they had no beasts of any kind. We passed on the other side and went on without hostilities. On going along we struck on the rocks. An hippopotamus rose near us, and had nearly overset the canoe; we fired on the animal and drove it away. After a great deal of trouble we got off the canoe without any material danger.'

The boat was equipped, as Barth was told by Chief Awab, with an iron hook for use against hippopotami, or canoes which came too near.

Then they came to Gao, or Gogo as it is named above by Barth. This city had been in decline since the collapse of the Songhai Empire, a decline accentuated by struggles which about 1770 had ended with control finally passing to the Tuareg and with the subjection of the Songhai people and the remaining Ruma. When Barth visited it in 1854 he found it a sorry remnant of its imperial past. An old man tried to give him information, apparently about Mungo Park, and to show him something in a house where, however, they were refused admittance, but the man was of weak understanding and Barth could not follow what he said. Apart from him Barth found the inhabitants sullen and uncommunicative, which he accounted for by the fact, 'as I shall mention further on, that they behaved rather treacherously towards the Christian who visited this place fifty years before'. Unfortunately this loose end is left untied in Barth's narrative.

Gao, or Gogo, we can probably identify with Amadi's Kaffo, as the name, transliterated from Arabic, has sometimes appeared as Kaogha or Kagho, and no other place-name along the river bears any resemblance to Kaffo.[2] Amadi said:

'We came to an anchor before Kaffo, and passed the day there. We had in the canoe before we departed from Sansanding, a very large stock of provisions, salted and fresh of all kinds; which enabled us to go along without stopping at any place, for fear of accident . . . In the evening we started and came to before an island . . . We passed the island and sailed. In the morning three canoes from Kaffo came after us, which we beat off.'

Perhaps this was the treachery Barth referred to. Soon afterwards Amadi was sent on shore to buy some milk, and two canoes went out to sell provisions to the travellers. On shore Amadi was seized, but seeing this happen Park threatened to kill the occupants of the canoes, whereupon Amadi was released. Then they bought provisions and made some small presents and departed peacefully. This incident must have reinforced Park's fear of being himself detained if he went ashore anywhere; his force was inadequate to rescue him.

Later, twenty canoes followed them and called out, 'Amadi Fatouma, how can you pass through our country without giving us any thing?' Park gave them some small items and they went quietly away. Further on, they came to a very difficult obstacle. Rocks barred the width of the river except for three passages through them. At this place they found some people they had seen earlier, on top of a large rock. Endearingly, Amadi says this '. . . caused great uneasiness to us, especially to me, and I seriously promised never to pass there again without making considerable charitable donations to the poor. We returned and went to a pass of less danger, where we passed unmolested.' This is unlikely to have been his normal route to the Hausa states, which were usually approached overland far from the Niger, and

Amadi probably really promised himself simply 'never to pass there again'!

His memory was selective, and he was surprisingly casual about the hazards of the river. In fact the travellers had had to find their way through not just one, but a whole series of rapids. Difficulties began at the hilly island of Ansongho sixty miles below Gao, which might be thought to be the place last described by Amadi, but for differences in the descriptions of how they passed it. The Niger divides into four channels, of which only a single narrow one is navigable. Here, Barth reflected, 'that heroic voyager from the north had to struggle with nature as well as with hostile men'. Chief Awab had told him that the boat stuck fast, giving the Tuareg a chance to mount a fierce attack, in which two of the whites were killed; this is evidently what Barth was alluding to in his comment on Chief Woghda's story about Bamba. But near Ansongho an old man who remembered Park's tall, commanding figure described how '. . . the tribe of Ide-Musa . . . attacked that mysterious voyager near Ansongho, where the river is hemmed in by rapids, but without being able to inflict any harm upon him, while the intrepid Scotchman shot one of his pursuers, and caused two to be drowned in the river.' This is another loose end left by Barth. (These are, incidentally, the only definite figures ever quoted for Tuareg casualties. Three Europeans were killed at 'Gharwalgaoo', according to Caliph Bello's records, but the facts remain unclear.)

After Ansongho, for some hundred miles, the river cuts its way through low, rocky hills, and its bed is frequently divided by many islands and rocks, the more dangerous when just submerged. Barth only saw the river from its banks, but Lieutenant Hourst of the French navy led a party this way in 1896 and gave the first full account of it. Several rapids soon after Ansongho caused Hourst's party anxiety but the worst was to come at Labezenga. With little warning they found water foaming over a rocky ledge right across the river, and, as the current swept them towards it, quick decision and steering were needed to head, just a few feet away from submerged rocks, into the only visible break over which the boat could drop and move on past the whirlpool below. Two of their three aluminium boats were damaged, and they sustained more damage further on.

The first Labezenga rapid was followed by a second and a third, which they spent hours reconnoitring before attempting them. There were more near Ayoru, now just over the frontier into the modern

Republic of Niger, and again at Kendaji, 70 miles below Ansongho, where Barth had sensed that there had been yet another fight. By then the worst was over, but confusing myriad channels and shallow, rocky places continued beyond Sinder. Park had had to detect and navigate the safest channels in his unwieldy wooden canoe, with no previous experience and, as far as we know, without local guides. All the time he had to keep a watch for hostile Tuareg, hindering him from landing on the banks to reconnoitre before entering rapids. It was an astonishing feat to get through at all, even though he may have had the advantage of a fuller river than Hourst and his party had.

At last Park and his companions came to the end of Tuareg country and were able to continue on their way quietly. Here the river flows, when high, more gently but at a rate of three knots or more. With fuller use of the sail, and the north-east wind to help them, they should have made rapid progress. The scene must have looked much as it does now at the same time of year, the river flooded out to a width of a mile or more, green with islands and ribbons of grass, some of it freely floating down, and green also along the banks, while a few yards up these gentle slopes, greenness gives way to the darker brown of cultivated land and the dull yellow of dried grass. In places, low ridges of dark and infertile ironstone stand back from the river. Small villages still appear in rapid succession down the river, but the city of Niamey with its bridge over the river did not then exist. After what they had passed through, it was a restful and liberating stretch of water.

Amadi said they stopped at Carmasse (?Karma, north of Niamey) and gave the chief one piece of baft. Then they went on and anchored before Gourmon (= Gurma, the west bank as a whole, rather than a place) and he was sent ashore with 40,000 cowries to buy fresh provisions. The expedition departed in peace and indeed the Chief sent after them to give warning of an army waiting ahead, enabling Park and his companions to pass on quietly. Barth found they had slipped past Say, the largest town in the area, entirely unnoticed.

About here the name of the Niger changes to the Hausa form 'Kwara', by which it is generally known for most of its remaining course to the sea. Further on they would have gone through a winding stretch between high banks, free from rapids, known as 'The W'. Soon, Amadi said, they

'. . . entered the country of Haoussa, and came to an anchor. Mr. Park said to me, "Now, Amadi, you are at the end of your journey; I engaged you to conduct me here; you are going to leave me, but before you go, you must give me the names of the necessaries of life, &c. in the language of the countries through which I am going to pass;" to which I agreed, and we spent two days together about it, without landing. During our voyage I was the only one who had landed. We departed and arrived at Yaour.'

They were by this time in present-day Nigeria, having travelled about 1,500 miles down-river from Sansanding, and being close on 2,500 miles from their starting-point on the Gambia. Guessing that they might have averaged 25 miles a day on the river, and accepting Amadi's original estimate of two months for the journey to Yauri, this brings us to the second half of January 1806. The earliest date ever given is one still in Ramadan, which ended about 22 December 1805, barely a month after they had sailed; this is improbable, however much we may allow for Park's unselfish but quite inappropriate haste to return to his family commitments. So is the longest estimate of four months, given by Isaaco.[3]

Amadi indicated that there were still four Europeans at Yauri, but his evidence stands almost alone on this. There were, as we have seen, reports of two or three being killed on the way and most of the stories of Yauri speak of only two or three Europeans there. Which figures are correct we cannot tell; such dates and numbers could not be expected to stand out in observers' minds for accurate recall years later.[4]

On a personal level the journey was an extraordinary feat of endurance against odds, showing great courage, tenacity of purpose, and skill in handling the boat. Park had maintained his resolution and brought his dwindling band through a whole succession of reverses and dangers, any one of which might have broken a man of lesser fortitude. But the question remains: did the voyage down-river have to be so bloody? His fixed resolution brought them through to Yauri, but it left a terrible trail behind him.

The most forceful condemnation of Park's conduct came from Major Gordon Laing. At In Salah, hundreds of miles north of Timbuktu, Laing sustained a verbal assault from one of the Tuareg who had been wounded in a fight with Park's boat and was ready to take an oath '. . . that I am no less a personage than the late *Mungo Park*, the Christian who made war upon the people inhabiting the banks of the Niger, who killed several and wounded many of the Tuaric . . .' Laing went on, 'How imprudent, how unthinking! I may even say how selfish was it in Park to attempt making discovery in this land, at the expense of the blood of its inhabitants, and to the exclusion of all after communication; how unjustified was such conduct! What answer am I to make to the question which will be often put to me? – What right had you, or if it was not you, What right had your country-man to fire upon and kill our people?'

Laing was a forthright man given to strong opinions, not always consistent. Earlier in his journey, firing off a volley against the parsi-mony of the British Treasury, he had written scathingly of Park's *weakness* on his first journey: 'I do not feel inclined as an Agent of a Government like England to be indebted to the King of Sego, or any other African Chief for a few shells to save me from starving as poor Park was . . . better by far, that English men should remain at home, than come into a country like this to excite commiseration and con-tempt . . .' When he condemned Park's use of force he had only a one-sided picture and could not justify such a confident verdict, so sweepingly ruling out the obvious answer of 'Self-defence', or the plea that each attempt to open communications was rewarded with an am-bush laid down-river. What Laing might have said if, after visiting Timbuktu, he had been able to return safely home, we may never know.[5]

These caveats having been entered, Laing's charges still call for serious consideration, especially as they were endorsed by the balanced and scholarly Dr. Barth, who admitted Park's courage. He believed the Tuareg attack on Laing to have been due to a desire for revenge for Park's acts, as well as to the love of plunder. But he never made clear what were his exact grounds of complaint against Park. He did not, despite his own experience, allow for the tangled politics of the area, nor for the misleading impressions of Timbuktu that Park had been given by Africans. On his own presentation of the facts, Barth could hardly have accepted Laing's tendentious statement that it was Park who 'made war' upon the Tuareg, even if he believed that Park had provoked the Tuareg attacks on him. None of his evidence sug-gests either that there was any peaceable approach to the travellers, after they had left Timbuktu, which they rebuffed.

The root of the complaint must therefore be that Park should have embarked upon these unknown waters at all without first making effective contacts, for after that it was too late. Both ordinary prin-ciples of law, and policy, with a view to future visits, pointed to a need

11. Timbuktu, from an engraving in Dr. Henry Barth, *Travels and Discoveries in North and Central Africa*, IV (1858)

12a. Rapids on the River Niger, at Awuru

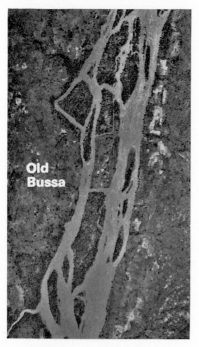

Old Bussa

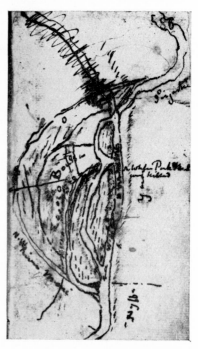

12b. Aerial view, October 1958, of the Niger at Old Bussa, showing almost the same area as 12c

12c. Captain Hugh Clapperton's sketch-map of Bussa, marking the location of Park's death

for such contacts, and Barth seems to have felt that Park showed himself insensitive to understandable fears. He accepted that Park did try to make contact at Timbuktu, and that the Tuareg had already started preparing to attack him. In the brief interlude between that attempted contact and the first clash with the Tuareg, Park had the choice of trying again and more boldly, at considerable risk to the whole boatload, it must have seemed to him; or following Laing's advice and going home; or taking a chance that nothing dreadful would happen if he did go on.

To us it must seem that, in choosing as he did, Park judged the situation wrongly, but if we dispense with the wisdom of hindsight, it is not crystal clear that he deserved castigation in such terms as Laing used. Laing himself was bold, and took chances; whether Park went beyond boldness to unthinking imprudence is a matter for fine judgement. It is difficult to make such a judgement when so little is known of the precise circumstances in the short critical period. There is also reason to think that, haunted by his responsibility for the earlier disasters of his expedition, his judgement may by this time have gone awry. There can be little doubt that what happened *arose from* Park's failure to make effective contacts at, or very near to, Timbuktu. Laing could be right in interpreting this failure as something worse than miscalculation, but, on the available evidence, I return to this Scotsman's charges a Scottish verdict of Not Proven.

CHAPTER XXX

'Or perish in the attempt'

From Yauri to Bussa

——— ∞ ———

Shortly before reaching Yauri Park must have taken note that the river turned due south, after running south-eastwards from near To-saye. He had, no doubt, finally discarded by then two theories in which he himself had never believed: that the Niger ran across Africa to join the Nile, and Rennell's theory of its ending in a lake or swamp in 'Wangara'. He must also have realized that the 'Mountains of Kong' were imaginary. In ignorance of the mountain chain in Cameroun, he might still have thought it possible that the river turned eastwards again, to emerge as the Congo, but a more natural expectation was that it would fall into the Atlantic in the Bight of Benin, a fact which it took Europe another twenty-five years to prove. His conduct is consistent with such a belief, which would have suggested that he had little further to go; for example, he apparently did not send any letters from Yauri, as he had told Banks he would do.

One story, on which Richard Lander placed much reliance, described the visit of three white men to Yauri. Of the leader of the party it said, 'He was a very tall and powerful man, with long arms and large hands, on which he wore leather gloves reaching above the elbows. Wore a white straw hat, long coat, full white trousers, and red leather boots. Had black hair and eyes, with a bushy beard and mustachios of the same colour.' In all of the literature there is no other description of Park's person as full as this. The Hausa word probably used could be translated as 'dark' rather than 'black' and, even though the known portraits clearly show grey hair and light-coloured eyes, in other respects it seems to be a good description. The account of his clothing is so strikingly similar to that given later by Chief Woghda to Barth, as to suggest that the religious mallam who spoke to Lander really had seen Park at Yauri. His long gloves were probably worn to protect his hands, as he was steersman of the boat.[1]

The two-day stop, on which Amadi taught Park some Hausa

words, was near enough to Yauri for the people there to hear of it and
to wonder what the visitors were up to, according to Joseph Dupuis.
He also said that the King or Emir (the thirtieth such, Muhammadu
Albishir Dan A'i) came down several miles from his capital to a point
near the waterside in the hope that the Europeans would disembark
to visit him.[2] Amadi described how well they were received there:

'I was sent on shore the next morning with a musket and a sabre, to carry to
the chief of the village [near the waterside, not the inland capital], also with
three pieces of white baft for distribution. I went and gave the Chief his
present: I also gave one piece to Alhagi, one to Alhagi-biron, and the other to
a person whose name I forget, all Marabous. The Chief gave us a bullock, a
sheep, three jars of honey, and four men's loads of rice. Mr. Park gave me
seven thousand cowries, and ordered me to buy provisions, which I did; he
told me to go to the Chief and give him five silver rings, some powder and
flints, and tell him that these presents were given to the King by the white
men, who were taking their leave of him before they went away.* After the
Chief had received these things, he enquired if the white men intended to
come back. Mr. Park being informed of this enquiry, replied that he could
not return any more.† Mr. Park had paid me for my voyage before we left
Sansanding: I said to him, "I agreed to carry you into the kingdom of
Haoussa; we are now in Haoussa. I have fulfilled my engagements with you;
I am therefore going to leave you here and return." Next day (Saturday)
Mr. Park departed, and I slept in the village (Yaour).'

   In fact, Park was probably disappointed to find that the main Hausa
states lay quite far away to the north and north-east, with Yauri only
on their fringe and chiefly inhabited, apart from the ruling class, by
non-Hausa peoples. Hornemann could have told much more of these
states had he lived to return to England.
   Another story gives some idea of the pleasurable excitement of the
people at this unique event, and also Park's strange response. It comes
from the Arabic manuscript given to Hutchison at Kumasi (now in
the Republic of Ghana) in 1817, and it has a ring of authenticity
about it, in spite of its unidentifiable naming of the Niger (in this area
called the Kwara) and the curious inclusion of a woman in the party.
It begins thus:

* Translator's note: 'The King staid a few hundred yards from the river.'
† Translator's note: 'These words occasioned his death; for the certainty of Mr.
Park's not returning induced the Chief to withhold the presents from the King.'

'In the name of God, the Merciful, the Compassionate:

'This document emanates from a territory in Hausaland called Yauri. We witnessed an event, the like of which we have never seen nor heard, in the river called K.ü.ḍ. While we were sitting down, we hear the cries of children: "We have seen a ship, the like of which we have never seen before." And the Sultan of Yauri sent forth his lieutenants with a cow, a sheep and all kinds of food, in great abundance. The ship carried two white men, one woman and two slaves – the white men hailed from the race of Christians. And the Sultan of Yauri asked them to come out to meet him, but they refused and proceeded . . .'[3]

Meeting the Emir on shore was not all they refused. Lander said they also refused his advice to leave the river and proceed more safely by land, so that the riverain peoples would not ill-treat them – 'This evil report was considered as the effect of jealousy and prejudice; and, ignoring the prudent counsel of the Sultan of Youri, the ill-fated adventurers proceeded . . .'[4]

This refusal was understandable, as it was the river above all they were interested in. Two stories cap it, however, by saying they further refused the offer of a guide, and certainly it is astonishing that they left without one.[5] Now there would be nobody to interpret, advise, buy provisions, or carry gifts. Park's hastily acquired smattering of Hausa might help him to buy provisions for some way down the river, but it could not serve the purpose of any communication beyond this. Without a guide, the dangers were immeasurably increased. Park's strange decision on this, setting the scene for final tragedy, can be partly explained if he believed he was already near journey's end, but it really does suggest that the tensions and troubles of the year since he left England had impaired his judgement. Yauri was no Ludamar or Tuareg country, but a state comparable to, say, Bondu or Kaarta where he had previously entrusted himself safely to local kings. His suspicion had grown beyond reason. It would not be surprising if the Emir was 'irritated', as Joseph Dupuis expressed it, by such behaviour and disregard for his rights and dignity.

If we may take the liberty of transferring Abdel Gassam's story from Timbuktu, where it does not fit, to Yauri, where it makes perfectly good sense, it tells us the same and adds some more:

'. . . the sultan sent to them one of his chiefs, and they held a parley. The Christians complained that the people wanted to rob them. The sultan was kind to them, and gave them supplies. Notwithstanding this, they went off suddenly in the night,[6] which vexed the sultan, as he would have sent people with them, if they had not been afraid of them a little: and he now sent boats after them, to warn them of their danger, as there were many rocks in the belly of the river, all pointed. However the Christians went on, and would not suffer the sultan's people to come near them . . .'

The rocks did not come at once, except at a small rapid at Tsulu quite near Yauri, which was not difficult to pass at that time of year when the water was high. Otherwise it was a broad and placid stretch of river, populous on the Yauri side but unoccupied bush to the west (apart from the large and fertile island called Fogge) until they came near to Bussa, seventy miles south. Near there, the river narrowed between low hills, and islands and occasional rocks would have begun to suggest further dangers ahead.

Meanwhile Amadi was back at Yauri, his duty done and with no sense of anything amiss. According to him:

'Next morning, I went to the King to pay my respects to him; on entering the house I found two men who came on horseback; they were sent by the Chief of Yaour. They said to the King, "we are sent by the Chief of Yaour to let you know that the white men went away, without giving you or him (the Chief) any thing; they have a great many things with them, and we have received nothing from them; and this Amadou fatouma now before you is a bad man, and has likewise made a fool of you both." The king immediately ordered me to be put in irons; which was accordingly done, and every thing I had taken from me; some were for killing me, and some for preserving my life. The next morning early the King sent an army to a village called Boussa near the river side. There is before this village a rock across the whole breadth of the river. One part of the rocks is very high; there is a large opening in that rock in the form of a door, which is the only passage for the water to pass through; the tide current is here very strong. This army went and took possession of the top of this opening. Mr. Park came there after the army had posted itself; he nevertheless attempted to pass. The people began to attack him . . .'

Three months later Amadi was not only released but was also given a slave woman. Then he learnt from a slave captured from Park's canoe what had taken place, and also that the only object recovered was a sword belt, which had been made into a girth for the Emir's horse.

Amadi's firm assertion that Yauri attacked Park because of this false accusation, is the most puzzling part of his whole narrative, for it is in flat contradiction to almost all of the other credible evidence.* None of the other accounts suggest either that Yauri was directly involved at Bussa or that any advice was sent to Bussa, which was a separate state, to attack him.[7] Only Joseph Dupuis' account supports Amadi on this, saying that a Yauri force was indeed sent, but only to bring Park back, and the commander was punished when it was learnt what had actually taken place. The whole weight of the other evidence – and particularly its detailed nature – is against Amadi here. Yet all the earlier part of Amadi's story, although it has odd gaps, is corroborated in essentials, and it would seem strange to brand him as a deliberate liar on this one point. If only the Landers had made some comment after visiting Yauri in 1830!

It is, in fact, an insoluble question unless entirely new evidence ever comes to light. Various people have guessed at a solution, and we can do no more. Some of Amadi's second-hand information about Bussa was certainly wrong or confused. We may surmise that that was true of what passed at Yauri as well. The Emir was 'vexed' or 'irritated' when told of Park's uncivil departure; he did imprison Amadi; and he also sent horsemen or boats, or perhaps both, in pursuit, but too late. All that Amadi did was to dramatize a little by claiming to have been present when the departure was reported, and to have heard what was said. The outcome was a vivid scene, factually wrong concerning the basis for the Emir's action and its purpose, but not intentionally so, apart from one small bit of embroidery. Those who prefer may try some other way to straighten the record.

There never was at Bussa anything like Amadi's huge rock right across the river, with an opening like a door. Indeed it could only have been a very unlucky accident that would cause the party to strike rocks there after they had successfully navigated so many worse places earlier. From April to July, when the water is low, the passage before Bussa could be very hazardous, as the Landers saw in 1830, but

---

*Taking it as an established fact that Park reached Bussa in his boat, Items 1, 3, 4, 6, 9, 11 (unless its location is changed), 29, and 30 in Appendix III fail to meet this requirement; Items 12 and 31 were sheer local invention; and Items 7, 14, 26(?), 32, and 33 which represent his death as purely accidental can be rejected in that respect because they would make the attitudes found at Bussa by Clapperton and the Landers inexplicable. The rest tally in essentials, apart from the puzzle over Amadi's story, with its sole support in Item 10. Even those stories which are rejected on this tend to overlap on secondary points with the more credible accounts.

earlier in the year little danger was evident, for example in late January or early February, which was probably when the boat arrived.

This has led to the common belief at Bussa that Park struck rocks in the Bubaru rapids fifteen miles below the town. These rapids are very dangerous, with a twisting safe channel, but not at all like the place Amadi described. Clapperton and the Landers were shown a particular spot in the eastern channel of the river just opposite Bussa town. Clapperton marked it on a sketch-map (Plate 12c), and when he later saw the Bubaru rapids he said of them, '. . . even if Park and Martin had passed Boussa in safety, they would have been in imminent danger of perishing here, most likely unheard of and unseen'.[8] The evidence overwhelmingly supports the Bussa location.

Omitting the large rock with its door, and the Yauri army, Amadi's version of the end otherwise agrees with the other sources. I prefer to quote, however, the fuller description, pieced together by Richard Lander from the various stories he and Clapperton had heard, of what ensued when Park with his one, two, or three companions reached Bussa:

'Their strange-looking canoe was observed by one or two of the inhabitants, whose shouts brought numbers of their companions, armed with bows and arrows, to the spot. At that time the usurpations of the Falatahs had begun to be the general talk of the black population of the country, so that the people of Boussa, who had only *heard* of that warlike nation, fancied Mr. Park and his associates to be some of them, coming with the intention of taking their town, and subjugating its inhabitants. Under this impression, they saluted the unfortunate Englishmen from the beach with showers of missiles and poisoned arrows, which were returned by the latter with a discharge of musketry. A small white flag had been previously waved by our countrymen, in token of their peaceable intentions; but this symbol not being understood by the people of Boussa, they continued firing arrows, till they were joined by the whole male population of the island,* when the unequal contest was renewed with greater violence than ever. In the meantime the Englishmen, with the blacks they had with them, kept firing unceasingly amongst the multitude on shore, killing many, and wounding a still greater number, till

---

* In 1830 Lander realized with surprise that Bussa was not on an island. Clapperton's Remark Books show that, confined to his hut by sickness, he had incorrectly preferred an account which made into a branch of the Niger what another rightly described as a tributary. Lander's 1830 unpublished Journal also shows that the people of Bussa were alarmed by the visit in 1826. 'Unequal contest' is not obviously appropriate to a few men with firearms against many men with bows and arrows!

their ammunition being expended, and seeing every hope of life cut off, they threw their goods overboard; and desiring their sable assistants to swim towards the beach, locked themselves firmly in each other's arms, and springing into the water, instantly sank, and were never seen again.'

According to Richard Lander, two slaves, badly wounded, managed to swim ashore, and were still at Bussa when he was there in 1826, but they were kept away from contacts.

Lander and his brother found in 1830 that there were Fulani (Fellatahs) living peaceably in the area with their cattle, as they had done for many years, and it was not true that the Bussa people had only *heard* of them. Nor are the Fulani as light-skinned as most Europeans, including Park himself. Nonetheless it is not as implausible as it may sound that Park's party was suspected of some connection with them. Just two years earlier, in February 1804, a Jihad or Holy War had begun 300 miles north of Bussa, when Shaikh Othman dan Fodio had aroused his fellow-Muslims, predominantly Fulani, to purge the Hausa states of practices contrary to Islamic Law, and the Caliphate was founded then. In the very same dry season as that in which H.M.S. *Joliba* arrived, but evidently later on, the Shaikh's forces invaded first Yauri and later the northernmost fringes of Borgu, the country headed by Bussa, as described by the Shaikh's son Muhammadu Bello in his book *Infaqu'l Maisur*. Rumours of Fulani movements and preparations could well have been wafting in and creating an air of tension at both Yauri and Bussa, causing a wary eye to be kept on unknown visitors from the north. Maybe Park was eventually caught up, in such an indirect way that he could hardly have known of it, in the effects of an Islamic movement like those that, at one time or another, affected most of the areas he had visited.[9]

If they were not mistaken for Fulani, then could they be Arabs, possible Fulani allies? Alternatively, how could Europeans be arriving from the north, when everyone knew they traded on the coast far to the south? Without an interpreter Park could not explain himself. Perhaps the people at Bussa did try to warn him of the rapids downstream, with gestures which were misunderstood, as several accounts suggest, and from there it would have been a short step to weapons being brandished on both sides, then let loose. The Bussa people claimed that Park had fired first, Lander suggested the reverse, but at bottom, whoever began it, there was probably simply an outburst of mutual suspicion caused by inability to communicate.

In their haste not all the stores had been thrown overboard to lighten the boat, and Lander said that the remainder were eagerly taken to Bussa. For days there was great feasting and rejoicing, 'but it happened that before their revelries were well over, an infectious disease, whereof they had not previously had the most distant idea, raged in the island, and swept off the Sultan,.[10] with numbers of his subjects . . . those who had been most active in the destruction of the strangers were cut off to a man, expiring in great agony'. Hastily everything (but again, not quite every thing) was burnt, and sacrifices offered, and the pestilence left them, but as news spread to neighbouring countries accusing fingers were pointed at Bussa. This redounded to the benefit of later travellers, for everyone then said, 'Do not hurt the white men; for if you do, you *will perish like the people of Boussa*!' This story has also been generally ignored, but it has a ground in fact, however it may have been magnified in the telling. There is evidence of a virulent disease which came westwards from beyond Lake Chad about this time, and which led to Bussa people evacuating the island of Kainji south of Bussa.[11]

More was seen by the Landers than is suggested above, but only Anderson's hymn-book and the *Tables of Mendoza*, both later taken back to Britain, have certainly survived to this day. At Yauri the Emir owns a silver-topped staff, possibly from Park's expedition. At Bussa the Emir has a ring formed from a large silver medallion, bearing the head of the British King George III, an inscription by now polished to illegibility, and the royal arms on the reverse. It was long associated with Park but is now known to have been struck in 1814 and to have been the gift of the Landers in 1830.[12] The journal of the voyage down the Niger is, unfortunately, extremely unlikely to be found now.

Park went in his own time under the description, 'the African traveller'. He never claimed to have 'discovered' the Niger, as if 'nobody' had seen it before. Had he been able to complete his journey it would have been a true exploration, for whilst most West Africans knew something of the Niger, there is no record of anybody's previously following its whole course from Bamako to the sea. It might be thought that the knowledgeable Caliph Bello, who was aware of British conquests in India, and who could confound Clapperton on ancient Christian heresies, withheld information about the river from Clapperton for political reasons, but his *Infaqu'l Maisur*, written for local eyes, confirms that he did not have a clear knowledge of its lower course.

Ironically, had he returned, Park would have been forced to report that, apart from the lower Niger below Bussa (the part he never actually saw), the river was not the great highway into the interior for which he and his sponsors were seeking, because of the rapids.

As it was, his second journey at first helped not at all to elucidate the mystery of the Niger. The names 'Yaouri' and 'Bousa' had already appeared on d'Anville's map, but they were still thought to be much nearer to Timbuktu than they are, with all that Amadi narrated after that place packed into a mere hundred miles. The various theories about the river continued to be propounded and argued, and even more were put forward. Ten years after the catastrophe of Park's expedition another attempt was made, aiming to test the Congo theory by simultaneous approaches from the Gambia and the mouth of the Congo. It was a fiasco at the Congo end, and a long-drawn-out failure at the other. But then, during the successful Denham–Clapperton expedition of 1822–4 from Tripoli, what was known of Park's second journey provided the vital clue. Whilst at Sokoto, Clapperton learnt where Yauri and Bussa really were. After returning to England, Clapperton hastened to return via Badagry on the coast to Bussa, fixing another position on what Park's journey had shown to be the same river as that recorded by him from Bamako to Silla. This in turn led to the Landers' definitive solution of the problem in 1830. Very soon, in 1832, Macgregor Laird, a Merseyside shipbuilder and merchant, in person led two of the earliest steamships to cross the seas in the first outsiders' venture into the Niger. 40 out of the 49 Europeans died, mostly from fever, but Richard Lander from a wound received in an affray.

For all that, it may be said that in Park's travels the histories of Europe and the *interior* of West Africa touched briefly, and then went their separate ways, and the same was true of his successors for a long time to come. Only on the navigable lower stretches of the Niger, the Senegal, and the Gambia was there any intensive European penetration before the Scramble for Africa at the end of the century. It was 1854 and another five expeditions later, the intervening ones having all suffered heavy losses, before Macgregor Laird's expedition demonstrated the full value of quinine against malaria, losing no lives at all. Even then further development was gradual. We have seen that grandiose plans of military intervention were afloat as early as in Park's time, but in the unlikely event of their having been adopted then, they would probably have achieved little positive result, with disastrous losses in men from disease.

In other continents Europeans went on with annexations, but for a long time Africa seemed to be a special case. After Britain's legal abolition of the slave trade in 1807, the year after Park's death, interested parties in Britain, many of them burdened with a sense of historical guilt because of that trade, groped for a policy towards Africa. They debated and tried out the naval suppression of the trade, treaties for its suppression in Europe and Africa, legitimate trade, the development of agriculture, conversion to Christianity, education, or, rarely amongst public voices, simply leaving Africa alone. All except the last had one thing in common, whether humanitarian or self-interested in aim, that they involved the Europeans taking the initiative, thus embroiling them further, for better and worse, in the affairs of Africa. This tendency was, however, checked by the belief that 'The only hope of improving the interior is by African influence,' to quote Macgregor Laird,[13] a view also powerfully urged by missionaries, especially the Church Missionary Society under its Secretary, Henry Venn. It was late on before the flame of Social Darwinism fused together the humanitarian, the trading, and the imperial impulses into a conviction of racial superiority. Then Macgregor Laird's peaceful steamships and quinine joined with more recently developed precision weapons to open new possibilities and, spurred on by new economic needs, promoted a sudden forward movement of European conquest.

Seen from the other end of the telescope the way ahead was, therefore, less sharply laid out than appears looking from our end. Until late in the century the British Government resisted – although with some exceptions – increases in its direct African responsibilities, and a growth of trading and other relations on a footing nearer to equality seemed just as possible, if not more so. In 1854 when Barth was at Timbuktu and the news of the French capture of Ouargla in northern Algeria came through, his belief was that 'Even in the event of the greatest success of the French policy in Africa, they will never effect the conquest of this region.'[14] After his time changes followed at a pace nobody could foresee, and within forty years French troops had occupied Timbuktu, whilst the British were getting set to seize the whole of Nigeria. For so long did it remain unclear to what use the work of Park and his successors would be put.

Had history unfolded the other way, the outcome would have been more consistent with Park's limited aims of 'rendering the geography of Africa more familiar to my countrymen, and in opening to their ambition new sources of wealth and new channels of commerce'. As in other political matters Park himself, if the question had ever been squarely posed to him, would probably have been determinedly neutral as to whether Britain should rule African territory, regarding it as outside his province, and a matter of state policy to be decided by those responsible. This apolitical neutrality left him free to concentrate on the geographical aims that most interested him, although also making him more amenable to being used by those who had other objectives, in his time or later.

As far as we can tell, Park's neutrality was reflected back by Africans in the interior on the whole keeping open minds as to what his extraordinary visits might portend, whilst their history continued to develop on its own lines. Many no doubt considered the alternatives: there might be exciting new possibilities of trade, as Mansong of Segu perhaps half-believed; or, so little about the Europeans being known for sure, they might fear invasion, as Caliph Bello of Sokoto did by 1826, for that reason advising the Masina Fulani to expel Major Laing; or again, the visits might lead nowhere. Most of the interior states probably then felt secure enough in their distance from the coast, so that a wary friendliness must have appeared the wisest policy to follow, leaving all options open.

On another level, Park's journeyings can be looked upon as an individual epic. In this light, we can only regard his second journey as a brave but tragic and misguided failure. His early life and his first journey gave him an ambitious goal and the faith that he could achieve it, but he had also learnt to dread captivity and to see too simple a solution in the caravan principle. The long wait between expeditions had brought family responsibilities and the need to grasp his one opportunity, now or never. The 'now' proved untimely, and the resulting disasters undermined his strategy, but not his resolve and fortitude. He fell back within his natural reserve, and failed to take the limited opportunities he had to make his passage in peace. Encountering unforeseen opposition when he had pushed on optimistically beyond the point of no return, he had repeatedly to use force in self-defence, in strange contrast with the humane and conciliatory line of action he had always pursued before. Finally, under all the strain, suspicion overcame his judgement and his vision was constricted to the narrow line of the river going onwards to its distant end. He spurned the means of communicating with those through whose countries he must pass, and the final outcome was all but inevitable. It was truly the course of his life which prepared his own death for which, if Dr. Lawson remembered correctly, he had been ready ever since he had lowered his brother-in-law into his grave at Sansanding.

It would be a pity if this failure obscured his genuine achievements, especially on his first journey, above all his human understanding and his showing that between Africans and Europeans there is no difference in 'the genuine sympathies and characteristic feelings of our common nature'. His observation may sound trite, but wherever racism exists it has not yet been fully learnt. Superficial differences often set bounds to kith and kin narrower than the extent of the human race. Park's view implied that the needs of this common human nature make equal demands in all countries to be heard and met. Park had the intelligence and good sense, and was sufficiently free from preconceived theories and axes to grind, to be able to see humanity in Africa much more truly than many men, often cleverer and more original, who came after him.

There is a tailpiece to Park's story, in Hutchison's manuscript, which links it to our day:

'Later, the body of one of them was carried by the water to the town of Kanji, in the territory of the sultan of Wawa, and when the sultan of Wawa heard the news he buried it in his land. As for the other body, we saw not; perhaps it sank to the bottom of the water, but God knows best.

'This is a correct record of the account from the mouth of Sharif Ibrahim.'

There is no tradition of this burial – of who knows which member of the party – on Kainji island, from which, as we have seen, the inhabitants fled soon after Park's death to try to escape a pestilence. Less than twenty years ago, Kainji village on the west bank enjoyed as tranquil a rustic life as could be found anywhere. Now the village is no more, and only the southern tip of the island can be seen, carrying the main distribution centre for electric power from the massive dam built across the island and commissioned in 1969, to supply much of Nigeria. The impressive town of New Bussa stands some miles from the dam towards Wawa. A lake stretches up-river seventy miles to Yelwa, the modern headquarters of Yauri Emirate, submerging both the Bussa of Park's time and a more recent town. All the islands and rapids of the lower Niger are also covered; only one rapid is left, at Awuru, with a by-pass canal, below the dam. Those further back, down which Park had come earlier, are unaffected, but in the area between Yelwa and Bussa all the old landmarks have gone. Only with a chart could one now discover where Mungo Park's journey on earth and water ended.

APPENDIX I

Sources of information about Mungo Park's life

———— ℞ ————

Lewis Grassic Gibbon's biography (1934) included some general and cryptic observations, and Peter Brent's *Black Nile* (1977) has a bibliography, but otherwise no indications of source materials have previously been given. Naturally, as Gibbon said, the *Travels* and the *Journal* remain the major sources. The two were combined in the second edition of 1815, together with the Biographical Memoir by John Whishaw,* some Addenda to it, and some Appendices written or collected by him, also Isaaco's and Amadi Fatouma's Journals, and finally Major Rennell's Geographical Illustrations of 1798.

From the Colonial Office Whishaw obtained the originals of the documents relating to the second journey.[1] He also had some letters and other papers from Park's family, Banks, Dickson, and Sir Walter Scott. My efforts to locate these papers, which have never been alluded to since Whishaw used them, have been unsuccessful. The Arabic manuscripts of Isaaco's and Amadi Fatouma's Journals have also disappeared.[2] Whishaw inquired for any remaining 'fragments' relating to the first journey, but he was rebuffed by Park's brothers, and Dickson told him that manuscript notes left at his house had been mislaid or destroyed.[3]

Whishaw's editing, however, shows every sign of care, and this is borne out by available copies of some letters he quoted, and more especially of the English translation of Amadi's Journal and the concluding part of Isaaco's, copied direct from the Freetown, Sierra Leone, office in October 1812 by Lieutenant Sibbald, R.N.[a]

Lord Liverpool, Colonial Secretary when Isaaco's Journal was received, for some reason selected the anti-slavery African Institution to publish Park's *Journal*. The Committee thought that the Government might wish to omit

---

* John Whishaw (1763–1840) was a barrister and a Commissioner for Auditing the Public Accounts. He was a friend of Wilberforce and Sir Samuel Romilly. He became a Director of the African Institution in 1813; soon afterwards he took up the editing of Park's *Journal* after Zachary Macaulay and the Secretary, Thomas Harrison, had failed to make progress, He was elected a Fellow of the Royal Society in 1815, and later became a Fellow of the Geographical Society, successor to the African Association, founded in 1830.[6]

some parts,[4] but after reading it Wilberforce advised that he saw nothing that need be suppressed.[5] In the absence of the original manuscripts, we can take it that we probably have a complete edition of the official documents, and of most but not all of the private letters that Whishaw had.

Whishaw himself knew the limitations of his work, which were due to the circumstances of publication. Lord Liverpool had ignored those who might have been thought to have a prior claim: Sir Joseph Banks, on behalf of the African Association, and also the Park family. Both had plans for publication, the latter having received an offer of £1,000 from an Edinburgh publisher.[7] (They eventually received more.) Banks retired in dudgeon after Liverpool's successor, Lord Bathurst, believing that concurrent publications would serve no useful purpose, asked him in October 1812 to come to an arrangement with the African Institution.[8] When Alexander Park approached him in June 1813, Banks replied stiffly, telling him of the Government's decision: '. . . disappointed as I have been in my attempt to serve the Family by the interference of a set of Gentlemen with whom I have little acquaintance . . .,' he nevertheless wrote highly of Wilberforce and referred Alexander to him.[a]

The family and Banks were therefore suspicious, first whether the greatest financial benefit would be secured for the family, and secondly whether material might not be used for controversial ends. Banks was soon corresponding amicably with Whishaw over financial matters, but only after Whishaw sought ducal intercession in September 1814 did Banks give him papers and general help, which Whishaw acknowledged.[a] It was probably Banks who sponsored him for membership of the Royal Society in 1815.

The Park family's suspicions seem never to have been entirely overcome. Adam Park, in a letter to Alexander, advocated co-operating with Whishaw to a limited extent, but only 'Now that it is perhaps not in our powers to prevent this measure . . .', and he suspected an attempt to probe Mungo's opinions on the slave trade.[a] The materials Whishaw obtained from this source were indeed 'slight and scanty',[a] and most personal letters were withheld from him. Some simple facts, dates, etc., he was given were incorrect.

H.B.'s *Life* of 1835 has considerable additional material, obtained from relatives and friends, about Park's life in Scotland, and there are some new details in the anonymous 1838 *Life and Travels* published by Chambers, of Peebles origin. Of the later biographies, few have anything new. Joseph Thomson (1890), whose book is marred mainly by bowdlerizing, political and otherwise, quoted some previously unpublished letters and some details supplied by the Andersons at Selkirk. Lewis Grassic Gibbon (1934) saw an interesting private collection from which he was not allowed to quote, but the practised eye can detect a few points deriving from unidentified sources, as distinct from his own insertions to fill gaps or to colour his portrait of Park. Much of his critique boils down to his dislike of religion and of an eighteenth-century style. Stephen Gwynn's straightforward and balanced book (1934) also has a little new material, as does Peter Brent's *Black Nile* (1977).

Also available are the scattered Banks papers, especially the Dawson Turner copies in the British Museum of Natural History, the British Library, Selkirk Public Library (where a significant collection of Banks's and Whishaw's letters was found inside a fine copy of the *Travels* by Mr. J.B.Baxter in 1971, when he was preparing for the bicentenary celebrations), the Sutro Papers, and the Historical Records of New South Wales. The African Association's records are an invaluable supplement, and Rennell's various writings show how the geographical problems appeared at the time.

Light is thrown on Park's personal life and background by documents in Register House, Edinburgh, the National Library of Scotland, Selkirk Public Library, the Selkirkshire Antiquarian Society (possibly this is the collection Gibbon saw), and in private hands. The Anderson family's collection seems to have been divided up, and some of it may have been lost. Craig Brown's *History of Selkirkshire* and the *Proceedings of the Berwickshire Naturalists Club* also help. The University of Edinburgh records tell us something of Park's university career. Ships' logs in the National Maritime Museum and the East India Company papers throw light on his voyages.

The background to the 1805 expedition can now be enlarged from the Camden Papers and the Selkirk Public Library collection and from more thorough use of the Public Record Office papers. Park's diary of the 1805 voyage to the Gambia is in the British Library.

These and other sources are acknowledged in the notes on each chapter. The sources of information on the last stages of his 1805–6 journey are discussed in Chapter XXVII, and the accounts of his death are gathered together in Appendix III.

Park's final expedition

Membership and after-effects

———— ⧼⧽ ————

MEMBERS

The following were the members of the expedition. All of the dates from 1 May 1805 onwards should probably be read as one day later, as explained in Chapter XXV.

NAME	LAST HEARD OF
Officers	
(Captain) Mungo Park	Died at Bussa early 1806.
(Lieutenant) Alexander Anderson	Died of dysentery at Sansanding, 28 October 1805.
Lieutenant John Martyn, R.A.C.	Died at Bussa early 1806.
George Scott (Draftsman)	Died at Koomikoomi of fever, 15 August 1805.
Other Ranks of the Royal African Corps, Seamen, and Carpenters	
Private (unnamed)	Died at Kaiai between 22 and 26 April 1805.
Private John Walters	Died following epileptic fit, after Kussai, 15 May 1805.
James (Carpenter)	Died of dysentery, 8 June 1805
Private Hinton	} Left behind, 17 June.
Private Sparks	
Private Rowe	Left behind, 20 June.
William Roberts, Carpenter	Left behind, 22 June.
Private J.Cartwright	Drowned in the river Senegal (Ba Fing), 27 June.
Private Shaddy Walter	Died, 28 June.
Private Baron	Lost, 28 June.
Private Bloore	Lost, 29 June.
Private Roger M'Millan	Died of fever, 2 July.
Private J.Bowden	Failed to turn up, 18 July.
Private Francis Beedle	Died of fever, 21 July.

NAME	LAST HEARD OF
Corporal Powal	Died of fever at Bangassi, 26 July.
Private M'Inelli	
Private Frair	
Private Thomson	Left behind at Bangassi, 27 July.
Private Hercules	
James Trott, Carpenter	
Private William Allen	Left behind, 30 July.
Private William Hall	Failed to turn up, 5 August.
Private Lawrence Cahill	
William Cox, Seaman	Failed to turn up, 6 August.
Private Michael May	Died, 9 August.
William Ashton or Alston, Seaman	
Private Bird	Failed to turn up, 11 August.
Private Dickinson	Failed to turn up, 12 August.
Private Jonas Watkins	Died at Koomikoomi, 14 August.
Sergeant M'Keil or M'Keal	
Private Purvey	Failed to turn up at Bamako,
Private Samuel Hill	19 August.
*Private Thomas Dyer	Died of fever at Maraboo, 6 September.
Private Seed	Died at Samee, one of fever, the
Private Barber	other of dysentery, 24 September.
Private Marshall	Died at Sansanding, one of fever,
*Private W.Garland	the other of dysentery, 2 October.
Private Joseph Mills	Died from wound in ankle (?), at Sansanding, early November.
Private Thomas Higgins	Reported sick by Martyn; probably mad on leaving Sansanding, and died after Timbuktu.
Private Abraham Bolton	Died either on the way to, or at,
Private John Connor	Bussa.

African Helpers

Isaaco	Reported by Major W.Gray in the Khasso area near the Senegal, 1820.
Isaaco's wife and child, and an unstated number of 'Isaaco's people'	At Sannanba, 1810.

*One of those listed from Dyer down to Garland must have been the fourth carpenter.

NAME	LAST HEARD OF
Amadi Fatouma	Seen by Isaaco at Sansanding, 1810.
Three others in the boat,	Two killed at Bussa? One captured
described by Amadi as slaves	and kept at Yauri, or two at Bussa?

AFTER THE EXPEDITION

MUNGO PARK'S FAMILY

The effects on Park's family took a long time to work themselves out. James Dickson had to apply in April 1806 for the first £1,000 promised by the Government to Mrs. Allison Park and due over a year earlier.[2] He applied again in December 1807 for the £3,000 payable if Park was not heard of by that July.[1] The moneys were duly paid.[2]

Park's will was proved in the Prerogative Court of Canterbury on 14 December 1812, but assessed for legacy duty at 1% in 1825, possibly because of complications over a separate trust fund set up in 1816 for his children with the proceeds of his *Journal*; this would have ended in 1825 as the last of the children came of age. The assessment showed net assets amounting to £2,079 15s 7d., of which £331 12s 4d. was due to his wife on the unexpired portion of their marriage settlement.[a]

Alexander Park wrote to Banks in 1813 that the family found that 'with all their economy in the management of their affairs, they much doubt it will not be in their Power to give them a liberal education without applying to Government for assistance . . .'[3] Mrs. Park had apparently continued to live with the children at Foulshiels, and could hardly have used up all of the £4,000 from Government and her other assets so soon. Possibly Alexander had induced her to invest some, as he did, in a bank which collapsed in 1814. He died on 1 June 1814, at Selkirk, insolvent, and his farmer brother Archibald was bankrupted.[4] Sir Walter Scott got Archibald a post in the Customs Department at Tobermory, Isle of Mull, where he died on 9 August 1820.[5] Adam died at Gravesend in 1846. The eldest sister Margaret probably died at Croydon before 1837 when the civil registers begin, her husband James Dickson having died there in 1822. The second sister, Mrs. Jean Thomson, lived until 1851, the same year in which John died at Foulshiels; he had continued as tenant of the farm after his mother died on 28 March 1817.[6] The youngest sister Isobel was married three times: to John Anderson in 1807 (died 1809), to Archibald Buchanan of Glasgow in 1812 (who supplied some of Whishaw's information, including the memorandum on Park's views on slavery), and later to a Mr. Dalgleish of Glasgow.[7]

Allison died in 1840 in Edinburgh, after living there, it seems in some want, since about 1820.[5] The eldest son Mungo, who had qualified as a surgeon, after being educated out of his share of the trust fund,[5] died at the age of twenty-three in Trichinopoly, Madras, shortly after arriving in India in 1823.

The second son, Thomas, studied science at Edinburgh University and then became a naval lieutenant. Taking three years' leave of absence, he had himself landed at Accra from a ship bound for the Pacific in June 1827, so as to search for news of his father. He told his mother of his plans only after his arrival there. He spent three months preparing himself, learning the Ashanti language and making a trial excursion of fifty miles into the interior, observing the local geology and writing about it to his former Professor, Robert Jameson. He dismayed the small European community by resolutely separating himself from it and living in the African town. He was said to have tried to harden himself by taking long walks scantily clad in the heat of the day, and to have anointed his head and body with clay and oil. According to one account, he took a local wife.

Thomas finally set off in September, and probably died, aged twenty-four, on 31 October 1827 at Yansong, said to be 140 miles inland. The accounts of his death are almost as varied as those of his father's. Some attributed it to illness brought on by his privations (with rather an air of 'We told you so'). Most involve some combination of a tree and a festival. In two stories he was said to have been poisoned for having climbed a sacred tree to watch the festival, in one version because he ignored warnings against so doing, in the other despite his having been given permission by all concerned, including the 'fetish priests'. More probably, as in the fullest account, it was an ordinary tree he climbed in order to watch the festival of new yams, and he injured himself badly in a fall when coming down after a long day in the hot sun, having unwisely tried to quench his thirst with palm wine. All of his property was sent down to Accra and handed over to the British authorities, but for one item. When Richard Lander arrived back from Sokoto at Badagry, 100 miles east along the coast, on 21 November, he learnt of Thomas Park's death through their shirts getting mixed up in the laundry![8]

The daughter Elizabeth married a Welsh landed proprietor called Meredith, but by 1934 no descendants of hers were traceable.[9] The last son, Archibald, born after his father had left home for the last time, became a colonel in the Indian Army and lived until 1867, and it is through him that the Park line and name have continued.

Mungo Park is commemorated by plaques on the partly restored shell of Foulshiels, and on his house and the site of his surgery at Peebles, by a statue in Selkirk, and by monuments at the site of Pisania in the Gambia and on Jebba Island, Nigeria. The monument in Selkirk is at one end of the High Street, facing the Andersons' house and Lawson's Manse. A meeting to adopt measures for its erection was called on 20 December 1841, but it was not until 2 March 1859 that it was formally inaugurated. It was improved years later by the addition round the base of sculptures by Thomas Clapperton of Galashiels.[a]

Colonel J. Willcocks, acting in Lugard's absence as Commandant, West African Frontier Force in Borgu, proposed erecting a monument at Bussa in 1898, but the Colonial Office found the proposal premature, as the area was not yet under British rule.[10] In 1911 a proposal was made to erect a monument at Forcados on the coast, a place quite unconnected with Park or even with the Landers' journey in 1830. After the 1914–18 War the Governor, Sir Hugh Clifford, revived the proposal for a monument, but suggested Jebba Island in the Niger, then the most accessible site near to Bussa. About £1,000 was raised by public subscription and the obelisk, commemorating both Mungo Park and Richard Lander, was completed in 1929. It was built by the Public Works Department to a design donated by Messrs. Thomas and Edge.[11]

ALEXANDER ANDERSON

Little is known about him except what is recorded in Park's *Journal*, in two letters, quoted in the text, from Park to his father, and his own letter to his father from Kaiai in April 1805. Apparently he was unmarried. After his death at the age of 33, £1,000 was paid to his father, who died in 1816. Four of the latter's sons practised as surgeons: Alexander, John, Andrew, and Thomas. The last-named took over his father's practice, became a Burgess of Selkirk in 1808,[a] and died at Selkirk in 1850, having been much loved locally. He also had surgeon sons, one being Dr. Henry Scott Anderson, at one time Provost of Selkirk, who died in 1890.

LIEUTENANT JOHN MARTYN

His family apparently came from Castlebar, Co. Mayo, Ireland. His sister, Sarah McAlpine, unsuccessfully petitioned the Colonial Office in 1808 asking for back pay and sale of his commission.[c] In 1810 a further claim was made.[b] As late as December 1814 his brother, Robert Martyn, a colonel in the Austrian Army, wrote to Banks asking for his help. John's will had left his property to his brother Andrew, but Andrew in turn had died in 1808, leaving it to Mrs. McAlpine, who Robert said was rich, while a sister, Dimney, was unprovided for. Banks judiciously regretted he could not help.[12] Colonel Martyn and a brother petitioned the House of Commons, and a memorandum of 1808 was then turned up in the Colonial Office, authorizing the issue of John's pay up to August 1807 to his legal representative.[c] He was to receive double pay whilst with Park.

GEORGE SCOTT

Scott was born 10 October 1779, the son of William Scott, tenant in Singlee near Selkirk, and his wife Margaret.[13] Other known facts about him are given in the text; he was aged twenty-five when he died. His brother appealed to the Colonial Office for assistance in 1808.[c] In 1810 another approach was made, and on consulting Cooke, then at the Foreign Office, it was found that double a lieutenant's pay had been agreed upon.[c]

OTHER RANKS OF THE ROYAL AFRICAN CORPS, SEAMEN, AND CARPENTERS

These unfortunate men were not of a sort to leave many records, except possibly in Courts Martial or Civil. Nothing is known of them prior to the expedition, apart from a few comments on some of them in the *Journal*. None of those left behind on the journey was ever heard of again. Mrs. Cox obtained £40 'as of the Royal Bounty' in 1810.[b] I hope the other widows obtained something also.

ISAACO

He was a trader, probably including slave-dealing, operating between his home on the Gambia and the upper Niger. There is no evidence that he ever went farther east than Sansanding. He has been described as a 'priest', but the only authority for this seems to be Maxwell's 1810 despatch to the Colonial Office.[c] Islam has no priests as such, but he may have been a local religious leader and teacher.

After delivering Park's *Journal* to Dean at Kaiai or Ainsley at Pisania in 1806 he was next reported early in 1810 on the Senegal coast. Maxwell seized the opportunity to send him up the Gambia and then inland in search of news of Park. He went with some of his family and an entourage. It is hard to trace his route in detail, but it certainly took him through Khasso and Kaarta and then down to the Niger at Nyamina. His family had been forced to move towards the coast by a Bambara (probably Kaarta) invasion. He found some of them not long after starting out, apparently in either Wuli or Bondu, including his mother who, however, had moved *inland* from her earlier home at Tabajang on the Gambia. At Daamana near Fort St. Joseph, one wife's relatives objected to her travelling with him, and they were divorced. He collected another wife and a sister he had left behind on (returning from?) his journey with Park over four years earlier, at Sannanba not long before he came to the Niger. Although a Muslim, he travelled with some live hogs in his baggage, and two were given to King Dacha (Dha) of Segu, a son of Mansong, as part of his present from Maxwell.

During his journey Isaaco suffered from thefts, defecting guides, and a prolonged detention with ominous signs of coming pillage or death, from Tiguin-Coro, the Fama of Kaarta, but he successfully played on the King's fear of Segu. Such things could happen to a well-known African trader as well as to a lone stranger like Park.

Isaaco's Journal has often – starting with Whishaw – been regarded as a tedious and unnecessary exercise, but it has its own interest. It was kept on Maxwell's express instruction, '... should the immediate objects of the voyage unfortunately not succeed, that it may not be altogether useless'. Maxwell also said, 'I have every reason to be satisfied with the Character of the Person whom I have employed. He is well acquainted with the Country, and has engaged to proceed if necessary to Tombuctoo and Katsina ...'ᶜ Isaaco was paid $700 or £175 through Dr. Heddle at Gorée; his receipt is in the British Library.[14]

Isaaco said that the Fama of Segu was so distressed on hearing from him of Park's death that he sent an army to avenge it. Finding that the place where Park had died was a very long way off, the army stopped beyond Timbuktu, and the Fama ordered them to exact vengeance instead from the nearest Fulani, those in Masina. The Segu rulers seem to have been adept at such improvisation of motives; probably they wanted to chastise the Fulani any-way.

Isaaco sent a man to Yauri, who purloined Park's sword-belt which had been made into a horse girth, but he does not seem to have brought back any information. This exploit took eight months, which Isaaco presumably used profitably in trading.

Major Peddie, originally in charge of the next West African expedition, contacted Isaaco and expected him in Senegal in 1816.[15] Then Peddie died and the expedition made several unsuccessful starts. When it eventually pene-trated to Bondu, the new leader, Major Gray, encountered Isaaco at Baquelle on the river Senegal in June 1819. He volunteered to go ahead of Gray and find some of his party. Gray noted that he was lame and lent him a horse; perhaps this lameness dated from the crocodile's attack when he was with Park. They parted after some time but met again in April 1820. Gray be-lieved Isaaco would have served him well but decided against employing him because of one drawback – at the time he was *persona non grata* with the kings of both Kaarta and Segu, and he was hoping to use Gray to be restored to favour.[16]

Isaaco seems to have attracted improbable footnotes. Gray has one saying, 'Properly called Siacco.' (His name would now be written Isiyaku.) James Jackson has another in his book, 'Isaaco was a Jew, not a Moor'! In fact he was a Serahuli.[17]

AMADI FATOUMA

Little is known of Amadi Fatouma beyond what is shown in his account of the voyage down the Niger. Park did not mention him in the *Journal* he sent back from Sansanding, and referred to him only in his last letter to Banks, the gist of which is given in Chapter XXVI. He was engaged, on Isaaco's recommendation, very shortly before the party set off from Sansanding. Park said in the letter: 'I have as yet had only two conversations with my guide, and they were chiefly occupied in adjusting money matters; but I have no doubt that I shall find him a very useful fellow traveller.' Even his name would be unknown if Isaaco had not met him again.

Isaaco found him at Madina, a village a few miles down-stream from Sansanding, on 3 October 1810. 'I sent for him; he came immediately. I demanded of him a faithful account of what had happened to Mr. Park. On seeing me, and hearing me mention Mr. Park, he began to weep; and his first words were, "They are all dead." I said, "I am come to see after you, and intended to look every way for you, to know the truth from your own mouth, how they died." He said that they were lost for ever, and it was useless to make any further enquiry after them; for to look after what was irrecoverably lost, was losing time to no purpose.'

Isaaco then returned to Sansanding and, as he instructed, Amadi went to him there the next day to tell him what he knew concerning Park; then they parted.

Eight months later, after the sword-belt had been brought from Yauri, Isaaco had to explain to the King why he had no further reason to stay at Segu, having learnt all he could about Park's death. In his explanation he said, 'Amadi fatouma being a good, honest, and upright man, I had placed him with Mr. Park; what he related to me being on his oath, having no interest, nor any hopes of reward whatsoever; ... being certain of the truth of what he had said, ... all these reasons induced me to proceed no farther.'

That was the latest information recorded about Amadi, apart from Campbell's, Duncan's, and Toutée's dubious stories (see Appendix III, Items 6, 29, and 30).

Stories of Mungo Park at Yauri
and of his death at Bussa

———— ∞ ————

These are given in the chronological order in which they were reported. The Bowdich, Denham, Clapperton, and Lander narratives are available in reasonably accessible published sources, so they are only summarized here; the background to their writings is given in Chapter XXVII.

THE CHARLESTON COURIER

1. From Charleston, South Carolina, U.S.A., 1 July 1806:
'MUNGO PARK – We are sorry to communicate to our readers, the death of this enterprising and indefatigable traveller . . . they had penetrated about 1500 miles into the interior to a place called Sego, which MR. PARK had described in his former Book of Travels. – The number of his attendants had been reduced by sickness and death to three, exclusive of himself; – the King of this place, after carrying him into every part of the city, which is walled in and considered the largest in Africa, and shewing him every curiosity which it afforded, had cruelly and brutally murdered him, together with his attendants. This intelligence is furnished us by a gentleman recently from the Rio Pongus, who received the information from traders from the interior country, and on whom reliance might be placed.'

THE TIMES

2. 10 July 1806: 'A letter, it is said, has been received from the River Gambia, stating, that Mr. MUNGO PARK, the traveller, and his retinue (two or three excepted) have been murdered by the natives in the interior of the Country. This story is stated to have been verified by the arrival of the persons who escaped the massacre, at Widah.'

Note: On 1 September 1806 *The Times* quoted a summary of the Charleston report. On 20 January 1807 Park's death at Segu was reasserted; on 12 January 1808, and on 19 May, 14 June, and 8 November 1810 reports of his being still alive were published; on 15 October 1811 it was said that he was believed to be dead, but on 4 April 1812 that he was possibly still alive. On 13 August 1812 an inaccurate account of Maxwell's communication was published, and on 3 September the last part of Amadi Fatouma's Journal was quoted. On 20 May 1816 a slight possibility of Park's being alive, based on Robert Adams's encounter with a slave woman at Wednoon (Wadi Nun) in Morocco, was inserted.

JOHN HILL

3. A correspondent of the British and Foreign Bible Society in West Africa (quoted by permission of Miss K.J.Cann, Archivist). In a letter from Gorée on 9 August 1808, he merely repeated the 'uniform belief' that Park had been murdered. On 28 September 1809, writing from Sierra Leone, he referred to reports from the Senegal, to which he was not inclined to give much credence:

'They state, however, that he had actually passed Jenne in his boat with Lieut. Martyn, & a Private alive & with him, when the King of Jenne sent a party after them with orders to drown them in the Joliba.'

ALEXANDER COURT

4. British merchant at Mogador, Morocco, from 1805, in touch with traders going to Timbuktu. Banks quoted him (C.O. 2/2, 3 October 1811) as saying:

'Mr. Park and his Company with the exception of one Black were murthered by the Foulbers, a Race of Black Mahometans living towards the Country of Musky or Moses, and near Henbara [probably Hombori, 130 miles south-east of Timbuktu] which is situate between Tombuctoo and Houssa and not very distant from the third cataract on the Niger ...'

AMADI FATOUMA AND ISAACO

5. Most of Amadi's account has been quoted in the text. The end, from when the Yauri army took up position on a high rock in the river at Bussa, reads as follows:

'Mr. Park came there after the army had posted itself; he nevertheless attempted to pass. The people began to attack him, throwing lances, pikes, arrows and stones. Mr. Park defended himself for a long time; two of his slaves at the stern of the canoe were killed; they threw every thing they had in the canoe into the river, and kept firing; but being overpowered by numbers and fatigue, and unable to keep up the canoe against the current, and no probability of escaping, Mr. Park took hold of one of the white men, and jumped into the water; Martyn did the same, and they were drowned in the stream in attempting to escape. The only slave remaining in the boat, seeing the natives persist in throwing weapons at the canoe without ceasing, stood up and said to them, "Stop throwing now, you see nothing in the canoe, and nobody but myself, therefore cease. Take me and the canoe, but don't kill me." They took possession of the canoe and the man, and carried them to the King.'

Isaaco said his wife and sister, when found at Sannanba in 1810, assured him 'that they had seen Alhagi Biraim who told them that Mr. Park was dead and that he saw the canoe in which he died in the country of Haoussa; to which country he, Alhagi, had been, and to the place where Mr. Park died.' Isaaco added that the relations of several travellers who had passed the same country agreed with Amadi's account.

In 1813 Lieutenant-Governor MacCarthy of Senegal heard a similar story, but this attributed Park's death to the Moors. However, he attached as limited a credence to it as did his informant, an Ambassador from Kaarta (C.O. 267/36).

CAPTAIN THOMAS CAMPBELL

6. Leader of the expedition from the west coast after Major Peddie died until his own death in June 1817, when Major Gray took over. From a letter from Senegal, 20 May 1816 (N.L.S., MS. No. 2835, f. 175):

'When I was at Goree I was informed by a man brought from the Gambia, that Park was not dead or killed but was robbed by Amadou Fatouma of the greater part of his goods and obliged in consequence to leave the River, that Park should not have proceeded at the time he did as Mansong was then unwell, and the likelihood of the Crown being vacant or rather disputed, gives rise to great mischief and bloodshed in those Countries. That had Mansong lived he would have sent in search of Park and found him if in life or severely revenged his Death – It is needless to enlarge on such stories . . . There are I am told some of his Papers preserved in the Palaver House at Sansanding.'

THOMAS BOWDICH

7. At Kumasi in Ashanti in July 1817 Bowdich met a learned Moor from Timbuktu, who said he had seen three white men and some blacks suddenly appear in a vessel with masts at Bussa. They traded peacefully, and passed on and fended off attempts to warn them of sunken rocks. After striking these rocks they tried to swim and were drowned. Another Moor confirmed this.

8. Hutchison stayed in Kumasi after Bowdich left and brought back an Arabic manuscript. Both Appendix II to Bowdich's book and J.G.Jackson's *An Account of Timbuctoo and Housa* give two translations, by Abraham Salame, Arabic translator to the British Government, and by Jackson. A third, by Professor S.Lee of Cambridge University, is with the original manuscript in the British Library (Add. MSS. 18390). There are differences between the three. A new translation by Professor A.M.Al-Hajj, Bayero University, Kano, is used here by his kind permission. The first and last parts are quoted in the text. The middle portion reads:

'. . . And the sultan of Yauri asked them to come out and meet him, but they refused and proceeded to the land of Bussa, which was greater than that of the sultan of Yauri. Thence, while they were sitting majestically in the ship – as if they were the sovereigns of upper Kü.ḍ. – and shouting loudly to the people of Bussa, they came upon a huge rock and the ship was trapped. The men and women of Bussa gathered together with all kinds of weapons but the ship could not free itself from the rock. And the man in the ship killed his woman and threw all his belongings into the river through fear . . .'

HAGI (AL-HAJJ) MAHOMET ALIBALI

9. A Moroccan merchant, as reported by 'W.S.C.' who had met him on a Mediterranean voyage in 1820. He said he had lived for 25 years at Tim-buktu and as far as he could – with difficulty – recollect, the events described occurred about 1809 (from *Blackwood's Magazine*, 1821, pp. 158–9):

'. . . I asked him whether he had ever heard of any Christians visiting Tim-buctoo? He said that he did recollect of a boat (*una barca*) manned by Christians, advancing towards Timbuctoo by the river. The king, hearing of its approach, sent a canoe to inquire regarding their object, and to demand duties. A dispute ensued, in which the Christians fired on the Timbuctons, killing one and obliging the others to retire, who however did so only to await an opportunity of revenge. The Christians then rowed to the shore, at the foot of a high mountain, and disembarked there, leaving the boat un-guarded. The tide falling soon after, the boat was left ashore.

'The Timbuctons thought this a good opportunity for revenge, and climb-ing up the mountain, they rolled large stones upon the boat, leaving it totally useless.

'In this helpless predicament, the Christians wandered for some time among the mountains in the greatest distress. Unfortunately, however, their visit, the catastrophe, and their presence, united in exciting the imaginary fears of the Timbuctons. The king found it necessary to call a council, in order to consider the most effectual means of preventing those consequences which these fears had for their object. The general opinion there was, that they were spies, and that, if allowed to escape, they would, in all probability, re-turn with an army to take possession of the country, and inflict some dreadful calamity upon the inhabitants. Under this impression, it was resolved, that they should be immediately taken and put to death; a resolution which was carried into effect. The merchant drawing the side of his hand across his throat, signified what had been the end of these unfortunate adventurers . . .'

JOSEPH DUPUIS

10. Visited Ashanti on an official visit for the British Government in early 1820. From his *Journal of a Residence in Ashantee*, London, 1824, Part II, pp. CIX–CX:

'. . . every sheikh of a tribe looks either for a present or a visit by which he may confer the sacred rights of hospitality, and receive the stranger's acknowledgments. Without these formalities it is by no means safe to pass from one district to another, unless the caravan is of sufficient magnitude to afford protection to itself. I cannot help thinking that the misfortune which befel Mungo Park was owing to the neglect of these indispensable precautions ...' (Dupuis then went over Park's journey to Yauri, using Amadi Fatouma's account.) 'The story of Mr. Park's death was no secret with any of the Moslems in Coomassy, and it happened precisely as Mr. Bowdich has related, which, in point of fact, agrees with the journal of Isaaco. The capital of Youry is distant from the river a short day's journey, and it is said, that when the king sent provisions to the canoe, he entreated by message that the white chief visit him on shore, and he would meet him near the waterside, an intention which that sovereign put in practice, but was irritated at finding the canoe would not wait, and had already gained an offing from the port; for Park, anxious, no doubt, for the prosecution of the voyage, quitted his anchorage without thinking it incumbent on him to pay his respects to the king, although the public curiosity or suspicion was excited by his detention two days on the river in gleaning information of Amadi Fatouma. It is the opinion of the Moslems, that no present was sent in return for the provisions, and if so, the conjecture of Park's editor, that they were withheld from the king by the chief, is well founded. When the king sent his army to Boussa, the Moslems say it was done to bring the white men back by force, but their destruction was never meditated; and the king, when the catastrophe was related to him, punished his officer with fine and imprisonment.'

MAJOR DIXON DENHAM

11. Leader of the Borno expedition from Tripoli in 1822–4. The account he heard from Abdel Gassam, son of a Fulani Chief of Jenne, has been quoted in Chapters XXVIII–XXX.

12. On 7 August 1824 Denham heard a tale of a man with a white beard who was said to have lived three years at 'Gusgey on the Quolla', having no means to go on, and he died there.

CAPTAIN HUGH CLAPPERTON
Nos. 13–15 relate to the 1822–4 Borno expedition.

13. Heard on 20 March 1824 from Mahomed Gomsoo, the Chief of the Arabs in Sokoto, who said (in summary) he was at Yauri when Park's party arrived – he appears to confuse Bussa and Yauri (probably a misunderstanding by Clapperton) – and that Park and his one companion would not wait for the Sultan of Yauri to visit them and give them a guide; they were assailed when the boat struck rocks and they jumped overboard; this was reported by a horseman *to* Yauri, where a book was in the Sultan's hands. On the same day

Caliph Bello told Clapperton that the boat caught on rocks when the water was low.

14. In a letter to Horton, Colonial Office, 6 June 1825 (C.O. 2/16 Part 2), Clapperton said:

'It may be some satisfaction to know, that I ascertained from Bello, beyond all doubt, that the late Mungo Park perished not by hostile attack, or intended attack of the natives, but by mere accident, owing to his ignorance of a ledge of Rocks, which crosses the Quorra and forms a great fall or Cataract, down which he was carried and his Boat was upset. The place I have marked on the Chart, from the information of Persons from Youri.' A note on the letter says no chart was enclosed.

15. From Appendix VIII to Clapperton's Journal (translation of a document in C.O. 2/16 Part 2, by Salame):

'Hence, be it known that some Christians came to the town of Youri, in the kingdom of Yaoor, and landed and purchased provisions, as onions and other things; and they sent a present to the King of Yaoor. The said king desired them to wait until he should send them a messenger, but they were frightened, and went away by the sea [river]. They arrived at the town called Bossa, or Boossa, and their ship rubbed [struck] upon a rock, and all of them perished in the river . . .

'And they agreed, or arranged among themselves, and swam in the sea [river] while the men, who were with [pursuing] them, appeared on the coast of the sea [bank of the river], and fell upon them till they went down [sank] in it.'

Nos. 16–22 are from the records of Clapperton's second expedition,
when he visited Bussa and nearby Wawa, and corresponded with Yauri

16. Wawa, 23 March 1826: Having previously heard various 'insubstantial accounts', he was now told by the 'Governor's headman' that there was no fight but that the white men drowned in trying to get ashore after their boat struck rocks. The people of Bussa who ate meat from the boat all died, 'because it was human flesh'. Three days later the headman said, '. . . the natives did shoot arrows at them but not until guns had been fired from the boat'. The next day the Governor 'related to me nearly the same story'.

17. (a) At Bussa, 31 March 1826, in a conversation with the Sultan:

'I next inquired of him after some white men who were lost in the river near this place twenty years ago. He seemed rather uneasy at this question, and I observed that he stammered in his speech. He assured me he had nothing belonging to them; that he was a little boy when the event happened. I said . . . that with his permission I would go and visit the spot where they were lost. He said no, I must not go; it was a very bad place . . . I then asked him if he would allow me to inquire of the old people in the town the particulars of the affair, as some of them must have seen it. He appeared very uneasy, gave me no answer, and I did not press him further.'

(b) Next day, at Bussa:

'Every one in fact appeared uneasy when I asked for information, and said it had happened before their remembrance, or that they did not see it. They pointed out the place where the boat struck, and the unfortunate crew perished. Even this was done with caution, and as if stealth; though, in every thing unconnected with that affair, they were most ready to give me what information I asked; and never in my life have I been treated with more hospitality or kindness.'

18. A letter received by Clapperton from the Sultan of Yauri on 14 May 1826 said, '. . . that not the least injury was done to him at Youri, or by the people of that country; that the people of Boussa had killed them . . .', the white men jumping overboard and the blacks being killed in the boat.

19. At Koolfu, in Nupe country east of the Niger, on 17 June 1826, a man gave Clapperton an eye-witness account, which he thought the most correct story he had then heard. The Sultan of Bussa was said to have taken them for the advance guard of a Fulani army and called his people from neighbouring towns to attack them. There were two white men and two blacks. Those who ate meat from the boat died.

20. Appendix II to Clapperton's Journal contains an account copied in Arabic from the Sokoto records, translated by Salame, which was referred to in the text above. It was roughly correct about their direction of approach to the Niger and their losses, and it ended:

'They proceeded towards the east till they arrived at Boussa; but the inhabitants fought and killed them, and their ship is to this moment there. This is the substance and truth of the case.'

21. In the Introduction to the Journal there is the translation of an Arabic document from 'The Sharif of Bokhary', possibly the 'Bakkanee' where Hornemann died. It says there were two freemen and two slaves; that the event happened in the month of Rajab [in 1806, September–October]; that the boat 'came to a narrow place or creek, into which they pushed it, and remained there three days; but the people of Boossy, having observed them, assembled and went and fought them for three days'. After throwing their goods overboard, the white men jumped into the river and drowned.

22. Also in the Introduction are translations of some Arabic letters to and from Clapperton. To 'The Lord of Boossy' he referred to 'his brethren, who were slain by the people of your country'. To 'The Lord of Yaoury' he referred to 'the Christians who were seized by the people of Boossy'. The reply to this said he should inquire at 'Boossy' for 'the cause of the destruction of

the ship and your friends (and) what happened between them of evil'. The writer knew nothing of the cause. Another letter (the addressee's name is illegible) said, 'I have written to the Lord of Boossy about the Christian book, whose owner was destroyed by the inhabitants.'

RICHARD LANDER

23. Returning after Clapperton's death, on 3 September 1827 Lander was told by the Chief of Wawa that they had not thought white men were good when Park and his followers were drowned at Bussa. The same day a mallam claimed to have seen three white men at Yauri and to have accompanied the leader and one other three times to visit the Sultan, to whom they gave a valuable present. They had arrived in Ramadan (April). They refused the Sultan's advice to proceed by land; when he heard of their death he was much affected, but was powerless to punish those responsible. A pestilence swept off the king and many people at Bussa; this was attributed to a judgement of the white men's God.

24. In his own book, *Records of Captain Clapperton's Last Expedition to Africa*, Vol.I, pp.145–9, Lander referred to the 'shame' displayed at Bussa over the events, and then gave his own reconstruction of them, largely based on Items 19 and 23. The main part of this is quoted in the text.

RICHARD AND JOHN LANDER

25. On 20 June 1830 the King of Bussa referred to 'the deplorable event' which had happened when he was a very little boy.

26. At Yauri, on 27 June 1830, with the water low, they were told it was about the same time of year that Park arrived. His pilot was paid off and he returned to his own country. Park had a 'companion and three white boys', and several other men chained into the canoe. 'When the accident happened at Boossa by which they lost their lives, it is said they preferred being drowned, to avoid, as they imagined, a more dreadful death.'

27. Next day the chief of the Arabs and 'Prime Minister to the Sultan' told them Park had remained in his canoe and sent a messenger to Yauri with a present which was reciprocated.

28. The Landers' questions to the Sultan of Yauri about the book and papers he had told Clapperton he had, brought emphatic disclaimers, on 29 June and 6 July 1830, of any connection with such things.

JOHN DUNCAN

29. From the *Journal of the Royal Geographical Society*, Vol.16 (1846), pp.157 et seq.:

'In consequence of information received from a Mohammedan priest respecting the murder of Park, I travelled to [Adofoodiah in Dahomey] ... I also met a Tripoli merchant I had seen at Egga when with the Niger expedition. Amadi Fatouma was, it appears, the principal [cause?] of Park's death. Having complained to the King or Chief of Yaouri that Park had discharged him without paying him his full wages, Park was interrogated upon the subject, and of course indignantly denied the charge; whereupon an attempt was made to detain the canoe, which was at the time moored to the bank by a piece of rope. Park, said my informant, cut off the hand of one of the people attempting to detain the canoe. This was the commencement of the affray, which ended in the traveller's death . . .'

(Duncan continued about a white man coming from Constantinople four years later in search of Park's papers. There is a fuller and slightly different version of this story in his book *Travels in Western Africa*, 1847.)

COMMANDANT G.J.TOUTÉE

30. Commandant Toutée sailed up the Niger to Say, well above Yauri, in 1895. In a letter quoted in his *Dahomey, Niger, Touareg* (Paris, 1897, pp. 267–8), whilst describing John Duncan as generally '*le plus cynique imposteur*', he supported Duncan's account of Park's death. His own boatman, who was well respected in the area, when at Yelwa in Yauri Emirate, '. . . ended by showing me the tree to which was attached the white traveller's boat when he was killed. Mungo Park's boat, cast off after his death, was indeed lost in the rapids of Bussa, but he was no longer in it when it capsized' (Author's translation).

Lieutenant E.A.L.Hourst, passing down-stream the next year, echoed Toutée's assertion, but not from any independent inquiries.

CAPTAIN E.A.LENFANT

31. Captain Lenfant said that on his visit to Bussa in 1901 he heard a legend that Park was assassinated by the Kamberi people on the orders of the King of Bussa, but the then king said he did not know about the matter. (*Le Niger – Voie Ouverte à notre Empire Africain*, Paris, 1903.)

MR. J.C.O.CLARKE

32. Mr. Clarke, District Officer (see Michael Crowder's book *Revolt at Bussa*), noted down the following story in a Bussa Divisional Office file in 1913, without comment:

'When Kisaran Dogo was "King" of Boussa, a white man came down the Niger in a canoe. He gave Kisaran Dogo a large coin. When Neda his daughter was about to marry he had the coin attached to a ring as a wedding gift for Neda. Neda did not accept the present, stating that she preferred slaves, which were given to her. Kisaran Dogo kept the ring, which has been worn by every Sarkin Boussa since that time. The white man (Mungo Park?)

stayed a few days at Boussa and then started down the Niger; the same day his canoe was capsized in the rapids of Bubarro between Malali and Garafini. It is said that when the next day broke night immediately came on again. Ex-Alkali Lowal of Yelwa was at that time eight years old, so this would be 70 or 80 years ago.'

There is a marginal note against the penultimate sentence, '*Aka yi dere biu*', the Hausa for 'there were two nights'.

Note: The Governor of Nigeria, Sir Hugh Clifford, communicated this to the Secretary of State for the Colonies in 1920, together with information he had received from the Astronomer Royal, that there had been a large partial eclipse of the sun at Bussa, just before sunset on 16 June 1806, and a total eclipse visible at or near Bussa at noon on 29 November 1807, neither of which fitted the story well. Clifford said he had caused further inquiries to be made but could not obtain any further information. Published in the *Geographical Journal*, Vol.LVII, 1921, pp.130–32.

DR. CAMERON BLAIR

33. Dr. Cameron Blair wrote in the *Geographical Journal*, Vol.LXXV, 1930, pp.95–6, in reaction to a passing suggestion that local hostility had caused Park's death:

'In July 1901 I was quartered on Jebba Island with the 1st. Bn. Northern Nigeria Regiment. At that time there were living at Jebba two aged natives who gave a vivid account of Park's end, as related to them by their respective fathers, who had been actual witnesses of it. These two old men were most indignant at the belief current among the Europeans that Park's end had been due to the hostility of the natives. Their account of the affair was like this; News got about that a white man in a canoe was coming down the river towards Boussa; the natives knew that he was a stranger who was probably unaware of the existence of the rapids and of the consequent danger awaiting him thereat; they therefore turned out (some of them mounted) and made their way up the river-bank until they met the canoe; they signalled him to halt, but he, mistaking their friendly signals for hostile ones, pushed on and met his death by drowning in the rapids. Their tale sounded true, for remember the facts; We know Park had never passed up the river; had he done so, the natives were bound to have known; it was therefore evident that the white man was necessarily a stranger who was in great danger, and they proceeded to warn him of his danger. A stranger going downstream in a dugout canoe and ignorant of the peril he was approaching, as Park was, was going to practically certain death. Had the natives been hostile, they would have passively awaited his end in the rapids.'

Bibliography of principal works consulted

———— ✿ ————

I. PARK'S WORKS AND BIOGRAPHIES

Travels in the Interior Districts of Africa, Performed in the Years 1795, 1796 and 1797 by Mungo Park, with Geographical Illustrations of Africa by Major Rennell, London 1799.

The Journal of a Mission to the Interior of Africa in the Year 1805 by Mungo Park, with an Account of the Life of Mr. Park [by John Whishaw] (including Isaaco's and Amadi Fatouma's Journals and, in the second edition, some additional material with the Account of the Life) London 1815.

The Life of Mungo Park, by H.B., Edinburgh 1835.

Life and Travels of Mungo Park, anonymous, Chambers, Edinburgh 1838.

Life and Travels of Mungo Park, anonymous, Parker, London 1838.

The Life of Mungo Park, anonymous, Newman, London 1849.

Mungo Park and the Niger by J.Thomson, London 1890.

Mungo Park by T.B.Maclachlan, Edinburgh 1898.

Mungo Park by W.H.Hewitt, London 1923.

Niger: The Life of Mungo Park by Lewis Grassic Gibbon, Edinburgh 1934.

Mungo Park and the Quest of the Niger by Stephen Gywnn, Bristol 1934.

Black Nile by Peter Brent, London 1977.

II. BRITAIN

A History of the Scottish People 1690–1830 by T.C.Smout, London 1960.

The History of Scottish Education by James Scotland, London 1969.

History of Selkirkshire by T.Craig Brown, Edinburgh 1886.

The Life and Times of George Lawson, D.D. by Rev. John Macfarlane, Edinburgh 1862.

Life of Sir Walter Scott by John Gibson Lockhart, Edinburgh 1837–8.

The Reign of George III, 1760–1815 by J.S.Watson, Oxford 1960.

III. THE AFRICAN ASSOCIATION, AND PREVIOUS KNOWLEDGE OF AFRICA

Description de l'Afrique et de l'Espagne by Edrissi, Amsterdam, 1969 edition.

History and Description of Africa by Leo Africanus, Hakluyt Society edition, London 1896.

A New General Collection of Voyages and Travels by Thomas Astley, London 1745–7, reprinted Cass, London 1968 (includes major parts of Jobson, Moore, and the French writers about the Senegal basin).

An Account of Timbuctoo and Housa by James Grey Jackson, London 1820, reprinted Cass, London 1967.

Proceedings of the African Association, London 1810, reprinted Dawsons, London 1967. (Annual volumes published before 1810 also consulted.)

Records of the African Association, 1788–1831 by Robin Hallett, London 1964.

The Penetration of Africa to 1815 by Robin Hallett, London 1965.

Sir Joseph Banks – The Autocrat of the Philosophers by H.C.Cameron, London 1952.

The Life of Sir Joseph Banks by E.Smith, London and New York 1911.

The Banks Letters: A Calendar by W.R.Dawson, London 1958.

A History of the Gambia by J.M.Gray, Cambridge 1940.

The Golden Trade of the Moors by E.W.Bovill, London 1957; 2nd edn. 1968.

Image of Africa by P.D.Curtin, London 1965.

IV. FIRST AFRICAN JOURNEY

History of West Africa, 2 Vols., eds. J.F.A.Ajayi and Michael Crowder, London 1971 and 1974.

History of Islam in West Africa by J.Spencer Trimingham, London 1962.

Haut-Niger-Sénégal by M.Delafosse, Paris 1912.

Histoire des Bambara by Louis Tauxier, Paris 1942.

Saga of the Niger by Richard Owen, London 1961.

Mandingo Kingdoms of the Senegambia by Charlotte A.Quinn, London 1972.

V. AUSTRALIA

Sir Joseph Banks: His Relations with Australia by G.Mackaness, Sydney 1936.

Historical Records of New South Wales, Vols. III and IV, Sydney 1895–6.

The Fatal Impact by Alan Moorehead, London 1966.

VI. THE SLAVE TRADE

History of the Abolition of the African Slave Trade by Thomas Clarkson, London 1808.

Capitalism and Slavery by Eric Williams, 2nd edition, London 1964.

The British Anti-Slavery Movement by Sir Reginald Coupland, London 1933.

African Memoranda by Philip Beaver, London 1805.

VII. SECOND AFRICAN JOURNEY

Historical Records of the Royal African Corps by J.J.Crooks, Dublin 1925.

History of Sierra Leone by Christopher Fyfe, Oxford 1962.

Mission to Ashantee by Thomas Bowdich, London 1819.

The Journal of Friedrich Hornemann's Travels and The Letters of Alexander Gordon Laing edited by E.W.Bovill, Hakluyt Society edition, Cambridge 1964.

Travels in Western Africa by W. Gray and Staff-Surgeon Dochard, London 1825.

Travels and Discoveries in Northern and Central Africa by Major Dixon Denham, Captain Hugh Clapperton and the late Dr. Walter Oudney, London 1826.

Journal of a Second Expedition into the Interior of Africa by Captain Hugh Clapperton, to which is appended the Journal of Richard Lander, London 1829.

Captain Clapperton's Last Expedition to Africa by Richard Lander, London 1830.

Explorations and Adventures on the Niger by Richard and John Lander, London 1832.

Travels through Central Africa by René Caillié, London 1830 (English translation).

Travels and Discoveries in North and Central Africa by Heinrich Barth, Ph.D., D.C.L., London 1857.

Timbuctoo the Mysterious by Félix Dubois, New York 1896 (English translation).

The Exploration of the Niger by E.A.L.Hourst, London 1898 (English translation).

ARTICLES

Gentleman's Magazine
Annual Register

Geographical Journal
Transactions of the Linnean Society
Proceedings of the Berwickshire Naturalists Club
Notes Africaines (I.F.A.N., Dakar)
Nigeria Magazine
Royal Commonwealth Society *Library Notes*
The Times
Dictionary of National Biography (D.N.B.)

MANUSCRIPT SOURCES
(showing abbreviations used in the Notes)

Public Record Office, London – Colonial Office Records (C.O.); War Office Records (W.O.).

British Library, London, Additional Manuscripts (Add.MSS.).

British Museum (Natural History), London: Dawson Turner copies of Banks correspondence (D.T.C.).

National Library of Scotland, Edinburgh (N.L.S., MS.No.).

Scottish Record Office, Edinburgh, Parish Registers and Register of Wills.

Foreign and Commonwealth Office, London, India Office Library and Records – East India Company Records.

National Maritime Museum, Greenwich: Ships' Logs.

Royal Botanic Gardens, Kew, London: Banks Papers.

Royal Geographic Society, London – Sutro Papers (copies of Banks papers in Sutro Library, San Francisco, California, U.S.A.).

—Records of the African Association (copies of papers in the University of Cambridge Library).

University of Edinburgh Library.

Selkirk Public Library.

Selkirkshire Antiquarian Society.

Wilton Lodge Museum, Hawick.

Letters in the possession of Mr. G.Ogilvie and the Revd. R.I.Johnstone.

Kent County Records Office: Camden Papers.

Notes

———— ∞ ————

References have not generally been given to material included within the covers of the second 1815 edition combining the *Travels*, the *Journal*, and other items as indicated in Appendix I, or to material derived from the works referred to at the head of a chapter. Abbreviations are indicated under 'Articles' and 'Manuscript Sources' in the Bibliography.

Except where indicated, the sources cited have been little used in biographical writings about Park.

CHAPTER I
MUNGO PARK'S HOME COUNTRY

See Section II of the Bibliography, especially Smout and Craig-Brown.

CHAPTER II
FAMILY AND EDUCATION

I have drawn here on works in Section II of the Bibliography, H.B.'s *Life*, the Scottish Parish Registers, and inscriptions on gravestones (an unreliable source of information; for example, they would show Mrs. Anderson as having been 59 when she bore her last child). Mr. E.N.Bilton has supplied some information about Elspeth Park's family. The error in Mungo Park's birth date was pointed out in the *University of Edinburgh Review*, 1971, by Professor George Shepperson. The University's Matriculation Register and Library Borrowing Register have also been referred to, by permission of the Librarian.

1. Stephen Gwynn, *Mungo Park and the Quest of the Niger*, p.34.
2. N.L.S., MS.No.9609, folio 11. Archibald and his family also figure in MSS.Nos.3888, 3892, and 3906, as well as in J.G.Lockhart, *Life of Scott*, and elsewhere.
3. Information kindly made available by Mr. J.McIntyre.
4. *Proceedings of the Berwickshire Naturalists Club, 1876–8*, p.14.

5. Lewis Grassic Gibbon, *Niger: The Life of Mungo Park*, especially pp.13 and 24; and H.B.'s *Life*, p.5.

6. Revd. John Macfarlane, *The Life and Times of George Lawson, D.D.*, from which all the information concerning Dr. Lawson is derived. He was Professor of Divinity, teaching intending Ministers of his Church, as well as parish Minister of Selkirk.

7. This supposition was also made by Gwynn, op. cit., p.109.

8. *Life and Travels of Mungo Park*, anonymous, Edinburgh, 1838, p.1.

CHAPTER III
'FIRST STEP OF THE STAIR OF AMBITION'

Particulars of James Dickson are derived from the Parish Registers, the Biographical Memoir, and the D.N.B. The sketch of Banks's career is based on the biographies cited in Section III of the Bibliography.

1. *Transactions of the Linnean Society*, Vol.II, pp.286–92.

2. Gibbon, op. cit., p.23.

3. Private communication from Mr. E.H.Cornelius, the Librarian, Royal College of Surgeons of England.

4. Gibbon, op. cit., pp.25–6. For both letters, see J.Thomson, *Mungo Park and the Niger*, pp.42–3; Dr. H.S.Anderson, owner of the letters in 1884, quoted the second as being addressed to Alexander (*Proceedings of the Berwickshire Naturalists Club*, 1882–4, pp.300–304). Gwynn, op. cit., p.110, was correct on that but misdated the letter to after the Sumatra voyage. The originals have not been traced.

CHAPTER IV
FROM GRAVESEND TO THE DEAD LAND AND BACK

Based mainly on the log of the *Worcester* in the National Maritime Museum, Greenwich, also to be found, with the accounts ledger, in the India Office Library and Records, references L/MAR/B/278 L and CC. Bencoolen, as it was when Sir Stamford Raffles was Lieutenant-Governor around 1818, is described in *Raffles* by Maurice Collis, London, 1966, and *Raffles of Singapore* by Emily Hahn, 1948. Its cession is treated in *The East India Company, 1784–1834* by Cyril Henry Philips, Manchester, 1961.

1. N.L.S., MS.No.10782, f.180 (previously unpublished).

2. Dr. J.M.Brydone, *Mungo Park and the Brydones of Selkirk*, London, 1963, p.3.

3. Wills in Scottish Records Office, Edinburgh, Register of Wills; Mungo Park senior's in Dalrymple, Vol.267, pp.464–7, and his son's in Vol.12, pp.780–83. Professor Shepperson drew my attention to these and to Park's marriage contract.

4. D.T.C., Vol.XI, pp. 77–8.

CHAPTER V

'RESCUING THE AGE FROM A CHARGE OF IGNORANCE'

I am much indebted for background information to works listed in Section III of the Bibliography. Reference has also been made to the Association's original records.

1. On the identity of Wangara, see E.W.Bovill, *The Golden Trade of the Moors*, 2nd edn., Ch. 14. From Bambuk and nearby Bure the name moved on with settlers to other places, or to other gold-bearing sites.

2. R. Pagéard, *Un Mystérieux Voyage au Pays du Bambouc, 1789*, in *Notes Africaines*, No.89, January 1961, pp.23–7, for the journey of the unknown Englishman *before* 1789. Job ben Solomon is the subject of Douglas Grant, *The Fortunate Slave*, London, 1968.

3. A British Governor of Senegambia also heard hints of an eastward-flowing river; see Hon. F.R.Rodd, 'Rennell's comments upon the Journeys of Park and Laing to the Niger' in *Geographical Journal*, Vol.LXXXVI (1935), pp.28–31.

4. P.D.Curtin, *The Atlantic Slave Trade: A Census*, University of Wisconsin, 1969, p.221.

5. J. Sinclair, *Memoir of . . . the late Rt. Hon. Sir John Sinclair*, 1837, Vol.2, p.204. Apparently based on Shabeni (see Ch. VI).

CHAPTER VI

'USING MATERIALS OF SO COARSE A KIND'

General sources as for Chapter V. Shabeni's report is given in full in James Grey Jackson, *An Account of Timbuctoo and Housa*, 1820. Much of it is quoted in R.Hallett, *Records . . .*, pp.104–116. Rennell's 1790 map referred to here is substantially different from the 1798 map published with the *Travels*, and the 1802 map in the Association's collected *Proceedings*, 1810.

1. Speech of Mr. Stanley in House of Commons, April 1791, from T.Clarkson, *History of the Abolition of the African Slave Trade*, Vol.II, p.280.

CHAPTER VII
'IT IS A SHORT EXPEDITION'

As in the previous chapters, I am indebted to the Association's *Proceedings* and to Hallett's books.

1. *Transactions of the Linnean Society*, Vol.III (1797), pp.33–9. The Librarian kindly allowed me to inspect Park's manuscript.

2. Previously unpublished letter held by Selkirkshire Antiquarian Society.

3. Richard Owen, *Saga of the Niger*, p.36. In 1958–9 Owen traced Park's route, the early part on foot, and met the author at Bussa. His account of the present condition of Jillifree, Pisania and other places is used in Chapters VII–IX.

CHAPTERS VIII–XIV
PARK'S FIRST JOURNEY IN AFRICA

My account here is based mainly on the *Travels*, supplemented by the Association's *Proceedings*, especially for 1797 and 1804. For historical sources, see Section IV of the Bibliography, and Gray and Dochard's *Travels* (1825).

CHAPTER IX
'BEFORE ME A BOUNDLESS FOREST'

1. For correspondence of Banks, Laidley, and Willis, see Dawson, *Banks Letters*; Dawson MS.46.25–6; C.O.267/10, p.145; and the Sutro Papers, 385, 394–5, and 397–8. Some of it is contained in the 1797 *Proceedings*.

2. J.F.A.Ajayi and M.Crowder (eds.), *History of West Africa*, Vol.I, p.420.

CHAPTER X
'FOR FEAR SOME ACCIDENT SHOULD BEFAL ME'

Uses Charles Monteil, *Les Khassonké*, Paris, 1915. In his dating of Khasso Mansas, Monteil apparently overlooked Park's statement that Demba Sego Jalla died soon after Park's visit; see Monteil, pp.24–30 and 46–7.

CHAPTER XI
'A LONELY CAPTIVE, PERISHING OF THIRST'

1. N.L.S., MS.No.786, f.11. Scott's previous letter to Whishaw is in Selkirk Public Library.

CHAPTER XII
'THE GREAT OBJECT OF MY MISSION'

1. Estimates range from low proportions of the population up to two-thirds, for various times and places. See John Grace, *Domestic Slavery in West Africa*, London, 1975, and Allan G.B.Fisher and Humphrey J.Fisher, *Slavery and Muslim Society in Africa*, London, 1970.

2. M.E.Mage, *Voyage dans le Soudan Occidental, 1863–66*, Paris, 1868, p.631.

3. Biographical Memoir, Appendix III. Young's letter is in Selkirk Public Library. Cahill's communication is given in the 1804 *Proceedings*.

CHAPTER XIII
'STILL UNDER THE PROTECTING EYE OF PROVIDENCE'

1. R.A.Adeleye, *Power and Diplomacy in Northern Nigeria, 1804–1906*, London, 1971, p.164.

2. E.A.Ayandele, *African Exploration and Human Understanding*, Mungo Park Bi-Centenary Memorial Lecture, University of Edinburgh, 2 December 1971.

CHAPTER XIV
'LONG NUMBERED WITH THE DEAD'

1. Sutro Papers, 387, quoted in Hallett, *Records*, p.162.

2. Original letter displayed in Old Court House, Selkirk.

3. Gibbon, op. cit., p.249, quoting from an untraced source.

4. See Rennell to Banks, 22 October 1797, in D.T.C., Vol.X(1), pp.201–203, and Banks to Chalmers, 21 October 1797, in Add.MSS.22900, f.355.

CHAPTER XV
'THE WARMEST APPROBATION OF THIS ASSOCIATION'

1. Earl of Ilchester (ed.), *The Journal of Elizabeth, Lady Holland*, 1908, Vol.I, p.172; and Gibbon, op. cit., p.254, quoting from an untraced source.

2. D.T.C., Vol.X(2), pp.229–30; and Kew manuscript B.C.2/189, Crown copyright, reproduced with the permission of the Controller of Her Majesty's Stationery Office, and of the Director of the Royal Botanic Gardens, Kew. Particulars of Edwards mainly from D.N.B. The *Abstract* and the *Geographical Illustrations* were in the 1810 *Proceedings*.

3. The Committee minutes of 31 March 1798 and those of the General Meeting of 26 May 1798 are quoted in Hallett, *Records*, p.162 et seq.
4. Specimens in the herbarium, listed by Robert Brown (see Ch. XVI).
5. *Proceedings of the Berwickshire Naturalists Club*, 1882–4, pp.399–401.

CHAPTER XVI
'OF A VERY CLOSE MIND'

See Section V of the Bibliography. Some of the official correspondence is in C.O.201/14 and 202/5. Copies of the correspondence of Banks, Park, and Dickson are in D.T.C., Vol.XI, between p.71 and p.101. The originals of two letters are in Selkirk Public Library. Some of them were published in the *Historical Records of New South Wales*, and two in Peter Brent, *Black Nile*, p.111.

CHAPTER XVII
'IT HAS NOTHING TO RECOMMEND IT, BUT TRUTH'

1. Royal Botanic Gardens, Kew, manuscript B.C.2/204, and D.T.C., Vol. XI, pp.84–5, 113–15, and 181–2.
2. Biographical Memoir, Appendix III. Young's letter of 9 November 1803 is held by Selkirkshire Antiquarian Society.
3. H.B., *Life*, p.153.
4. Sutro Papers, 478–81.
5. Association records, quoted in Hallett, *Records*, pp.265–6.
6. From minutes of the meeting, quoted in Hallett's *Records*, pp. 166–70. The version in the 1810 Proceedings was substantially edited.
7. Rennell to Sullivan, 17 October 1802, in C.O.2/1.
8. *Gentleman's Magazine*, August 1799, pp.680–81; and *Annual Register*, 1799, pp.489–96.

CHAPTER XVIII
'NEITHER WITHIN MY PROVINCE, NOR IN MY POWER, TO EXPLAIN'

See Section VI of the Bibliography.
1. Quoted in R.Coupland, *The British Anti-Slavery Movement*, p.36.
2. George Hibbert, M.P., *Substance of three Speeches in Parliament on the Bill for the Abolition of the Slave Trade in February and March 1807*, pp.24–5.

3. Letter in Selkirk Public Library.

4. Bryan Edwards, *The History, Civil and Commercial of the British Colonies in the West Indies*, London, 3rd edn., 1801, Vol.III, p.226 et seq.

5. *The Times*, 7 April 1797.

6. Hibbert, op. cit., p.88.

7. *The Times*, 4 April 1798.

8. Edwards, op. cit., Vol.II, p.101 et seq. Put forward as one set of views amongst others, they appear to be finally endorsed by Edwards.

9. N.L.S., MS.No.582, f.613.

10. Christopher Fyfe, *A History of Sierra Leone*, Oxford, 1962, pp.105–11.

11. In *A History of the Upper Guinea Coast, 1545–1800*, Oxford, 1970, Walter Rodney maintained that no true slavery was there discernible before the trans-Atlantic trade began, but this opinion is not generally accepted concerning the inland societies.

CHAPTER XIX
'MY LOVELY ALLIE'

H.B.'s *Life* is the fullest for this period, with some details also in Craig Brown and the Biographical Memoir (which quotes parts of Park's letter to Banks of 31 July 1800 and Banks's letter to him of October 1801, but not verbatim).

1. Sutro Papers, 478–81. Nicol told Banks he had tried to contact Park on 8 May but had missed him 'of course'.

2. Thomson, op. cit., p.175. He was evidently in touch with Allison's nephew, Dr. H.S.Anderson, and others at Selkirk.

3. Scottish Records Office, Register of Deeds, Vol.12, pp.775–80.

4. N.L.S., MS.No.3219, f.191, and No.582, f.613, previously unpublished.

5. N.L.S., MS.No.5308, f.425, previously unpublished but cited by Ayandele, op. cit.

6. D.T.C., Vol.XI, p.217.

7. Park's draft is in Selkirk Public Library.

8. Private communication from Mr. E.H.Cornelius, Librarian of the Royal College of Surgeons of England. Previously stated by Professor Shepperson in the *University of Edinburgh Review*, 1971.

9. Letter with Selkirkshire Antiquarian Society. Published in the *Proceedings of the Berwickshire Naturalists Club*, 1880–82, pp.300–304, and in Thomson, op. cit., pp.179–80.

10. Original in Selkirk Public Library, copy in D.T.C., Vol.XII, pp.265–6. Quoted in Hallett, *Records*, p.213.

11. H.B.'s *Life*, pp.154–5. Both it and the 1838 anonymous (Chambers) *Life* incorrectly date the move to 1800, but Dr. Marshall died on 12 September 1801.

CHAPTER XX
THE RELUCTANT SURGEON

General sources as for Chapter XIX.

1. Thomson, op. cit., p.184. The story was told by Dr. H.S.Anderson.

2. J.G.Lockhart, *Life of Sir Walter Scott*, and John Ruskin, *Fors Clavigera: Letters to the Workmen and Labourers of Great Britain*, Vol.IV, Letter XCII. Penultimate sentence from Biographical Memoir.

3. Manuscript note on p.158 of the British Library copy of H.B.'s *Life*, but my efforts to trace this poem have been unsuccessful.

4. Robert Brown, *Africa and its Explorers*, 1892, p.210.

5. Hornemann's Journals (1802) and Rennell's 'Geographical Illustrations' are in the 1810 *Proceedings*.

6. Proceedings for 1805, in the 1810 collection, and G.F.Lyon, *A Narrative of Travels in Northern Africa*, 1821, p.133.

7. Add. MSS.30262–1.

8. D.T.C., Vol.XIV, p.161.

CHAPTER XXI
'ANOTHER TRIP INTO THE CENTRE OF AFRICA'

1. C.O.267/10 for the Association's memorandum. Add. MSS.38233, f.94 for Banks to Liverpool of 8 June 1799; quoted in Hallett, *Records*, pp. 211–12. The Board of Trade did not even formally note the memorandum (B.T. 5/11 and 12).

2. For information on military plans see C.O.267/6, 7, and 18, W.O.1/351, W.O.4/192, and W.O.6/149. See C.O.2/1 for Banks's letter of 1 August 1802, Sullivan's memorandum of 12 August 1802, and related correspondence. Also see R.Mauny, *Guide de Gorée*, I.F.A.N., Dakar, 1954.

3. Sullivan to Banks of 13 October 1802 is in Selkirk Public Library; previously unpublished.

4. Royal Commonwealth Society *Library Notes*, New Series No.102, June 1965, and a letter from Stevenson to John Bowring of 25 May 1824, quoted by permission of the Society's Librarian. Relevant correspondence from Col. (later Lt.-Gen.) Stevenson is also be to found in C.O.2/1 and C.O.267/23 and 43; the Camden Papers in Kent County Archives, quoted

by permission of Marquess Camden and Kent County Council, Ref.U. 840, Papers O.26/1–10; and the Addington Papers in Devon Record Office, quoted by permission of Lord Sidmouth. C.O.55/62 indirectly throws light on the Ceylon aspect, mentioned in the Camden Papers.

5. D.T.C., Vol.XIV, p.162, with Banks's reply at p.163; the draft is in Selkirk Public Library.

6. Quoted from Gwynn, op. cit., p.161 (original not traced). That 1804 is correct, not 1805 as in Gwynn, is shown by the references to Sullivan and to Allison being at Peebles.

CHAPTER XXII
'FREITS FOLLOW THOSE WHO LOOK TO THEM'

1. See H.B.'s *Life* on Ombark Bouby. Receipts for his services, at 5s. per day from 1 January until December 1804 are displayed in the David Livingstone Memorial, Blantyre, Glasgow, quoted by permission of the Warden (copy in N.L.S., MS.No.10708, f.143) and in Add. MSS.42581, ff.253–6. His letter to Mrs. Park of 8 December 1804 is held by Selkirkshire Antiquarian Society, and that to Banks of 15 February 1805 is in Add. MSS.37232-K, ff.60–61, with Banks's outline reply noted on it. The spelling of his name has varied, but he signed himself as shown.

2. Camden Papers, Ref.U.840, Papers O.25/2/1–5.

3. Royal Commonwealth Society *Library Notes*, New Series No.72, December 1962, with a letter of 23 May 1853 to Miss Erskine by an unknown writer who had known Mrs. Thomson.

4. N.L.S., MS.No.786, f.11, for Scott to Whishaw of 24 April 1815, the gist being quoted in the Addenda to the Biographical Memoir. See also Lockhart's (1837–8) or Allan's (1834) *Life of Scott*.

5. Gwynn, op. cit., p. 157, the first published reference to the housemaid's story.

6. Park to Williamson of 29 January 1805, quoted by permission of the Librarian, Chambers Institute, Peebles. A different part was quoted by Gwynn, op. cit., pp.161–2.

CHAPTER XXIII
'HIS MAJESTY HAS SELECTED YOU'

Park to Camden of 4 October 1804, and Camden's instructions of 2 January 1805, are quoted in full in the Biographical Memoir.

1. Park to Anderson of 26 September 1804, quoted by permission of Mr. G.Ogilvie; previously unpublished.

2. P.R.O.30/8/119 Part 2; previously unpublished.

3. Add. MSS.37232, ff.54–5, copy in D.T.C., Vol.XV, pp.140–41, more fully quoted in Hallett, *Records*, p.216.

4. The Biographical Memoir did not say Rennell had held discussions with Park before the memorandum was submitted, as in Whishaw to Wilberforce of 7 April 1814 in C.O.267/39.

5. See D.T.C., Vol.XV, pp.242–4 for Banks's notes of discussion with Camden on 18 December 1804.

6. Camden Papers O.210A, pp.16–20 and O.25/2/6.

7. D.T.C., Vol.XV, p.171.

8. N.L.S., MS.No.582, f.614, and Ayandele op. cit.

9. George Fraser to Cooke of 28 May 1805 and 5 July 1805 in C.O.2/2 and M.Shedden to Cooke of 12 January 1805 in C.O.267/23.

10. W.O.6/149.

11. W.O.6/22 for Camden to Park of 2 January and 4 January 1805 and Cooke to Park of 19 January 1805. Camden to Lloyd of 2 January 1805 and Cooke to Lloyd of 24 January 1805 in C.O.268/6. Only the first item has previously beed cited.

12. Quoted by permission of the Revd. R. I. Johnstone; previously unpublished. The uncle was presumably his mother's brother, Mr. Hislop, see Brydone, op. cit., p.4.

13. C.O.2/2 for Park to Cooke and Capt. Hammersley to Cooke, both of 23 January 1805.

14. N.L.S., MS.No.5319, ff.220–23.

15. Logs of H.M. Sloop *Eugenie* by Commander Charles Webb and Lieutenant Younger, in the National Maritime Museum, Greenwich; I have used these for some other details of the voyage.

CHAPTER XXIV
'THE UNDERTAKING WORTHY OF THE BEST OF GOVERNMENTS'

Based largely on Park's report to Camden of 26 April 1805, in Add. MSS. Eg.3009, ff.30–46. Also uses J.J.Crooks, *Historical Records of the Royal African Corps*. The Biographical Memoir quotes most of Park's letters home.

1. C.O.2/2 for Park to Camden of 12 March 1805.

2. C.O.267/23 regarding the capture of the Spanish ship, and C.O.267/32 for Memorial of 18 April 1808 by Mr. McAlpine, citing Martyn's will and attaching the Garrison Order (also paraphrased in Crooks, op. cit.).

3. C.O.267/23 for State of Detachment Return of 25 June 1805; evidently Gorée had not been reinforced either locally or from England. C.O.268/6 for Cooke to Lloyd of 24 January 1805, mentioning the removal of stores.

4. *Cruize in the Channel and the Last Voyage of Mongo Park to Africa*, 1814. My attention was drawn to this by Mr. C.Finlayson, Keeper of Manuscripts, University of Edinburgh Library.

5. C.O.2/2.

6. Three specimens were described in Appendix V to the Biographical Memoir. Park's report to Camden and notes inside Mendoza's *Tables* refer to the accuracy of the watch.

7. *Life* . . . (Chambers), pp.78–9.

8. Selkirkshire Antiquarian Society hold Anderson's letter. Scott's letters are quoted by permission of the Warden, Wilton House Museum, Hawick; they were published in the *Transactions of the Hawick Archaeological Society* in October 1905.

9. Information supplied by Miss H.J.Martin.

10. D.T.C., Vol.XV, p.365.

CHAPTER XXV

'THUNDER, DEATH AND LIGHTNING – THE DEVIL TO PAY'

The account here is based mainly on the *Journal* and the Biographical Memoir. The original letter from Badoo to Banks is in Selkirk Public Library. I have given my own form to medical comments, which I gratefully acknowledge, by Professor E.H.O.Parry, until recently Professor of Medicine, Ahmadu Bello University, Zaria, now at the University at Ilorin; they are based on tenuous evidence which makes retrospective diagnosis especially hazardous.

1. Major L.Darwin in *Scottish Geographical Magazine*, Vol.XXVIII, 1912, pp.134–6.

2. N.L.S., MS.No.3278, f.58.

3. T.Bowdich, *A Note . . . on a Geographical Error of Mungo Park*, appended to *An Account of the Discoveries of the Portuguese in Angola and Mozambique*, London, 1824. Park's later latitudes are more accurate than Bowdich's amended ones.

4. Add. MSS.37232, f.62. Near-by places were mentioned in the *Travels*.

5. J.S.Gallieni, *Voyage au Soudan Français . . . 1879–81*, Paris, 1885, pp.127–9.

6. Gibbon, op. cit., pp.293–4. The *Observer* of 31 August 1806, *The Times* and the *Morning Post* of 3 September, and *Bell's Weekly Messenger* of 7 September. All misdated the letter from Sansanding to 10 November 1804 instead of 1805; Park wrote on 10 November 1805 to Heddle, as the latter told Dickson, and Heddle probably also wrote to Banks. Dickson was surprised by the letter in *The Times*. (See Dickson to Banks in Selkirk Public Library, copy in D.T.C.Vol.XVI, p.318, also Add. MSS.37232, f.67).

CHAPTER XXVI
'LONELY AND FRIENDLESS AMIDST THE WILDS OF AFRICA'

This is based mainly on the *Journal*.

1. Gray and Dochard, *Travels in Western Africa*, pp.345–6. The Governor of Bamako died while Dochard was there. Regarding the date of Mansong's death, see Louis Tauxier, *Histoire des Bambara*, p.101.

2. Félix Dubois, *Timbuctoo the Mysterious*, pp.322–5.

3. Source as in Ch. XXIV, Note 8.

4. Original of 10 November 1805 (last part missing) in Add. MSS.33230, f.37. Published in *Life* . . . (Chambers), p.88, and summarized in Addenda to the Biographical Memoir. Gibbon, op. cit., p.299.

5. Add. MSS.37232, f.63, dated 1 November with postscript 4 November. Previously only partly quoted.

6. N.L.S., MS.No.3278, ff.60–61.

7. Clapperton, *Second Expedition*, entries for 14 May and 17 June 1826; Barth, *Travels*, 3 June 1854. See *The Narrative of Robert Adams, a Sailor*, London, 1816, p.69, for an (improbable) description heard from a slave woman of 'Kanno' at Wadi Nun in Morocco, of the boat being rowed with oars.

CHAPTER XXVII
THE QUEST FOR MUNGO PARK

See Section VII of the Bibliography.

1. Webb to Camden of 31 July 1805 in C.O.267/23.

2. D.T.C., Vol.XVI, p.146, Banks to Marsden, wrongly copied as of 12 October 1805, as it refers to Jackson to Banks of 21 September 1806, at pp.320–21.

3. Add. MSS.37232, ff.62 and 66, and D.T.C., Vol.XVI, pp.259–64.

4. Allison Park to Dickson, 12 April 1806, in C.O.2/2.

5. Regarding Mrs. Thomson, see Chapter XXII, Note 3. The story about Park's mother is in Gwynn, op. cit., p.2.

6. See Appendix III, Items 1 (located for the author by Dr. R.Taylor Cole) and 2.

7. Add. MSS.30262–1, f.40, where neighbouring items relate to Dickson. Written on the back of a letter from Park beginning, 'Dear Sir, I have left this enclosure with Dr. Heddle . . .'

8. John Anderson to Fraser of 10 July 1806, and Fraser to Shee, Under Secretary, of 12 July 1806, in C.O.2/2. Windham to Lloyd of 12 July 1806 in C.O.268/6. Lloyd to Windham of 10 October 1806, in C.O. 267/23 (my emphasis).

9. Maxwell to Liverpool of 8 March 1810, in C.O.267/33. Maxwell to Liverpool of 10 December 1811, in P.R.O.30/26/102, the date of receipt being shown in C.O.324/69.

10. Article by F.P. in *The Philanthropist*, Vol.IV, 1815, pp.201–19.

11. D.T.C., Vol.XVII, pp.296–7, Sutro Papers, 710–2, and *The Times*, 4 April 1812.

12. Lander to Hay from Fernando Po, 7 January 1831, in C.O.2/18, p.33.

13. *Proceedings of the Berwickshire Naturalists Club*, 1882–4, pp.300–304. Also notes kept with the book by Mr. G.Ogilvie.

14. See Appendix II concerning Thomas Park. Quotation from Lander's unpublished Journal (p.97, 20 June 1830) in the Wellcome Institute of the History of Medicine, by courtesy of the Wellcome Trustees.

15. Although a number of the accounts were cited by Jean Rouch in the second of three articles, '*Les rapides de Boussa et la mort de Mungo Park*', in *Notes Africaines*, Nos.43–5, published in 1949–50 by I.F.A.N., Dakar.

CHAPTER XXVIII
'A BOAT CAME HAVING CHRISTIANS ON BOARD'

Draws especially on Dubois' *Timbuctoo the Mysterious*, Caillié's *Travels*, Ajayi and Crowder's *History of West Africa*, Barth's *Travels*, and Charles Monteil, *Une cité Soudanaise: Djenne*, Paris, 1932.

1. Clapperton's *Second Expedition*, Appendix II.

2. Barth's *Travels*, entry for 25 June 1853.

3. Denham's Journal, entry for 23 June 1823.

4. See Appendix III, Item 3.

5. *The Letters of Gordon Laing*, p.312.

6. See Appendix III, Item 9.

7. Jackson to Banks of 21 September 1806, original in Selkirk Public Library, copy in D.T.C., Vol.XVI, pp.320–21. The version in Jackson's own *Account of Timbuctoo and Housa*, p.319, is mutilated and says it was received in Mogador in March, not sent from Kabara then.

8. Court to Banks of 25 May 1810, original in Add. MSS.37232, copy in D.T.C., Vol.XVIII, pp.35–9.

9. Fitzclarence, *Journal of a Route across India, through Egypt to England, 1817–18*, London, 1819, p.497.

CHAPTER XXIX

'THE FIXED RESOLUTION TO DISCOVER THE TERMINATION OF THE NIGER'

This uses Amadi's Journal, Hourst's *Exploration of the Niger*, and entries in Barth's *Travels* under the datelines 20 June, 27 September, and 1 December 1853, and 24 March, 25 April, 10 and 24 May, 3, 14, and 20 June, and 11 and 18 July 1854.

1. Court to Banks of 2 December 1806 in D.T.C., Vol.XVI, pp.338–40. It was inaccurate about how they arrived at Segu; it said twelve Europeans sailed from there, four being killed near Timbuktu, where the speaker acted as interpreter with the King of Soudan; and that he left them in July 1806.

2. See William D.Cooley, *Negroland of the Arabs*, London, 1841, reprinted Cass, London, 1966, pp.109–10.

3. Different positions are taken here on timing and casualties in Park's party from those in the author's article 'The Death of Mungo Park at Bussa' in *Nigeria Magazine*, no.72, March 1962. The confusion in Item 23 in Appendix III, which places Ramadan in April 1806, is probably due to Lander. Isaaco's estimate, at the end of his Journal, was apparently given in response to a question.

4. In Appendix III, Items 8, 13, 19, 21, and possibly 26 all say there were two Europeans at Yauri. Caliph Bello's record and two of Barth's stories imply the same, only Barth's story from Ansongho supports Amadi in saying that the party passed unscathed.

5. Laing's *Letters*, pp.254–5 and 294–5.

CHAPTER XXX
'OR PERISH IN THE ATTEMPT'

The items referred to are in Appendix III. I am indebted to Professor M.A. Al-Hajj of Bayero University, Kano, for permission to use his translation of Item 8.

1. From Item 23. Mr. J.Mungo Park owns H.Edridge's miniature of Park (reproduced on the book jacket) and another miniature possibly of him. Miniatures derived from Edridge are owned by Mr. G.Ogilvie and the National Portrait Gallery. T.Dickinson's engraving from Edridge, used as the frontispiece of Park's *Travels* (see Plate 7), is the best-known representation of Park, but another engraving by R.Bell was used in H.B.'s *Life*. Thomas Rowlandson's watercolour (Plate 9) in the National Portrait Gallery dates from shortly before Park set off on his final journey. Mr. J.W.Ritchie owns a portrait by Sir Henry Raeburn, plausibly but not certainly identified with Mungo Park.

2. Unpublished M.A. thesis of Dr. Mahdi Adamu, 'Yawuri – A Hausa Government in Decline', at Ahmadu Bello University, Zaria, for a list of Emirs of Yauri. This paragraph also uses Item 10.

3. See Item 8.

4. See Item 24.

5. See Items 13 and 15.

6. Item 13 also says that they left at night.

7. In *The Niger Explored*, p.30, E.W.Bovill gave no evidence to support his assertion that Yauri advised Bussa to attack Park.

8. Clapperton, *Second Expedition*, 2 April 1826. Bovill, op. cit., published a sketch in Clapperton's Remark Books in C.O.2/16 (see Plate 12c).

9. Pages 87 and 91 in an English version, *The Rise of the Sokoto Fulani*, by E.J.Arnett, Kano, 1922, deal with these campaigns. Arnett conjectured the Yauri campaign was in January 1806, but Yauri seems to have been undisturbed when Park was there. Murray Last in *The Sokoto Caliphate*, London, 1967, p.37, dates the expedition to the middle and late dry season. These facts support an early date in 1806 for Park's arrival. A translation of part of the *Infaqu'l Maisur* was published with Clapperton's account of the Borno expedition.

10. Probably Jibrin, great-great-grandfather of the present Emir of Borgu, Alhaji Musa Mohammed Kigera III, according to a king-list by Clarke in the same file as Item 32.

11. Private communication from Mr. J.E.Lavers, Bayero University, Kano, concerning the sickness. It is mentioned as a local event in Arnett, op. cit., p.92. Private communication from the Emir of Borgu regarding the evacuation of Kainji Island about 1807.

12. *Nigeria Magazine*, no.72, March 1962, p.62.

13. M.Laird to Lord Clarendon, British Foreign Secretary, 5 March 1855, quoted in Revd. Samuel Crowther, *Journal of the Expedition up the Niger and Tshadda Rivers*, 2nd edn., reprinted Cass, London, 1970, p.xii.

14. Barth, entries for 24 March and 24 April 1854.

APPENDIX I

SOURCES OF MATERIALS ABOUT MUNGO PARK'S LIFE

a indicates information from papers in Selkirk Public Library; copies of some of them are in D.T.C., Vols. XVIII and XIX.

1. Note at the front of C.O.2/2, and C.O.267/35 and 39.

2. Personal communication from Mr. Christopher Fyfe, former Government Archivist, Sierra Leone.

3. Dickson's statement is given in the Biographical Memoir.

4. Sutro Papers, 697–701.

5. C.O.267/35.

6. Records of the African Institution from 1813; Lincoln's Inn Admissions Register, supplemented by information from the Librarian; lists of Royal Society Fellows; Patrick Medd, *Romilly*, London, 1968; some official correspondence and letters in D.T.C., Selkirk Public Library, and C.O. files; register of deaths, London.

7. D.T.C., Vol.XVIII, pp.254–6, and Sutro Papers, 697–701.

8. Sutro Papers, 704–5.

APPENDIX II

PARK'S FINAL EXPEDITION, MEMBERSHIP AND AFTER-EFFECTS

a indicates information from Selkirk Public Library papers.
b indicates C.O.2/2.
c indicates the C.O.267 series, volumes 25, 32, 33, 35, and 41.

1. D.T.C., Vol.XVII, pp.73–6.

2. C.O.2/17, p.323.

3. D.T.C., Vol.XVIII, pp.254–6.

4. N.L.S., MS. No.9609, f.11.

5. Letters quoted by permission of the Revd. R.I.Johnstone.

6. Craig Brown, op. cit., Vol.II, p.298.

7. *Proceedings of the Berwickshire Naturalists Club*, 1882–4, pp.399–401.

8. Thomson, op. cit., pp.244–5; Lander, *Clapperton's Last Expedition*, Vol. II, pp.234–5; Robert Jameson, *Narrative of Discovery and Adventure in Africa*, Edinburgh, 1830, pp.362–3; James E.Alexander, *Voyage of Observation Among the Colonies of West Africa*, London, 1837, pp.181–2; *Bulletin des Sciences Géographiques*, Paris, 1828, Vol.13, pp.229–30; *The Times*, 14 May 1828; *Quarterly Review*, Vol.XXXVIII, 1828, p.112; *Notes Africaines*, I.F.A.N., Dakar, No.44, 1949, p.124.

9. Gwynn, op. cit., p.260.

10. C.O.446/1, pp.713–14.

11. *Geographical Journal*, Vol.LXV (1925), p.65; Vol.LXVIII (1926), p.456; and Vol.LXXIV (1929), pp.470–71.

12. Sutro Papers, 727–9.

13. Scottish Parish Registers.

14. Add. MSS.37232, ff.73–4.

15. N.L.S., MS. No.2835, f.175.

16. Gray and Dochard, op. cit., p.307.

17. N.L.S., MS. No.3278, ff.60–61.

Index

—— ଉଷ ——